'Can't remember the last time I read anything this gritty and compelling. Frazer doesn't write like an angel. He writes like a demon. *Scoundrel Days* is one of the finest Australian works in years.' **Brett D'Arcy, author of *The Mindless Ferocity of Sharks***

'With a poet's eye for locating the marvellous within the commonplace and a novelist's ear for the nuances and rhythms of natural speech, Brentley Frazer has crafted a unique narrative from the myths and rumours of life and a wild imagination. *Scoundrel Days* is fiercely original, inspirational, and will no doubt find a wide, varied readership.' **Anthony Lawrence, author of *Headwaters* and *Bark***

'A true artist's journey from blindness (or, what we call youth) into glimmerings of sight (coming of age). The writing is transcendent, and the writer lives in the tradition of the Beats, yet has managed to create something new through his use of the E-prime constraint.' **Venero Armanno, author of *Black Mountain* and *The Dirty Beat***

'Brentley's unconventionality, radicalism, aggression, schizophrenia, non-adaptability and sublimity with hallucinogenic scenes and pornographic moments is a bizarre mix of elements of neo-symbolism and post-romanticism, wrapped in a form of hypertext prose, and finds itself somewhere at the intersection of Burroughs, Breton, Rimbaud, Salinger and Ian Curtis.' ***Tribuna Magazine***

Brentley Frazer is an Australian author whose poems, prose and academic papers have been published in numerous national and international anthologies, journals, magazines and other periodicals since 1992. He holds an MA (writing) from James Cook University and authored *Scoundrel Days* as part of a submission for a PhD in creative writing at Griffith University. He is also a lecturer at Griffith University and the editor-in-chief of *Bareknuckle Poet Journal of Letters*.

www.brentley.com

Scoundrel Days

a memoir

Brentley Frazer

First published 2017 by University of Queensland Press
PO Box 6042, St Lucia, Queensland 4067 Australia

www.uqp.com.au
uqp@uqp.uq.edu.au

Cover design by Josh Durham, Design by Committee
Typeset in 11.5/15 pt Adobe Garamond Pro by Post Pre-press Group, Brisbane
Printed in Australia by McPherson's Printing Group

National Library of Australia
Cataloguing-in-Publication data is available at http://catalogue.nla.gov.au

ISBN
978 0 7022 5956 2 (pbk)
978 0 7022 5892 3 (ePDF)
978 0 7022 5893 0 (ePub)
978 0 7022 5894 7 (Kindle)

For my only Sunshine
~ ens causa sui ~

Contents

Part One
The Wreckers

Go! if your ancient, but ignoble blood
Has crept thro' scoundrels ever since the flood.
Alexander Pope

1

—January 1972. Soldiers. Blue heavy sheets flapping in the wind.

Mum ignores me awhile, fussing with a brush, and then says:

—The hospital had no roof. The cyclone blew it away. The army slung blue tarps across the rafters … But a newborn remembering birth? Impossible!

I watch her reflection comb her long auburn hair.

—Cyclone Althea destroyed Townsville, says her mouth in the mirror.

She wears her hair out now. Back in the city she wound it in a bun, spent hours smoothing down strays with lacquer. When Mum swims, she wears it loose. She doesn't swim often. Diving gives her migraines, since Dad ran her over with a tractor.

On the corner of Cassia and Acacia. Our house and the police station side by side, separated by a driveway and a narrow dead patch of lawn choked with bindii-eyes and goat's-head thorns. The white brick police station has a huge open-air skylight. The Acacia Drive side has a reception area, an office and a courtroom. The house side has a prison cell, two bunk beds with grey government-issue blankets, a sink and a stainless-steel toilet with no lid and no door. My bedroom window looks out to the reinforced wall of the prison. The shouts of drunken miners and the moans of sunburned truck drivers seep through the bricks.

Our house on stilts. Seven steps up to the veranda. We moved here right before my fifth birthday. The town has only one policeman: my dad, posted here from Townsville by his sergeant. Imagine hills of rolling grass and wild horses grazing on the banks of a slow-flowing river. Limestone mountains bursting up from the earth. Blue jagged rocks reaching into the heavens, shrouded by gentle mists. Now picture the opposite: a stopping point for tired travellers with dusty caravans on their way to Undara Volcanic National Park, a service town, two hundred kilometres inland from the coast.

Greenvale belongs to the nearby nickel mine. Queensland Nickel Industries laid it on for the miners and their families when they built the entire town in the early seventies. Golf greens and tennis courts. Olympic-size swimming pool, a library, a theatre, a school, a shopping centre and a pub. Kerbed streets and channelled gutters, sports oval with fifty-metre-high lighting towers, eighty-five houses, a police station and a drive-in movie cinema. Before that, nothing but the cattle which still roam through town, kangaroos, and yowies that roar in the night above the cacophony of the galahs. The galahs sound like your neighbour falling down the stairs forever, with an entire crockery set filled with boiling water.

2

The kids at Greenvale State School wear the same shirt. Pale blue, *Greenvale State School – Mining for Knowledge* written in white letters around an excavator bucket-wheel. My first day, in a big dumb hat with stupid shiny shoes and a huge bag with a plastic lunch box containing an orange which thumps and annoys the hell out of me when I walk. Inside I have a chocolate tin full of pencils and a ragged copy of *Tom Sawyer* with missing pages. The other kids wear jeans with dirty knees and go barefoot. They slouch and yawn as the teacher introduces herself as Mrs Crisp.

—Now, children, Mrs Crisp says, arranging some papers: Get up off the carpet and pick a desk. You'll sit there all year. I'll go into what you can, and what you *cannot,* keep in your desks later.

A mad scrabble of dusty kids in an eager fit bump and fight over the desks. I grab one as close as possible to the window, beside a strip of linoleum and a room-long stainless-steel sink which separates me from the bush and the creek through the glass. A boy with a crazy mop of orange hair slumps down at the desk next to me.

—Hello! I say, offering to shake.

—Fuck off, with ya pretty gaylord shoes, he says, rolling his eyes at my extended hand.

He has odd eyes. In the left, two colours fight for dominance, bleeding into each other like the edges of shadows: orange, matching his hair, and green, like the greenest blade of grass you've seen. His right eye, cold and black as a shadow itself, swallows the light from the window behind me.

So I stop wearing shoes to school. Walking home across the park, I kick a broken bottle and cut the webbing between my big and second toes. Another memory flashes like a punch in the liver. The slice through skin. A man wearing a green cloth hat tied under his chin and a white face mask with a wet patch from his breath. Someone holds me down with rubber hands. The man mumbles for a while. My mother's voice. The man wipes at me with a cold yellow liquid and with a pair of scissors cuts my penis.

At home from the park. After cleaning up the trail of blood that follows me through the door, Mum produces a box of cotton-wool balls, a sticking plaster and a bottle of the same yellow liquid, marked *Iodine*. As she dabs at the cut between my toes, I ask:

—Mum, what happened to my penis?

Picking up the bottle of iodine from the table and studying the label, I press on to fill the silence:

—I remember a doctor cutting me with shiny scissors, and a bottle of this iodine stuff. I remember screaming!

Ashen-faced, she tut-tuts at my foot, dabbing at the wound.

—In the showers at the pool you can see the whole tip of mine. The other boys have a hood-type thing. It wrinkles in the water.

Still fussing with my toe, she says:

—We believe in different things than those other boys. Dad has the same … She falters, trails off, composes herself: Jesus said those who *truly* believe will make the covenant to circumcise our sons.

—Circumcise?

—Ask your father about it. She rearranges the kitchen chairs to dismiss me.

Walking with a studied limp out through the screen door, down the steps, I stick up a middle finger to my little sisters, Jaz and Fliss, on the trampoline and cross the yard to the police station. I find Dad sitting at his desk, typing with two fingers, his police hat on a pile of papers. The air-conditioning circulates the smell of ink stamps, typewriter ribbons, boot polish and copy paper. My head swims. Dad never can spare time for anyone when he has paperwork to do, and he only does paperwork when someone sits rotting in the cells.

—Hey, Dad. I poke his shoulder.

He ignores me, tap, tap, tap, ding.

—Dad! I shake his arm. Nothing but the shouts of my sisters outside on the trampoline and a truck roaring by on the distant highway. I poke his ribs.

—Buzz off! he yells.

I back away and slip through the courtroom. The heavy vinyl-covered oak desks stink of linseed oil. Out into the jail hall the sun beats down through the skylight. The hot cement burns my feet. I smell piss in the heat and my stomach rises. I blink and focus on a set of filthy fat fingers gripping the prison bars. I can't see the rest of the man in the darkness of the cell. One of the hands disappears and then comes back through the bars holding a blue melamine cup. A gnarled mask scrunched around sharp predatory eyes aches out of the shadows. He opens his mouth to speak, revealing front teeth cracked, yellow and black:

—Get me some fucken water, kid. Water, fuck ya!

A string of drool oozes from his strips-of-liver lips, scabby and swollen. I stand out of his reach in the stretch of sun through the skylight and contemplate his blasted head. Clean shaven and traversed with scars, it lolls to one side like he has a broken neck. As he rocks back and forth, his head disappears from the light and reappears. He resembles a broken lamp, the bulb at an odd angle, flickering before it explodes. He reaches further through the bars to grab me. He drops the blue cup and it bounces on the concrete.

Dad told me melamine doesn't shatter. He showed me. He hit one of those cups with a hammer and said:

—See! Criminals can't commit suicide with the shards.

Suicide? A new word to me. Dad said sometimes people decide they don't have any reason to go on. Life gets too much, I guess. He told me suicide means someone intentionally takes their own life, a serious tone strumming in his voice. I pressed him of course and he said with a final full stop: the word derives from the Latin. A fancy word for self-murder. Dad rattles off definitions, like he memorised the dictionary:

—Murder: the killing of another human under conditions specifically covered by law. Boy, my job involves catching murderers and rapists and thieves and drug addicts and other low-life scum who'd sooner stab you in the guts than help you with your groceries.

The prisoner drools in the cage. I step further out of the gasping low-life's reach.

—Kid! Water, please, boy. The tap in here doesn't work. The shape points at the blue cup. I kick the cup. It bounces off the bars and hits the courtroom door behind me. The man glares at me with his anti-matter eyes.

—Get your own fucken water, scumbag, I spit at him.

Dad comes out the door and catches me mid-sentence. Too late – my mouth runs its course. He slaps the back of my head.

—Get the hell outta here, boy! he yells as I bolt from the jail block.

—

At dinner I ask:

—Dad, what does *circumcision* mean?

Mum drops her fork. It clatters on the table. She glares at me. Dad clears his throat, reaches for the wine bottle.

—Circumcision demonstrates to Jesus that us fellers follow the path, we know the truth, we've heard the living gospel. We know the way home. He takes a large gulp of wine, waiting for me to reply. I don't, so he continues: All the men Friends, and their sons, have undergone circumcision. I guess you could say as a pact. A pact with Jesus.

—Friends? A pact? None of my friends in school have it. You can't see their whole tip-thing.

Jaz laughs and baby Fliss flicks a glob of mashed pumpkin onto the tablecloth.

Mum sucks wind through her teeth and jumps up, sending her chair flying into the kitchen wall. She makes a dash to the sink and comes back with a dishcloth for the table. Dad fills his wine glass again and says:

—Those other boys won't get saved. The Angel of the Lord hasn't whispered the truth to them.

As Mum sits again, Jaz pushes a baby carrot around on her plate and says:

—Dad, do we know the truth?

—Jaz! Mum says: Behave yourself.

—Yeah, Dad! I pipe in: Who told us? And when? I don't remember. Can you tell us again?

—Don't you remember the meetings back in Townsville? Every Sunday, every Wednesday night, with the other Friends? Dad says, draining his glass and refilling.

—Yeah. I think so, but what friends? Jaz tries to hide the carrot under her fork.

—Other believers, Dad says, examining the label on the wine bottle.

—Anyway, I cut in: Today, when I sliced my foot, I remembered getting *circumcision*, and it bloody well hurt!

—Language! Dad yells, slamming his fist down on the table. His wine glass spills over. The off-white linen gulps the red like when friends meet: And you say *circumcise-d* – past tense! Rights his glass.

Mum stands, upsetting her chair again, strides across the kitchen and reaches down the Discipline Stick from atop a cupboard. A flat plank of pine with a handle shape cut into it, it has *Discipline Stick* painted in red capital letters, old homestead style, above a black and white cartoon of a boy bending over, his trousers around his ankles. The boy looks over his shoulder with tears in his wide comic eyes at a disembodied hand paddling his bum. Mum passes it to Dad.

—Where did you learn that language, boy? Dad holds the stick in his right hand, slapping it onto his left palm. Jaz starts crying, which sets the baby off.

—School! I shout above the racket. Sensing a beating anyway, I push my luck. Making a dash for the open front door, I yell over my shoulder:

—I also learned bugger, shit and piss!

—We'll lose this boy, Mum wails as I run across the lawn and leap the fence.

I pause on the other side and lean with a swagger up against the post. When I see Dad peering out the door, I shout:

—And I learned fuck from the scumbag in the jail! You don't like that, hey! Fuck. Fuuuuck!

—Why, boy, I oughta ... Dad rages from the veranda as I sprint up the footpath towards the park.

At school I have a habit of stretching my legs out under my desk to kick at the aluminium edging which separates the carpet and the linoleum. Mrs Crisp yells at me a thousand times to stop. Soon as she leaves, I kick at the edging again. This day, as she walks back in across the lino, the edging springs up like a silver snake and she trips right over it, falls headlong into the desks. Her left arm slaps down on the floor with a loud crack. She screams the same way baby Fliss did when she pulled a cup of tea off a table and melted her chest into her onesie. JJ looks on enthralled as Mrs Crisp bawls on the floor.

JJ and I hang around together now. It took him two whole years to talk to me. I don't notice his odd eyes so much anymore. I've never met JJ's dad. He drives trucks for the nickel mine. Mum doesn't like me hanging out with JJ because I go around to his house after school to watch *The Goodies*. Because of the stupid cult, Mum and Dad forbid television, smoking, drinking, dancing, jewellery, watching movies, cutting your hair if female and having a normal penis if male. JJ's mum has long straight black hair. She always goes barefoot, wears tight blue jeans with a wide flare at the bottom and looks pretty. We steal cigarettes from JJ's mum. *St Moritz – King Size Deluxe Menthols with gold band of authenticity!* it says on the packet.

I saved up four dollars washing the car and oiling the courtroom desks every Saturday to buy a flash new copy of *The Adventures of Tom Sawyer* by Mark Twain. It has a picture of Tom and Huck on the front and a Mississippi riverboat behind them. I swagger and smoke, like Tom. I reckon I started younger than him. Adults at the servo sure stare hard when they see a gang of seven-year-old boys puffing away. I also bought an authentic Barlow knife, which I carry at all times, like Tom. I've read the whole book a thousand times, except the missing pages. My new copy fixed that. I show JJ.

—Already read it, he says.

But I don't think he has. I have to explain to him, over and over, the motivations behind our escapades, which I base on Tom's adventures. I convince him that if you want to have a fulfilling life you need to create your own adventures. I practise what I preach, and I write everything down as well. Why else have adventures? He gets it, comes meowing outside my window in the middle of the night. I scramble out of bed and we sprint down the path into the public gardens, breathless, heads reeling with plots. The next day at school both of us fall asleep at our desks.

We start a gang one night in the park to protect ourselves from the prowler that heaps of people report to my father. This prowler, they say, also kills animals. A few people have reported finding household pets dead in bizarre circumstances. We call our gang The Wreckers, based on a film JJ loves called *The Wanderers*. He says if I think Tom Sawyer has clout, then I should go see this film. He asked the projectionist at the drive-in for the poster he has tacked up in his room. A bunch of mean dudes with greased-back hair all glaring into the camera, wearing beat-up leather jackets with cigarettes dangling from lips or tucked behind ears. A couple of them have shirts unbuttoned so you can see their chests. A few wear cool hats.

The other boys we let into our gang have to bring something to the table. We let Charlie in because his dad owns the pub and his mum owns the supermarket. Daryl can join because he says he can get us the green tobacco all the bikies like to smoke.

Here comes Ren, sweating from the climb to our gang headquarters on the hill behind the medical centre. Breathless, Ren says:

—Can I join The Wanderers?

—Wreckers! Dip-shit, JJ snaps: And *no*, fuck off, ya dome-head poofter! Ren has a dome-shaped head with stringy mouse-brown hair sticking up like fairy floss and a sore-looking welt above his left eyebrow from his habit of rubbing his face. He has episodes where he rocks back and forth saying *no-no-nooo*, swatting at the air around his head. Ren remains calm, but a darkness clouds his eyes.

—We should let him join, I say, watching his still face and stormy eyes.

—Fucken … why? JJ looks confused.

—He can take a beating.

Ren smiles. I've never seen him smile until now. I know him better than the other boys. Ren lives across the road. He comes over every day with his toys and doesn't take them home. Every day he has a black eye or a busted lip or bruises on his chin. An enormous collection of his Tonka trucks and Matchbox cars, marbles, even an expensive-looking telescope, overcrowd my bedroom.

—Ren, why do you leave your toys? I ask.

He sits there building a Lego supermarket, complete with shoppers pushing little trolleys. As he ploughs a red fire truck with real flashing lights through the shopping centre, mashing the plastic housewives into the carpet, he says:

—So I can play with them longer.

I know what he means. I climbed a tree to see into his yard one night. I saw Ren crawling around bleeding on the kitchen floor. A shadow moved, his dad smashing a collection of Matchbox cars with a hammer on the back steps.

A concrete driveway, suffering under the Australian sun, yawns like a cracked tongue between our house and the police station. You have to walk up the driveway to the front door. If I hear the rusty gate swing open, I stick my head out of my window to see who has come to visit.

The creaking gate wakes me. A pair of feet slap on the concrete. Wailing and banging on the side of the house.

—Help. *Help!* Officer cop, he raped and bashed me. Help! *Rape!* The voice chokes. I stick my head out of my window, trying to get a look at her in the shadow cast by the house. She sees me peering out and starts up some hellish wailing, bashing the wall with her fists. My parents stir and a strip of light blinks under my door. Footsteps down the narrow hall. A loud thump and much cursing as Dad cracks his shin on a table or something which Mum moved without him noticing. The veranda light comes on and reveals an Aboriginal woman wearing a white nightie splattered with blood, both of her eyes swollen shut. A strip of eyeball flickers around under one drooping lid, trying to focus on me as I look down on her. Dad emerges.

—Officer? Help. Me old man raped me with a bottle. Fucken broke inside … Help!

—Slow down … Let me get a look at you, Dad soothes. He leads her by the arm into the light.

Dad spies my head sticking out of the window, whispers to the woman and then shouts for Mum to call the doctor and an ambulance from Charters Towers. Dad and the bleeding woman disappear up the path into the police station.

I wake to the sound of water hitting the wall. I drag myself from my bed and look out. Dad has a hose, washing blood off the house.

—Dad, what did the screaming woman mean by *rape*?

—Rape? he mumbles, not looking up: The unlawful compelling through physical force, or duress, to have sexual intercourse.

—Unlawful. Sexual. Intercourse?

—Illegal fucking.

3

The phone rings. Mum picks up, listens awhile and says:

—Huh? Oh, okay, why don't you come over here? Oh … okay. She hangs up and says Dad wants to see me in his office. I drag myself over there. This hasn't happened before, ringing the house from ten paces away. I wonder what he caught me at. I find him in the courtroom, sitting in the judge's chair.

—Bren, I've got to talk to you about something important.

—Okay.

—I have to go and catch some deer poachers in the Maryvale Reserve.

—Oh.

—Most people consider this quite dangerous, so I have to tell you I mightn't come home. He looks into my eyes, puts his hands on my shoulders: Until I get home, you have to act as Man of the House. And if I never come back, you have to look after your mother, and your sisters.

—Never come back, Dad?

—Some persons do desperate things to avoid getting caught. They might kill me, boy.

—You mean, they might murder you, Dad? I say, my voice breaking.

He gives me a huge hug. Dad never hugs me. I don't remember another time he hugged me.

—Now go, help your mother. I need to get my weapons ready.

—Dad …

—Yeah?

—How do you define a *person*?

—The books you read, and the people you meet, he says, oiling his gun.

The next morning Dad has already left. Mum sits in the early light at the kitchen table. She doesn't hear me coming down the hall. Rays through the curtains catch her face; tears stream down her cheeks. She looks ten years older.

No JJ meowing tonight. I strike out alone into the sleeping town. Everything sparkles, covered in dew. Fog swirls around the fences. Owls and night-birds screaming in the gardens. Toads on the footpath. Outside the pub on Redbank Drive I see a figure slouched in the phone box. I recognise Ren and knock on the illuminated booth.

—Ren!

He doesn't acknowledge me. I push the door of the booth. It folds inwards, hits him in the back. He turns on his heel, facing me eyes wide, vacant, pupils flickering like insects.

—Ren? I say, startled.

Nothing but the soft thud of moths hitting the bare neon bulb in the box. The bulb buzzes, responding to dusty wings. He thrusts an arm out of the phone booth. A dead cat hangs from his fist, knuckles white, squeezing hard on its neck. Intestines balloon from its mouth, along with some white stuff, like cauliflower. I run like a poodle encountering a wolf.

The news rolls through the town in the morning. The groundsman fished a tabby from the pool, every bone in its body smashed, guts out like someone squeezed it.

Dad comes home from the deer-poacher gig with a gaggle of scruffy, shirtless, tattooed men. He's chained them together with their arms tangled around each other. Dad drags the whole group of six out of the back of his police Toyota by pulling one of the men by the beard. I taunt the shit out of them as they sit glaring at me from the cells. I skip up and down, singing about the glory of freedom while going through their bags.

Dad has piled the men's belongings on the concrete outside the bars. He sits in the office typing. They have an armoury of weapons, sleeping bags, radios, and the skins and antlers of about twenty deer in various stages of stink and preservation. They have a huge plastic container of the green tobacco my gang likes to smoke. I call them a bunch of scumbags and criminals as I help myself to a handful. They also have a couple of dirty Orchy orange juice bottles with bits of garden hose stuck in the sides. It all looks pretty sinister. One of the lengths of hose has an aluminium-foil funnel full of green tobacco stuffed in the end. This must work as a pipe of some sort. We use corncob pipes, like Tom Sawyer. I steal a whizzer-looking bowie knife: a full-sheath blade with a stainless-steel bust of an Indian chief's head on top of an antler handle. One of the foul-looking men, who has no front teeth, snarls at me as I make my exit:

—Little cunt, I'll wring ya fucken neck for nickin me shit.

I turn back to the bars to ask him what he means by *cunt*, but as I turn I kick a rolled-up swag. My toe hits something hard. I stick my hand in and find a pistol. I figure Dad hasn't seen it, so I nick that too.

I show the gun and the knife and the green tobacco to the other boys in my gang. I say *my* gang, because I beat Daryl fair and square in a fistfight for the title. Daryl's dad belongs to a bikie gang. I don't know which gang – not that I'd name them if I did; Daryl and I steal stuff from their headquarters all the time. Anyway, Daryl stands a bit taller than me. He has long black hair parted in the middle. He also has a hard head – you can smack him full knuckles to the chin and he doesn't blink. I beat him by resorting to trying to choke him to death. I near broke my hands. Daryl respects me now. Says he thinks that I carry *the crazy gene*, one of those freaks born without fear. I want to take him along one night to follow Ren, show him what crazy means. I think I will tell him, but I bet he won't believe me.

I doubt I'll ever meet a better thief than Daryl. He'll nick anything not nailed down. He lifted a bottle of tablets from his dad's gang headquarters. They have a rickety busted-up shed in the scrub surrounded by rusted barbed wire and guarded by two docile Dobermans. Our hideout up on the hill behind the medical centre has far superior engineering. We built it out of stones, old sheet-iron and wrecked car doors, and we call it a fortress. The Wreckers meet at the stroke of midnight, either in the fortress for drinking rum, smoking and eating crap, or down on the school oval for general mischief.

Daryl turns up with these pills. He calls them *salt tablets*, claims that truck drivers use them so they can drive for days without falling asleep and killing themselves. I take a green one and a red one. Charlie takes two green ones. JJ refuses, even after we call him a poof. He says he tried them before and they made him not shit for a year. Daryl chews up five, two red and three green. He washes them down with a huge swig of Bundaberg Rum. Daryl. The wildest boy I know. I mean, besides Ren, but in a different way.

We whoop up hell in the town, smash some windows at the theatre, break into the school canteen and eat all the potato chips, plus about a dozen boxes of sultanas each. We break the lock on the school caretaker's gardening shed and mess up his tools and piss into the lawnmower petrol tank. Charlie finds a toolbox with a padlock on it. He breaks the lock off with a hammer and goes quiet over in the corner. The curiosity kills me. I feel like I can fly. I go over and find Charlie poring over a glossy magazine with photographs of two women licking each other between the legs. I grab the magazine from Charlie. He snatches it back and pushes me over.

—Get ya fucken own. The box has heaps! Eyes glued to the photos.

I get myself a magazine from the toolbox. It has a title in bubble-type writing: *New Cunts, No. 12 – October 1976*. Underneath the title, a picture of a woman sticking her tongue into another woman's …

—Hey, what do ya call a girl's bits again? Charlie breaks into my thoughts.

—My mum says you call it a *sninny*, I say.

Daryl, who has a copy of a magazine called *Oui*, says, laughing at me:

—A fucken *sninny*! They call it a *cunt*, ya gaylord! Look, on the front of the fucken magazine: *New Cunts*. Christ. Shakes his head: My dad has a couple of these, Daryl adds: I saw my uncle jacking off through the window. He had one of these too.

—Jacking off? I look up from a picture of a woman sticking her whole hand into another woman's cunt. Both women look at the camera, tongue on teeth.

—Yeah, I know about jacking off, Charlie says: I do it all the time. Feels good, man.

Daryl laughs, loud, and it echoes across the school oval, disturbs a flock of plovers sitting around in puddles from the sprinkler. He claps his hand over his mouth. We listen for a bit. Only the *chhk chhk* of the sprinkler and an occasional squawk.

—You actually *admit* to wanking! Daryl whispers.

—Jacking off … wanking … what? I ask.

—Wanking, or jacking off … Same thing, man, Daryl says.

Daryl says *man* a lot since he started hanging out with his uncle.

—My uncle Johnny told me, in the city, in Townsville, you can pay a woman and she'll let you growl her out. He said you can pay em and they'll rub you all over with erotic oil and then jack you off. He called it a happy ending.

—Growl out? You still didn't tell me what *wanking* means, man. I call him *man* to see if he notices. He doesn't notice, so I say it again:

—Man, tell me what the fuck wanking means, and growling out, now, cunt.

—Don't call me a *cunt*, man. You call women cunts, Daryl snaps, angry, glaring at me.

—Why do you call women cunts?

—Uncle Johnny said so, says you call women cunts coz they have cunts. He even told me a joke. It goes: What do you call a woman?

Charlie and I look at each other then back at Daryl. Charlie shrugs.

—A life-support machine for a cunt! He laughs out loud again, echoing across the oval. The joke goes over my head. I've never heard the words *life*, *support* and *machine* said together, until now.

—What about *growling out*? I ask.

Daryl thinks for a moment, lights a cigarette, shrugs:

—I dunno, man … I dunno. I'll ask Johnny and let ya know. Then, opening a centrefold: Look at this, man. Sweet as a nun's cunt on Sunday.

We realise JJ hasn't said a word for ages and look over. JJ sits on the lawnmower, one of those ride-on ones with the big comfy vinyl seats, with his penis out of his jeans, tugging at it furiously.

—What the hell! Daryl laughs extra loud this time: JJ, stop wanking in front of us, man. Put ya cock back in ya pants. Jesus!

—Cock? What do you mean?

—His penis, his *cock*, you wanker! Daryl shouts at me.

—I haven't got *my* cock in *my* hands, so how can you call *me* a wanker? I've never heard that word. My mum calls it a diddle.

—*Diddle!* What the fuck … kinda poofter word! Daryl yells, punching me in the stomach.

I lie in the dirt and oil-spills on the gardener's shed floor, winded, gasping for breath. I manage to stand again and see Charlie drooling over one of the magazines, trying to get his cock out. Charlie has the body weight of at least four normal kids. He eats stolen chocolate bars from his mother's supermarket, and he drinks rum like a normal kid drinks Coke. He has a lot of trouble getting his arm under his belly. He grunts and sweats and pulls on his cock until he falls over, huffing like he's run from the law. The wrinkled bit he has, which I don't, looks red raw, poking out from under his belly like a rat's nose peeking from under a stove. JJ, contemplating this scene, his cock hard and proud in his hand, says:

—I told ya about them salt tablets. I couldn't wank for a week, and, I swear, I didn't shit till Christmas.

After we finish laughing, Daryl, who's eaten five tablets, gets his cock out of his jeans and it looks kind of droopy. He slaps at it a bit but nothing much happens. He glances over at me:

—Maybe you should get yours out, man. Let's see if the salties have affected you.

So I pop it right out of my jeans through the fly and JJ gasps:

—What happened to your cock? You got no beanie!

—You've had a *circumnavigation*! exclaims Daryl.

—Circum*cisioned*, ya fucken idiot. Charlie's voice, shaking.

—Circum*cised.* I correct them all.

—They chopped off your beanie! JJ, exasperated.

—Jesus told my parents to get me circumcised … because the Prophet whispered us the living gospel. It fucken hurt, I say, examining the scar.

—

The next day in school we can't sit still. We ping around the room from the salt tablets until Mrs Crisp clues on we've taken pills of some kind and searches our bags. JJ, the wanker, has the entire bottle in his lunch box. *Amphetamines.* A new word. Mrs Crisp says having my Barlow knife at school, and the drugs, constitute illegal acts. I've broken the law. People will call me a criminal. It feels fantastic. Dad will lay into me with the Discipline Stick for a good twenty minutes. He'll lock me in the cell. As Daryl, JJ, Charlie and I sit in the principal's office, waiting for him to come down from teaching Grade Seven and serve us the cuts for having drugs in school, Daryl says:

—Hey, Bren, I asked Uncle Johnny what *growling out* means … He said it means licking a woman's cunt.

—Why would you lick a woman's cunt? I ask, remembering the pictures from the glossy magazines. I can smell the paper.

—Johnny said women love that shit.

—So, if women like it, why pay them so you can do it?

—I asked the same thing! Uncle Johnny says growling out a woman *rocks your world.* Then my mum screamed at him to stop filling my mind with filth.

—So licking a woman's cunt, women call that filthy, even though they like it? I say as the principal bursts in.

We each receive six lashes with a bamboo cane across our palms. Well, I get seven as the principal heard me say the word *cunt.*

—

Easter school holidays, 1980, I learn about hell. A huge rain monsoon makes it across the mountain ranges from the coast. All major bridges on the highway flood and Greenvale loses contact with the rest of the universe. The water level breaks every record, the town overrun by stranded truck drivers and busloads of tourists. The courtroom at the police station has seven families sleeping there.

One family with a caravan full of kids introduce themselves to us as *Friends*. These Friends come from the mysterious meetings back in the city before we moved to Greenvale – the first Friends I've seen in the flesh since we moved here three years ago. They have a Prophet with them. An important man, Mum says, scalping up her hair tighter than I've seen it. Mum reckons this bloke speaks for God himself. The rain caught them out while heading north to Cairns, via the mountains instead of the coastal route, for the unfamiliar scenery. The Prophet, named Bruce the Elder, has a sick mother in Cairns and the family of Friends agreed *kindly* to drive him the six hundred and thirty-two kilometres to see her.

These Prophets travel around the world without any possessions or money, living off their Friends. I overheard Dad call one of the Prophets a *tramp preacher*. I guess you could call them that, but they always look sharp and own nice things, and stink of expensive city-folk aftershave, not like tramps at all.

Anyway, this Prophet and the family of Friends move right into our living room. The family look pretty uptight. They have one son and three daughters. The boy comes into my room. I tell him to fuck off. None of the daughters looks like a potential Becky Thatcher, so I pay no interest. The Prophet, Bruce the Elder, calls me *boy* and *son* and *champ*, takes a real interest in what I say about anything. I will have to put up with this phoney shit for the entire Easter holidays. Rain torrents out of the sky. The government sends in helicopters with supplies for the town. No trucks can cross the swollen rivers. Mum and Dad call every Prophet a *Worker*, for reasons I can't comprehend. They don't work at all, just preach the whole time about hell and damnation, say the government has fooled everyone because they have evil intentions. Bankers have the Devil whispering by their bedsides.

We crowd around the Prophet in the lounge room while the rain belts down and the wind tears at the roof and trees cascade against the sides of houses. He reads from the Holy Bible, then starts on about how we should thank the Lord for choosing us and blah blah blah when he stops mid-sentence and points at a school photograph of me on the wall above Mum's piano:

—Except that one. He has the smile of Lucifer himself. He'll need some extra attention.

My mother gasps in horror. All eyes turn on me.

Later, sitting atop the garden shed with JJ, smoking a St Moritz, sipping rum, I see Bruce the tramp preacher sneak past in the shadows of the house and peek through the window, at the boy of the visiting family of Friends in the shower. JJ's sneaker squeaks on the tin of the roof and Bruce looks up. At that same moment the donkey Santa brought for Jaz at Christmas snorts and kicks in her pen. Startled, because he didn't see the donkey huddled up under the tarp that Dad had slung over a tree to give her some shelter from the rain, the tramp preacher scuttles back to the house.

4

I accompany Dad to a cattle station. A horse has sunk to her neck in a dehydrated dam. We go to see if we can help drag her out. Since that monsoon at Easter and all through the summer not a mist of rain has cooled the dust. We arrive and see the farmer already out in the mud, stroking the horse's head. Thrashing wild thing. She has wide eyes, sensing her doom. Sinking deeper, she snorts. When the farmer sees the police Land Rover come over the ridge of the dam, he stops and sloops towards us, knee deep. Green cracked clay on the edges of the dam lifts out towards the baking sun like a set of smashed dinner plates. The whole place smells like the inside of a fish tank when you clean it out.

The farmer and Dad tie a rope around the horse's neck to the tow bar of the four by four, but we can't get any traction in the broken clay on the banks of the dam. Raptors like question marks in rusted ironbark spires. The farmer squelches back out, puts the barrel of a .22 to the white diamond on the horse's forehead, pulls the trigger. Blood arcs a metre in the air, nostrils flare, final breath taken.

—'Bout a dozen more next dam over, mumbles the farmer.

All the cattle stations out here have names. Scattered along the Burdekin River you'll find Ups and Downs, Greenvale Station and Lucky Downs. Further north-east, above Mount Dora, you'll find The Valley of Lagoons.

North-west of Greenvale, out by Mount Esk, Conjuboy Station.

Dad takes the whole family to the slaughterhouse at Lucky Downs, to help out and share in the spoils. Lucky Downs has its own butcher shop. They prepare cuts and make sausages to sell to the town-folk. I'd describe it more as a slaughter shed on a little hill in a bone yard full of crows. Stone and wood, a corrugated-iron roof, concrete floors with half-pipe drains, and a little crane with a hook to hoist the beast. A farmer named Henry climbs the rails and stares down at a forlorn-looking cow. I scramble up beside Henry. The cow looks up at me; it moos helplessly as Henry takes aim with a bolt-gun.

—Senses its death, he drawls as he fires. The bolt hits the cow, centre of her head, and she drops to the floor. Henry scrambles back down, emerges on the other side of the pen with a cable in hand. He kicks the cow onto her back and grabs both of her hind legs, sticks the hook through the shins above the hoofs and yells out:

—Hit it!

A generator starts, the cable tightens and the beast in a river of her own blood floats out into the dressing room. They crank her up into the rafters, head down. Henry cuts her exposed throat. A frothy waterfall of blood pours out of the cow, pools on the concave concrete floor and runs into the half-pipe drains.

—Kids, get the buckets, get outside and get that blood down to the pit! Henry shouts at us.

We rush outside to a pile of ten-litre buckets and fill them with blood sluicing from the pipes sticking out of the wall. We pick our way among the bones of the thousand dead, shooing away the crows that scream at us, eyes, beaks and talons flashing. At the bottom of the little hill by a creepy pandanus tree and a rotten wooden fence we pour the blood into a deep trench. Black feathers float in the congealed mess. We race up the hill again, skipping over skulls glinting in the sun.

Driving around farms. Killing animals. Dad keeps me busy like this all through the day. Also, because he knows of my nocturnal activities, he takes me out at night shooting rabbits. We get home way after midnight and he has me up again in the dawn, helping fight bush fires or attending the scenes of car accidents or pulling marijuana plants from the bank of Redbank Creek.

Timothy's family tree has roots deep in these parts, since the 1880s droving days. We visit Timothy and his parents out on their cattle station, where I encounter a kid named Albatross. I've seen him around school. He attends sometimes, but the Aboriginal kids stick to themselves. Albatross's dad works as a ringer. He lives on the station. Albatross sits up in the rafters of the old sawmill, sneaking a cigarette, his gangly legs tucked up, bushy head hunched over like a skinny owl. I look for ant lions, little grey creatures that burrow down into the sawdust. They leave a dent where they tunnel in. I sit in the creaking shade of the shed, filling a jar with powdered wood, looking for an ant lion to trap. A voice comes from above:

—I saw your dad kissing Timbo's mum in the orchard.

I hide my fright and answer:

—Bullshit! Where?

I don't believe him. Albatross jumps down from the rafters into the sawdust. He leads me into the orchard and shows me the tree he sat in while he watched them kiss. Timothy says Albatross likes to spin yarns about the adults. I don't let on I know this. We climb and sit among the boughs and eat mandarins and tamarinds. Albatross lives among the trees of the orchard in a huge tin shed with an old bus parked up the side. His family sleep in the bus and hang out in the shed the rest of the time. The shed has loads of busted old comfy sofas with wobbly split-open arms and a huge antique table covered in beer cans and rum bottles. Everyone calls him Trossy for short.

—Your parents swing, Trossy says, drooling from the sour of a tamarind.

—What do you mean, swing? I say, wiping my eye from a squirting rind.

—Crispin, he says, meaning his older brother who's moved away to boarding school: Crispin told me most adults swing these days, at parties and stuff.

—They do have parties sometimes, I say, pondering this. I've seen melon balls, cheese platters, fondue and coffee liqueurs. Never seen a swing, though.

—

Trossy's Uncle Parky lives in an old bus too, way out in the bush on the banks of a huge cold river that flows out of the volcanic limestone mountains. The swimming hole up at Green River has a terrific swing. You get up so high you forget to let go sometimes. Uncle Parky comes into town to buy supplies and he always visits my dad. He looks nine thousand years old and stands about that many feet tall. When he smiles, he radiates wisdom. You can't help but listen to what he has to say, about anything. Because of the circumstances in which he entered the world, no one knows his age. Parky has the longest feet I've ever seen; his toes gnarl up and point in different directions. Dad said Parky has never worn shoes his entire life and broke all his toes kicking saplings on horseback in the dark. Everyone calls him Uncle Parky, though only Albatross can claim that fact.

Today Parky comes into the police station bending through an entrance no one uses. He huffs under a load of groceries, his Akubra beaten and filthy, the band on it not a sweatband but a band of sweat, a black cockatoo feather punched through the felt. He catches me at my dad's cop-desk, my hand in the petty cash box. Parky shouts out to my dad, laughs at me stuffing everything back into the drawer. He lets me think I've got away with it, then dobs on me.

Dad goes on about the hell I cause for the family, the trouble at school. Parky tut-tuts through his giant grey beard and looks at me out of his one good eye. I've heard the story a few times. When Parky's tribe chose him as witch doctor, they burned out one of his eyes with a red-hot stick, so he could navigate the dreaming. Way back in the droving days, Parky's tribe caught wind of the approaching cowboys who'd struck north from Charters Towers to claim land along the Burdekin River. For reasons unknown they stuffed Parky in a hollow log and disappeared into the bush. One of the cowboys, Timothy's grandfather, found Parky and waited with him by the log for three days. Parky's tribe didn't return, so he adopted him. Dad told me Parky looked about four when found by the cowboys way back in nineteen hundred and something.

Before you know it, my dad agrees I should accompany Parky and Albatross out to his bus on Green River. By doing so, I'll for certain learn some discipline.

—Some bush tucker and a few lessons in life from Parky will do you good, boy, Dad laughs, slapping my back.

As we arrive at Parky's bus house in the mountains by Green River, the sun slips beyond the horizon. I can't see a damn thing. Uncle Parky and Albatross say they can both see clear as day. They reckon I suffer from white-man blindness. I say, on account of their black skin, if they close their mouths, I can't see them at all. They consider this the funniest shit they've heard in years and deliberately melt into the darkness. I flail around in the moonless night like an idiot, tripping over logs and god knows what else.

Parky starts up a raging bonfire and goes walkabout. Albatross and I sit around smoking Noogoora burr. He says Noogoora burr holds a sacred place in Aboriginal witch-doctor ceremonies – Parky showed it to him. Albatross prepares it for smoking, boasting Parky has decided to teach him the ways of the Kuradji. We lounge around, puffing on the bitter stems. You have to toke it gently or risk burning the crap out of your lips. We marvel at the stars out here in the middle of nowhere, the Milky Way like a smashed windscreen on the road.

—What does Kuradji mean?

—It means *clever man*.

—Like a witch doctor?

—Parky doesn't like white man's words. You shouldn't call him a witch!

A twig snaps and Uncle Parky materialises by the fire with a half-skinned goanna. I blush red as the embers.

—I don't care if you call me a witch, little feller, but ya shouldn't smoke the Noogoora burr. It'll fuck with ya white-man mind.

Sleeping by the fire under the stars. Dreams of serpents and eagles and Uncle Parky. He walks on water and rides clouds around.

In the morning we eat cold goanna and drink billy tea. Parky has a smoke and then takes us boys up into a giant limestone gorge. He reckons it formed when lava exploded out of the mountain a billion years ago. As the lava cooled, it cracked open like the top of a cake in an oven. He points out a heap of caves, explains they guard the bones of his Kuradji ancestors. He shows us where to find fossils: perfect fern leaves and weird ancient fish skeletons frozen in limestone.

—Where we stand, boys, you won't find older land anywhere on earth. Parky points to a crag in a long broken length of rock: That rock over there has an entire legend attached to it, the legend of the Kunia woman. The Kunia woman got herself captured, raped and killed by a lizard man. If you know how to look right, her legs jut up – see those rocky outcrops in the distance.

We gaze off into the distance awhile, small among the clamour of birds, the song of the river.

By and by, in the gorge with the deep green lagoon, with the best swing in the world, we break for lunch. Uncle Parky says to have a swim while he nicks off and hunts for some bush tucker. He disappears in the trees on the ridge, and Trossy and I strip down. We kick about, stir up a jewfish and some turtles from under a floating log. Taking turns, we try to touch the bottom, clearly visible, but far deeper than it looks. We drift on our backs, shouting up at the cliff above the lagoon, sending echoes down the limestone gorge. After a while we decide diving sounds like a good idea. We clamber up through the trees and make it to the edge. Albatross dives off, leaving me on the cliff. He floats down below, egging me on to jump; then, he freezes and turns whiter than me. The colour in his face drains away like spilled ink in a sink and he shouts something incomprehensible. Thrashes about, near drowning himself.

—What? I yell down to him.

—Yowie! he screams, pointing up at me.

—What?

—Fucken yowie. HELP!

I've read about the fight-or-flight mechanism in the reference-only section at the library; the fear in his voice triggers it. I turn on my heel, ready to punch and run. Behind me towers a ferociously ugly creature covered in thick orange hair. Clumps of mud, broken sticks and gore matt and snarl and hang off it like dags on a sheep. It has dull grey eyes, a flat pushed-up nose, and teeth like an English bulldog's. It snorts and then roars. I vomit right in its face from the stench and terror. Projectile vomit, too – it hits the yowie right in the eyes. It roars again, louder. I run like a sinner to heaven and dive off the cliff. In mid-air, as I turn like a thrown cat to see if the thing follows, I see Trossy sprinting through the trees on the opposite bank, screams sending up flocks of birds.

Shadows stretch through limbs and over ridges. Parky appears with a skinned kangaroo. I holler down from the tree, tell him we saw a yowie and that Albatross ran off and hasn't come back. Parky looks concerned. He turns in a circle, stops, listens a moment and strides off into the bush. Alone here I won't sleep. I shat my pants when I vomited on the yowie, and my arse burns.

Right on the edge of night Parky returns, empty-handed. We huddle around the fire, waiting for Albatross. Parky gets mighty fidgety; he smokes cigarette after cigarette. A terror grows in me that Parky will disappear into the dark, leaving me as yowie prey. I will never feel comfortable in the bush again. Tugging at his grey nicotine-stained moustache, Parky says:

—White fellers don't usually see the yowie. What did it look like, boy?

—Ugly! I inch closer to the fire.

—Did it say anything?

—Huh?

—Did it speak? He lights another smoke, stretches out his legs so the flames flicker on his calluses and broken toes.

—No, it roared at me and I piss-bolted.

—Someone has died. He coughs. The tone of Parky's voice sticks a cold finger in my liver and I find myself trying to crawl onto his lap. He laughs, but not at me.

—The yowie comes to let us know someone in our family has passed. It doesn't eat people.

—Passed?

—She sings in the songline now.

—Who sings?

—Albatross's aunt. I think she passed over. The yowie came to tell him.

—What do you mean, songline? Passed over?

—She died, mate. Our people go to the songline on the other side, to sing with the ancestors.

One of the logs on the fire collapses into coals, sending up a shower of sparks, startling both of us. Parky rises to stoke the fire, then from the waterskin strapped to the front of his four-wheel drive he fills his billy. He slips out of the light; my heart races again.

—Where did you see it? he says, emerging again into the circle cast by the fire.

—On the cliff above the lagoon.

—The cold lagoon?

—Yeah.

—Ha! I'd worry more about the Rainbow Serpent who lives in the bottom of that pool!

—What!

—Big feller … 'bout three times the length of my bus.

5

The Wreckers loses a member. Ren has disappeared from school and the teachers say he's moved away. We size up David to take his place. Sometimes David turns up at school and sits in his cowboy clothes at the back. He lives out on Greenvale Station, the first pastoral lease in these parts, from which the whole town derives its name. He and his two sisters attend the School of the Air. They do most of their classes over a two-way radio. He stands a good foot taller than us and – unlike us boys who never wear shoes – he wears boots, proper horse-riding boots with the tall heel to stick through stirrups. He always wears a chequered collared shirt with pearl clip-buttons, and jeans with a man's belt done up to the last notch, because he looks skinny as a goanna. The extra length of his belt hangs to his knee. He has an Akubra hat and a cheeky-looking gleam in his eye.

I don't know when my sister fell in love with him, but she stands there in the playground when he comes to school, stares at him with a dreamy look on her face, like a sated kitten curled up in belly fur. I know she fell in love because I heard her telling her pet donkey, Smudge. Jaz always talks to her donkey, mostly about how much she hates me for playing jokes on her all the time. My favourite trick never fails. I get up on the roof above the pen Dad built to keep Smudge in at night. Sooner or later Jaz comes out and starts chatting away. I call out *Hey, Jaz!* She looks up and I dump a bucket of ice water in her face.

I go to Charters Towers with Dad. He wears his police uniform with the formal hat, not his bush one, so I know he has official business. Whenever this happens, he forgets I exist. I can go off into the town by myself and spend my money on whatever I damn well please. I find a store called Ye Olde Magic Shoppe. I love magic tricks. I purchase a fake pen that comes with a bottle of disappearing ink. On the label it has a picture of a bloke squirting ink on a tablecloth in front of a horrified waiter. I wander around Charters Towers for several hours, pushing my absence from Dad's watchful eye as far as possible. When I get back to the police station, he stands on the veranda talking to a cop with a whole bunch of stripes on his sleeve.

—Hey, Dad, check out the pen I bought. It has real ink and everything.

I aim the nib at him and squirt the whole chamber on his police shirt. It splashes over his shoulder and collar and runs down inside. The other cop looks like the horrified waiter on the label. Dad's face becomes a detached mask for a moment. As the ink evaporates, the mask wrinkles into a grin and the other cop laughs.

A policewoman runs down the veranda and says:

—Bob, an emergency call came in from Greenvale!

Dad hurries off and leaves me here with the head cop.

—Funny little bugger! he chortles and slaps my back.

Dad emerges and says we have to go. I have trouble keeping up with him as he strides to the Toyota. We speed off. He starts the siren to get through the town traffic. Out on the highway as we barrel towards Greenvale, Dad wears that mask again.

—What happened, Dad?

He stares ahead, ignores me, concentrating on the road.

—Dad?

—What? he says, fussing with the dial on the radio.

—Has something bad happened at home?

—Right now, I dunno.

—You don't know what happened?

—I don't know, he says and then sighs.

Nothing, for the next hour and forty-five minutes. I watch the minute hand on the dashboard clock turn all the way around as the trees and road signs flash past and the dull hum of four-by-four tyres on bitumen sends me into a trance. As we cross the Redbank Creek Bridge on the outskirts of Greenvale, the radio comes alive. Among the fuzz a shaky voice says:

—We can confirm that, Bob. The boy, David, from Greenvale Station has died in an accident.

Dad glances at me in time to see my face fall. As we pull in to the driveway of the police station, I try to imagine what Jaz will say to her donkey.

Jaz sobs her heart out for hours, her arm around Smudge's neck. Soon after, Jaz stops talking to her donkey and she stops skipping everywhere. She spends countless hours down the side of the house, bouncing a ball off the wall, talking to herself. She starts fighting with her friends at school. She comes crying to me in the playground with some story or another about what such-and-such a girl said to her.

We go to David's funeral in Charters Towers – the first time I've set foot inside an actual church. They've closed the casket. David fell off the back of a truck and broke his neck. I try to imagine what he looks like. Mischief gone from his eyes.

I don't want to ever love anyone … in case they die.

—

Change. Like the dread I feel when alone in the bush. Mum and Dad have spent the entire year drawing up blueprints for a house they want built in the city. This change feels like the finality of death that surrounds David's chair at the back of the class. Mum and Dad explain we have no choice but to pack up, say goodbye to Greenvale and return to Townsville, so I can go to high school. None of my friends have to leave town to start Year Eight. They have rooms reserved for them at a boarding school in Charters Towers. Most of them have already left, laughing and excited, making plans for all the capers they intend to get up to with their parents hours away.

—

We leave Greenvale forever today. I dreamed last night that JJ died in a solo gunfight. I went to his funeral. The whole gang huddled around. Charlie cried. In my dream Daryl stood for an eternity, staring down into JJ's grave. He had his long hair cut because he moved to the city and his new school wouldn't let him in class with his greasy locks. All of us boys chucked our old Wreckers gang jackets down onto the coffin. Those glorious jackets, filthy and loved, our gang name on the back in black Hobbytex.

As we roll out of town, the removal truck behind us, and strike out for the highway and a new life, I see JJ fishing off the Redbank Creek Bridge. I look out the back window as we pass. He gives me the finger, his mad orange hair like the setting sun.

Part Two
Deadly Nureyev

'All right, then, I'll go to hell.'
Mark Twain

1

January 1984, a week after my twelfth birthday. We roll into Townsville to our new house in the wet. Pouring rain for an entire month. We turn into Hazel Street in the middle of a new estate in the suburb of Rasmussen. Dad points out our new house. You can't miss it, though you can barely see through the belting rain. Our house and two more stand in the belly of an empty cul-de-sac. We gasp in surprise – on our new front mud puddle huddles a crowd of about forty people. We pull up as the removalist truck booms around the corner right on our tail. Mum winds down her window to get a good look at the crowd. Dad swears through his teeth:

—Shit, every bloody Friendly in town, come to welcome us!

He slinks out of the car, not bothering about the rain at all. Mum near has one of those conniptions I read about in Regency romance novels. She has her hair down, wearing a big floppy hat and sunglasses. She scalps herself trying to get her hair up under her hat. These apocalyptic nuts have come to judge her every move.

I jump out of the car and take off up the street. I have zero desire to get pawed at and hand-pumped by a bunch of religious zealots. I get away around the corner and hunch up under the eaves of a half-built house all abandoned and forlorn in the haze. I pull out a wet bent smoke and stand there cursing at the rain and the sky and God and everything because my matches have sogged through. A figure looms out of the mist, jumping puddles, puffing away on a cigarette.

—Oi! I yell into the wind. He comes closer, looking for my voice. When he spies me, he gets up under the eaves. I recognise him, one of the gaggle of Friendlies from our front mud puddle.

—Lookin for you! he says, lighting my cigarette for me with a wicked-looking zippo.

I take a puff and measure him up. We smoke in silence for a few minutes, and then he says:

—I heard a Worker talking about you. They say you get up to some real delirious shit, mad adventures and stuff.

I swell with pride.

—Joe, says the kid, sticking out his hand, but my mates call me Feral.

—Cool name! I say, jealous.

—Yeah, I chose my own tag.

—Your tag?

—Yeah. You don't have a tag?

—I dunno. What do you mean?

—What? You don't know this? Ya graffiti name. You know, ya tag … ya tag it on walls and shit.

—I've never graffitied … wait, no, I've carved stuff into desks and library chairs. You know, like girls' names.

—Yeah, like that, but ya use spray-paint or Nikko pens, or whatever, and ya tag ya name all over, and you get treated like a hero. Plus ya get to act all mysterious and shit, and listen to people wonder on about who has such balls, to go tagging up the place like that.

A car slushes around the corner, slow, an eye out for someone.

—Fuck! says Feral, panic in his voice: Me fucken dad. Cunt'll smell me smoking again. Fuck, man, ya got any gum?

I shake my head. He lurks on the other side of the waterfall sluicing off the eaves, gives me a slap on the shoulder, and then darts away into the rain.

I head back across the flooded cul-de-sac. I have to get myself a good tag. I pause to smash a couple of windows in a new house going up, and linger in the mud, dreading the Friendlies. This cult doesn't make friends for themselves; they make friends for Jesus. I don't know much about it;

no one will answer my questions. I've asked Dad a hundred times why he believes these people but he always answers with *behave yourself* or *don't act the fool.* They act like saints and ridicule worldly sinners. They have secret meetings in the house of an Overseer on Wednesday nights and Sunday mornings, and public gospel meetings to welcome the lost. Each region has an Overseer, a man or woman on the verge of sainthood, someone who does everything right but has succumbed to the ways of the world, like having wealth or falling in love.

Around Easter the tramp preachers descend on the flock. They come and live in the Friends' houses, make themselves right at home while they fish the neighbourhood strangers. *Fishers of Men*, they call themselves. During this time they hold missions to drive out devils and to impress those they've hooked. Then they *test* the meetings, call on their flock to take the final step and *profess* to follow no other than Jesus the King.

Once a year, around Christmas, they hold a mass gathering called Convention. Friends come from thousands of miles away and they all gather in a huge tent somewhere, to worship at the feet of the saints. Last holidays my grandma answered some of my questions. She said a man named William Irvine started his Ministry of Truth way back in eighteen-ninety-something, and he rejected all churches and established doctrines and all the laws of man. Grandma said God spoke to Mr Irvine direct, inspired him to preach the gospel. Grandma said Mr Irvine set about condemning the ways of the world, and everyone alive who hadn't heard his word faced an eternity in hell. Sure, she said, you can go right on reading the bible your whole life and you can primp up and wear your best Sunday silks and pray until your knee-bones end up flat as the good book itself, but unless you hear one of God's chosen Workers speak the living word with your own ears, you'll find yourself drinking a cup of hot bile with Satan himself in no time.

Grandma said I shouldn't call the chosen ones tramp preachers, because people say that as a term of derision. She said those who understand our path use the word Workers to describe the saints. She said I should pray to Jesus and thank him, for those born into the fold have a path to heaven less fraught with worldly vices. I asked Grandma what I should call the church with no name, to make it easier to explain to my friends. Even though she has spoken English most of her life, my gran sometimes struggles and reverts to the German she spoke as a child. *Die Namenlosen*, she whispered: *Die Namenlosen*.

I've made friends with a kid named Maz. I can see his two-storey house across the empty cul-de-sac. His mother looks pretty worn out all the time. Maz and I stay out late, shoplifting and raiding unlocked cars for change. We play *Space Invaders*. He says his stepdad has a son named Reuben who leads a street gang in Sydney. Maz says he met Reuben last Christmas holidays and Reuben blew his mind. Reuben's dad wants to get him off the streets and bring him north for a new start. Maz feels pretty proud he has a rad stepbrother.

2

Dad drives me to school the first day because of the rain. He dumps me at the gate. I swagger into the school grounds. I've never seen so many kids in one place in my entire life. Some of them look real rough buggers. Older kids, some with beards! I turn tail and saunter back out the front gate, check the old man hasn't clued on I plan to wag my first day.

I hightail it off in the direction of the skating rink down the street. I get about halfway along the outside of the fence and a car sharks over to the kerb. The door opens; Feral looks out. I peek in the car to get an eye at his old man: the creepiest fucker I've seen in my life. I've seen some creepy, real bad fellows too: deer killers, rapists, wife-bashers and assorted psychos. Feral's old man resembles a vulture. A vulture with massive pot-lid ears that stick so far out they appear translucent. You can see all the veins in them, like a mess of red electrical wires dangling in a wine flagon full of petrol. His eyes have a tangible reptile quality about them, not to mention the pink business shirt. What kind of man wears pink? I go to call him a poofter out of instinct and shock at seeing a grown man, hell, *any* man, newborn or nine hundred, wearing pink. But before I get a chance to do or say anything, Feral alights from the car, looking pretty eager to get away from his father.

Then, like someone poured him out of a grease-trap into a drain, his father slips out of the driver's seat, grabs Feral in a half-nelson, and smashes him down on the hood. He stands close enough for me to smell

Old Spice aftershave, even older old-man stink and … roasted chicken? His flabby skin hangs under his eyes like burned cheese and his forehead looks mega greasy like he's scrubbed himself down with a roast chicken.

—You got cigarettes in your bag, boy? Give me your bag, boy, he demands in a sleazy rasp. He rips Feral's bag off him, busts the zip as he yanks it open with his drumstick fingers. Sure enough, Feral has a pack of smokes in there: Marlboros. His dad snatches them out of the bag, his hand like a claw from one of those damn arcade games where you always lose. He gives Feral a real hard smack in the ear, drips back into his car and speeds off, showering us both with mud.

—Don't worry, Feral. I've got smokes and ten bucks. Let's go play some pinball in the city. This cheers him up. My apt private use of his secret tag-name in a moment of crisis to remind him of the important stuff gets well rewarded. He has a clippie bag of weed in his shoe.

We hide at the back of the oval, under a new building construction. Feral shows me how to make a bong out of an apple. We smoke a couple of cones each, and, feeling pretty tripped out, I lie down, listen to the rain on the leaky roof. I need a girlfriend. I need a tag. I think I'll tag with blue paint. I love the smell of blue paint.

A bell clanging in the school wakes me with a start. I passed out! Feral has already left. I scrabble around in the shadows for my bag and climb out of the building site. Then I scoot around the corner, shaking off concrete dust, and bump right into a stern-looking old woman with a bent-up nose and piercing, demon-keen eyes. She sniffs the air around me. Straightens her trousers.

—Name, she snaps.

—Name? I answer.

—NAME! she shouts in my face. I reel back, stunned.

—You fucken old … crow! I yell at her.

—WHAAAT! she screams, even louder, so that at least half the suburb hears. Vicious glee sparkles in her eyes as she grabs me by the ear and twists so that I buckle at the knees, physically at her mercy.

Turns out that I've just called the school's deputy principal a fucken old crow to her face. Mrs Hudson searches my bag, finds my pack of cigarettes, my Barlow knife and a copy of *New Cunts*. She rifles through a fat file and pulls out a sheet, smooths it on her desk. She reads my enrolment form and raises an eyebrow. My dad wrote his profession on there. I guess she saw the word *Constable* and got a thrill. She reads my dad's work number out loud to herself, picks up the receiver, hands it to me, dials the phone. It rings a couple of times. I hope he won't answer. He answers:

—Hello.

—Um … hi, Dad.

—What have you done now, boy? he sighs down the line.

—Erm … Mrs Hudson caught me smoking.

—Tell him about the weapon, Mrs Hudson grunts from her desk.

—Mrs Hudson says to tell you that I have broken the rules because I have my Barlow.

—What'll we do with you? Dad says, resigned.

—Tell him about the filthy magazine I found in your bag also! barks Mrs Hudson.

—Dad … I also have a porno mag.

Mrs Hudson grabs the phone from me and says into the mouthpiece, not even putting the receiver up to her ear:

—In plain English, sir, considering your son has done all this on his first day … well … twelve-year-old boys, in my years of experience, they don't do that sort of damaged stuff until much later, at least fifteen. Your son, sir, must classify as the worst, most despicable outright delinquent boy I've come across! Any parent who raises a boy like yours ought to just bow their head in shame.

Then she listens awhile, says uh-huh a couple of times and hangs up the phone. I don't know what my old man said to Mrs Hudson. She stares at the phone for a bit, then looks at me, sort of weary-eyed, and says as she shoos me out of her office with a dismissive wave:

—You better get along to class.

—

I've learned a lot this first week. Having a cop for a dad in high school doesn't make you cool like it does in primary school. It makes you the sworn enemy of every teenager by default. I resemble a walking bruise. Two boys try to *pole* me – a half-Aboriginal kid nicknamed Muddy and another kid named Clint, who has a pointy face like the foxes on my grandma's farm. Muddy has a tattoo of a marijuana leaf with a script which reads, *til death do us part.* He rolls up his shirtsleeve so you can see it. To pole someone you need three dudes: one grabs you by the arms and the other two grab an ankle each. Holding you horizontal and spread-eagled they run you at a pole. I say:

—You two fuckheads have mental problems. You need three dudes to pole someone.

I come to. Muddy knocked me unconscious with one punch. A full-on fistfight has happened. Feral and another boy with a spike haircut stepped in to help me. The spiked kid introduces himself as Harlan – Harley to his mates. Harley has a magnetism which makes him seem much older, and wiser. I feel like a moon in his orbit. Just as the moon keeps its distance from the earth, you shouldn't get too close to Harley. He brawls at school because of the deep scar he has right in the middle of his forehead. He told me his dad in a drunken rage one night smashed his face into a table. He also told me he fell over when he first learned to walk. Kids at school taunt him by saying he had a dick cut off his forehead, and he explodes.

3

I tell Feral and Harley about my gang, The Wreckers, back in Greenvale, all the masterful adventures we pulled off. I make it sound tough and romantic. I intend to persuade them to join my new gang – for protection, racketeering and general mischief, I say. They laugh at me. They belong to a *posse*, since way back in Grade Six, where they met. They reckon I seem pretty cool and have a good reputation and all, but they've never seen me do anything reckless or admirably illegal like their posse leader, Gigolo.

Everything in Townsville seems to have *Gigolo* written on it, and *HBK*, Heart Break Kids. I want to join Gigolo's posse but the boys say you can't *join*; he has to like your tag. You have to have a killer tag and know how to do proper graffiti writing or you get called *toy*. Also, you have to tag in rad places that command attention. I don't have a tag and have never tried to write graffiti style. They say I sure better learn how to do it and come up with a rad tag and get tagging if I hope to get noticed by Gigolo. Gigolo, the master of graffiti, breakdancing, and breaking and entering.

Since I arrived in this city my childhood freedoms have eroded. Greenvale had no Friendlies. I didn't realise the power the cult has over my parents, besides the odd glimpse into Mum's mental state and her obsession with knotting her hair. Cars don't even have to pull up outside our house anymore; she always wears her hair up in that bun which pulls her face tight as a face you make at your sister. Mum has turned stern and paranoid and vicious, and her migraines never go away. She has rictus smile. I imagine she doesn't sleep with her hair knotted, but she has it up when she goes to bed and she has it up at breakfast. Every Wednesday night and every Sunday morning I have to dress in over-starched long pants and a shirt and tie. A bloody tie! We have to go to this old couple's house for *meetings*. They look in their late hundreds. Their house smells like lavender, Old Tawny port and bones. Old people smell like bones. You can smell their bones through their thinned-out skin. The old coot stands up and he drones on about Jesus and the disciples. He rubs his palms together like a vacuum-cleaner salesman. Us kids sit there bored to death.

The bible provides me with fodder for my poems. I sit up in my room for weeks on end reading the bible for the good bits, writing wicked scenes of my own. I have a new hero: Lord Byron, even above Tom Sawyer. How I wish for a life like his. A genius, a ladies' man, a bare-knuckle fist-fighter. I hate getting into fights. I always end up bleeding the most. Mum says: *You'll ruin your good looks with all this brawling.* I don't have enough good looks to go losing any. I can talk my way out of a fight most times. Except with Muddy. Muddy doesn't follow any established patterns of aggression – not that I can determine, anyway. Most kids have a reluctance somewhere within them. They hesitate before smashing your nose flat. Not Muddy. He has all the reluctance of a snake you've stepped on in the bush. In between writing poems and reading I practise graffiti. I still need a tag.

The old man pipes up at dinner and says we have to go to Convention down in Brisbane, whether we like it or not. Of course the arseholes who organise this thing have scheduled it over Christmas. Dad says we shouldn't celebrate Christmas anyway. He says if you take away all the tinsel, Christmas belongs to the world of men, a cynical excuse to sell stuff to people. The Friendlies make their pilgrimage from every crag of Australia. If they don't go, then the Devil himself has held them back. I remember attending a few times in my single-digit years, before this habit I've developed of writing everything down in my notebook. I've looked into the hole sometimes, but those memories have funnel-webs. I've had enough of these fundamentalist apocalyptic freaks. Mum has our letter of invitation up on the fridge. Typed out with zero flourish: *Welcome Friends: Annual Convention December 23rd–27th 1984, Skyview Avenue, Rochedale, Brisbane*. It has a list of tramp preachers who've come from all over the world.

4

After thirteen hundred kilometres we roll through the front gates of an old farm on Skyview Avenue on the southern outskirts of Brisbane. I see about five thousand pretty girls milling about in sundresses and my interest picks up. A mayhem of cars have parked up on a grassy hill which looks down on the farm. The old man parks there, right by this fucken-rad-looking purple Cadillac, one of those with the huge fins and white leather seats. We lug our suitcases and sleeping bags and stuff down to the sheds. They've erected a giant circus-style tent in the middle of a field surrounded by trees. Off to the left sits a huge shed full of tables and chairs and people cooking at massive gas burners. A stable at one end of the grounds houses the females, a coop at the other for the males. A third shed, which looks far more comfortable, houses the Workers. So the old man and I say sayonara to the old lady and my two sisters, and go to find our beds.

Our shed looks like a dilapidated chicken roost. The windows don't have glass; they have chicken wire. The middle of the cavernous interior has king-sized double-decker beds. Dad and I pick one, on top near the end, clamber up the ladder, stretch our sheets across the huge mattress and lay out our good gospel clothes. Dad says he wants a shower so I take the opportunity to cut out and find a spot to smoke. I walk around the sleeping sheds, and the eating sheds, but can't find a suitable place, so head up to the car park. One end of the car park has a grove of shady trees that look pretty climbable.

Weaving in and out of the cars I notice one of the cutest girls I've seen in my life sitting in a tree. She has skin like marzipan and acres of chestnut hair. I walk right up to the tree and see her trying to hide a cigarette. I swagger some and pop a cigarette into my mouth and light up, winking at her.

—Hey, gorgeous! I say, and take a nice deep drag.

Bruce, the goddamn tramp preacher from back in Greenvale, raptures out of nowhere and grabs me by the scruff of the neck.

—Why, Brentley, he says with a sick chuckle: What a surprise … Still in the express lane to hell, I see … A black eye, too. How'd you get that? Fighting, I bet, like a mongrel dog. And he frogmarches me through the car park down the knoll to the sleeping shed, all the way saying:

—Sin originates in the thought. Sow a thought, reap an action; sow an action, reap a habit; sow a habit, reap a character; sow a character, reap a destiny.

We find my old man at the foot of our bed strangling himself with a tie.

—Caught your boy smoking, says the tramp preacher.

—Boy resists all attempts to control him, Dad grunts, clipping me on the head.

—Well, friend, we have missions planned in Townsville. We'll stay with you for a few months in the new year. I'll sort him out for you then.

—

Day one of five days of sermons. Nothing to look forward to. Maybe I'll run away. In a city this size they'll never find me. Mum and Dad hustle us out of the breakfast shed to the church tent to get some good seats before the rush. The tent has a thousand benches in it, arranged in concentric circles. The olds choose one near the middle, close to the stage where the damn preachers will stand and yack on about the end of everything.

—Thank god I brought a cushion! I say: My arse'll cave in on these damn benches! And I blow a bubble with the gum in my mouth. Pop.

Mum slaps me in the mouth, making the scab from where Muddy split my lip recently open up all over. I mop at the blood with the collar of my shirt. Mum says, with total ferocity between her teeth:

—You better not use the Lord's name in vain ever again, or so help me I'll smite you myself. Dabs at my collar and then my lip with a tissue.

We sit down and before long people mill in like willing victims. Here comes the family of that hellishly beautiful chick I saw sitting up in the tree yesterday afternoon. She sees me gawping at her and flashes me a little smile. Her family sit two benches in front of us. The tent fills up and a hush settles in as the Workers march down the aisle like they represent the coming of the Lord himself.

Sure enough, they drone on clear to lunchtime, on and on about Jesus for the whole morning, preaching against the seduction of indecent curiosities. Each word falls like a hammer on an anvil and rings in the air. Occasionally everyone stands and sings from *The Book of Hymns*. One thing makes the whole situation bearable: the cute chick keeps turning and smiling at me, and she doesn't care that everyone can see her. She keeps right on, turning and smiling, every five damn minutes or so.

At lunch, when everyone rises and bolts off, I pretend I've lost my favourite pen in the world and I lag behind. I slip a poem I wrote in the third hour when I felt ready to commit suicide from boredom into the pink notebook I saw the hot chick scribbling in. Her notebook has one of those *This Belongs To* stickers in it. She has written her name, with a love heart for the dot on the 'i's: *Billie-Jean*. Get fucked! Just like the song! As I lift the fly to get out of the church tent, I bump right into Billie-Jean.

—Oh … hi, Billie-Jean, I say, stunned at her beautiful mouth, the way her lips part, showing her teeth. One of her front teeth has a bit of an angle to it. She licks her crooked tooth.

—How d'ya know my name, Brentley?

—Well, shit. I asked … around. Wait! How do you know my name?

—Your sister told me.

—Which sister?

—Jaz.

Then Billie-Jean's dad comes into the tent and she goes with him over to their bench.

—

At dinner I can't see Billie-Jean anywhere, so I go back up to the car park, hoping to find her. I smoke about two thousand cigarettes and listen to Mondo Rock's 'Come Said the Boy' cassingle on my Walkman. The damn batteries run flat from rewinding it over and over. I get up to leave but then see her coming up through the car park. I hate that: I sit around for a month waiting for something and no sooner do I give up and rise to leave than it happens. I take off my headphones as she approaches. Heart racing.

—What ya listening to? she says.

—'Come Said the Boy'. I sound all breathless, dammit.

—I love Mondo Rock.

—Yeah, well, that song anyway.

—Gotta smoke?

—Yeah. I give her a St Moritz. Stupid hands shaking.

—Oh, I love St Moritz!

I light it for her.

—Wanna sneak out tonight? Give me another smoke? she says, eyeing my fresh packet.

—Sure! Damn lump in throat.

—Let's meet here, by the tree … No, even better, see that purple Cadillac over there?

—Yeah, coolest car I've ever seen.

—My dad owns it. He loves that thing. Mum says more than he loves her.

—Very cool car!

—Meet me there. We'll sit between the cars. I'll bring a blanket.

—What time? Sounding like I don't give a fuck.

—Um … midnight?

—K.

—K. See ya then, then, she says, and skips off.

I chew a piece of gum, and with my heart light in my chest go back down to the sleeping shed. I decide to have a shower and make myself presentable for later. About fifty naked fellows in there, all showing they've taken the knife for Jesus.

Dad knows I have a plan up my sleeve. I keep fidgeting and looking at my watch. He asks me why I've hung my jeans and jacket on the ladder. I say in case I have to go to the toilet in the night, which sounds pretty thin, and he says I can go to the toilet in my boxers. I move my jeans off the ladder, fold them up and leave them at the foot of the bed, before he does it himself and discovers my Walkman and packet of smokes. I've gone through three Walkmans, because every time my parents find me with one, they smash it up, saying they have the Devil all over them. You need some serious skills to steal a Walkman. Most stores have them in a glass case.

The old man gets out his bible and reads a bit, and then a bit more, so I get out my *Collected Works of Byron* and read awhile and fall asleep! Dad's snores jolt me from my slumber. Some weird shit, sharing a bed with your old man. I get down the ladder and put on my jeans. As I sneak out of the shed, some ancient fellow eyeballs me from behind his torch as he reads the bible, but I ignore him. I get outside and have a look at my watch with my lighter and it says 12.24! I sprint up to the car park but can't see a thing in the dark. After a bit of hunting I spot the tail fins of Billie-Jean's dad's Cadillac silhouetted like a memorial of grandeur against the sky. I skip over and find Billie-Jean sprawled on a blanket between the cars, looking at the stars.

—Hi! I say.

—Hi yourself. Thought you'd chickened out.

—Chickened out? An adventure like this, with the most beautiful girl I've ever met? I'd've shown up if God himself told me not to come!

—Okay … Mr Risk! She giggles: I love your poem. I read it over and over. Why did you call it 'Fleeing Eden'?

—Because the protagonist runs from love.

—Why?

—Because her youth and beauty makes him fear age and death.

—Oh … and you call me Paradise?

—Um … yeah.

—And what do you mean by my *garden*?

—Ah … I kinda ripped that off from the Song of Solomon.

—The song of … who?

—Solomon … You know, the porno chapter in the bible?

—The *bible* has porno?

—You should read it.

—I hate God … I hate this whole Convention … fucken hypocritical pervos.

—Wow. I think I love you.

She kisses me, hesitates, says:

—How far have you gone before … with a girl?

—Um …

—I've kissed a few boys, and I let one finger me at school camp last year.

I realise I have my mouth hanging open and feign a yawn. Billie-Jean thinks a bit, puffs on her cigarette and says:

—I've never had a boy do it, but I let my best friend growl me out once.

I swallow and in the quiet it echoes off the Cadillac fender. I manage to find my voice:

—Wow … I've seen pictures in magazines of girls doing that … but my dad said girls don't *really* do that stuff, only for money.

—Pffft … your dad knows shit. She snorts: Parents always lie, anyway.

Silence, for a while. An owl above us. Clouds shift and the moon flickers, paints the sleeping farm below the car park in a misty silver palette.

—I've never had a head job, I say.

—If you growl me out, I'll give you a head job.

—Deal!

She giggles and fumbles with buttons in the dark and slips off her jeans. I beg the moon to come out, so I can get a better look. The moon complies, reveals Billie-Jean looking self-conscious on the blanket. She has blue undies with a big pink and white butterfly on the front. She spreads her knees, looks a little embarrassed. I lie down, put my face right up close to her and take a nice deep sniff. She smells like rock melon! Like when you go out into the field and pick one early in the morning.

Intoxicated I pull aside the butterfly and lick her for a bit, put in a couple of fingers, finger and lick, pushing my tongue as deep into her as I can. She bucks against my face. She tastes a bit like rock melon too, salty sweet. She has some pubes, a fine honey down. Some hair in my mouth, but I don't care. I look up for a second and she has her t-shirt bunched between her teeth, biting. She pinches her left nipple. She has tiny tits, but – tits!

—Lick my clit, she says.

—*Clit?* I say, my voice muffled.

—Yeah, my clitoris. This bit. She opens herself up, pulls back. A little shiny thing like a parrot's tongue pokes out. I lick her clit. She squeals and, giggling, pushes me away.

—I could stay here for eternity and not give a damn about the rest of anything, I say and she laughs.

—Your turn! Sits up, tugs at my belt.

Now, this hasn't happened before. I've never shown a girl my cock, let alone put it in her mouth! This whole scene feels forbidden. I have a crazy anticipation coming over me. What if a saint sits up in the trees watching? She has me out of my jeans before I finish thinking that. She coos a bit, which makes me feel pretty good, and then she says:

—You have a beautiful penis!

Which sends me reeling, and I feel her breath on me and the warmth of her mouth and this solves everything. I feel alive, for the first time ever. She sucks me for about five minutes, stopping only a couple of times, to ask me if I can let her know before I come. I mumble:

—Uh-huh, sure!

Then, she stops and says:

—Wait.

—Huh?

—Do you wanna do it?

—Huh?

—Let's have sex. We'll say goodbye to our virginity together!

I wilt in pure shock.

—Oooh … don't go soft now! She looks disappointed.

—Let me lick you again then, I say, blushing.

—Sure! She lies back, pulls her knees to her chest.

The moon, the sweet, gleaming moon, lights up the entire scene and I spring to attention again. She giggles:

—Just stick it in. Let's do it.

She pulls me on top of her. She has her hand around me, guiding me into her. I feel the warmth and the wetness as she thrusts her hips up, pushing herself onto me. I melt into her, thrusting slow, trying not to let the top of my cock shoot off like a released balloon. She moves against me, our breaths becoming one.

—Oooh! she moans: Oooh …

I thrust like the Devil gone mad, overwhelmed at the sensation and the smell and the heat and the sounds and the wetness of it all. I explode and lose myself entirely, deep inside my new girlfriend, her nails clawing at my back. For some reason, about now I wonder where she got all her experience. I pop out of her with a loud farting sound. We both laugh until Billie-Jean says:

—Shit!

—What?

—Your come leaked out all over Mum's blanket … Shit … How much did you come? She holds up her fingers into the light, showing strings of silver.

—Um … I didn't even know I *could* come like that. When I jack … err, *normally* I only get clear stuff, not much.

—Wow, you near drowned me, from the inside! She stands up to reveal a huge wet patch on the blanket. More of my sperm streams down her inner thighs: Shit. I hope I don't get pregnant!

—Pregnant? The last time I felt such horror, a damn yowie roared in my face. Seeing myself as a thirteen-year-old father makes me ill in the stomach. But it would make me a hero in school if I got a girl pregnant. So I compose myself and say:

—What would we call it? If a boy, I reckon *Byron* would rule.

—Like fuck! I'd have to get an abortion before my parents found out. They'd kill me, and you too, probably.

—Abortion? I haven't heard that word before.

—Maybe I'll go see a doctor and get the morning-after pill, she says, chewing the inside of her mouth, looking worried now.

—The what? I light a St Moritz, hands shaking.

—It kills the baby before it starts growing, or something.

—How d'ya know this … stuff? I say, searching for the right word but only coming up with *stuff*.

—My friend got pregnant … from her dad … I mean, her dad's friend.

—What?

—Yeah, she says, looking sad.

And we talk on, until the sky starts bleeding and birds come down from the trees and shit on the cars.

I swap addresses with Billie-Jean. We swear frequent letters and undying love. The Convention ends in a blur. I can't eat; I can't sleep. I only want to hang out with Billie-Jean.

5

January 1985. Back in Townsville but happy I chose to live my life like this – an endless series of adventures with no plans, no place in particular picked for a destination. I drift along, digging everything floating by. I'll keep writing everything down as it happens.

I find Feral at the corner shops playing *Space Invaders* and smoking. I tell him I lost the old virginity and he can see from the sheer pride in my swagger I tell no lie.

Harlan left today. Lucky bastard's dad got a new job down in Brisbane. I miss the dude because I never have to worry about getting beaten up while in his company. I've seen him take out a group of nine, and they fought dirty, too – tried to hold him down and get on his chest.

Feral and I go out every other night murdering government buildings – graffiti speak for leaving no wall untagged. Schools, toilet blocks, parking garages, shop windows. *Feral* and *Mr Risk* sprayed everywhere.

Gigolo has noticed. Feral came around and told me the secret address of Gigolo's posse pad. He has a party on and he wants me there! Apparently Gigolo found a whole house, complete with furniture, television, kitchen stuff and everything. Every kid in Townsville treats Gigolo like a rock star. Everyone over the age of four and under the age of a hundred knows his tag. Every teacher and every cop in the universe wants to know Gigolo's real identity. But the kids keep it quiet like a wizard does his magic word. Kids say his parents met in an institution for schizophrenics. His father has a reputation as quite a fine painter of landscapes and his mother, an Aboriginal Australian, paints traditional-style dreamscapes. He became a ward of the state from birth and got passed around dozens of respectable government-approved families until his mischief, or his sexual escapades with their daughters, saw him moving on again. Everyone agrees no better thief exists. Once, so the story goes, he waltzed right out of an electronics store with a ten-piece stereo in a box the size of a refrigerator.

I arrive at one in the morning, which I hope looks hardcore, but in reality it took ages for the olds to fall asleep. I expect a dive, but the street, named Love Lane, has huge sprawling houses with well-kept lawns – except Gigolo's lawn; you could get lost in there, come to grief tripping over an abandoned mower or a lost tribe. Feral, who also had to sneak out, beat me here. He points out Gigolo. He looks like the pop star Prince. He wears a purple Sergeant Pepper vest over a white shirt with black lace cuffs, and leather pants with three pairs of braces: one hanging at his sides, one over his shirt how you usually wear braces, and the other pair wrapped around his legs and clipped onto silver ten-hole Doc Martens boots. He has a slightly hooked nose, which gives him a cut-out-of-marble look, and full lips. Kohl cakes his eyelids, and he's plucked his eyebrows, so they look elegant above his brilliant hazel-green eyes. Gigolo has serious star power. About a dozen girls crowd around him, where he sits at the head of a long table, holding court, smoking cones out of a skull bong. The stereo belts out 'Uprock', by Rock Steady Crew, as I walk right up.

—Gigolo … Mr Risk, I say. Calm, I sit.

Gigolo holds up his knuckles. I punch his knuckles.

—Where did you get the name *Mr Risk*?

—A nickname from a chick I rooted.

—I like it, he says and takes a hit from the skull bong. Then on the exhale he says, a slight static of menace on the edges of his words: You got smarts, bro? Taps out the cone, repacks and pushes the skull across the table towards me.

—Sort of, I say, toasting him with the skull: Nothing society will celebrate … a genetic system criminal. I have anti-authoritarianism in my genes. I pull a cone, do my damnedest not to cough.

Then Gigolo says, in a different voice, like putting a single on longplay:

—Despite what people may think of me, I have an agenda. They say graffiti, I say self-expression. They say vandalism, I say protest for my abandoned generation, defining my own style … forget everything the fucken establishment taught us, man.

—Yeah. Like Mods. I love Mods, making art, living free, dressing rad and getting kicks. Have you read that book *Generation X*?

The chicks look bored. I offer my packet of Saint Moritz.

—Generation sex? Gigolo lights a cigarette.

—No … X … potential not yet determined, like X in an equation.

—Sounds like maths … I fucken hate maths and why do you read books? Also, I hear you have a fucken pig for an old man. He stares at my eyes.

—Yeah … so, I have a pig dad. I get away with shit because I know what they look for … I see it as an advantage.

—Exactly, says Gigolo: Can you get pig stuff? Leans in.

—Like what? Trying not to lean back.

—Dunno … Nightsticks, cuffs, guns and shit?

—Fuck … no … He only has one gun and doesn't bring it home.

—If you can get some weapons, I'll make you my Sergeant at Arms.

—What does a Sergeant at Arms do?

—Looks after all the posse's weapons, gets bonuses, chicks, drugs-n-shit.

—Fuck … sign me up … I'll try … but why guns?

—I wanna start a proper gang. Proper gangsters have guns.

—My old gang had a bunch of guns. Wish I still had them.

—What gang?

—The Wreckers. Back in the town I grew up in. This dude named Daryl stole a couple of guns from his old man's bikie club. Also, I nicked a pistol from a poacher.

—You still got the pistol?

—Nah. We got busted on amphetamines in class and they raided our fortress and found all the stuff and the protected animals we'd shot and I got locked up.

—Locked up … what, in a boys' home? Gigolo looks real impressed.

—Um, nah. My old man's jail. He locked me in every night, for three years, to stop me sneaking out and causing havoc.

—*Really?* In an actual prison?

—Yeah, between seven at night and seven in the morning … because my gang got busted on drugs and with guns, and shit.

—Fuck! Guns and drugs, ay. You can join my posse.

Gigolo believes me, and that matters. People get belief and truth mixed up all the time. When people believe things, you know, inside of their heads, it makes stuff happen outside their heads.

—So, who does own this place? I ask, looking away to contain my excitement, admiring the graffiti on the walls and the unhinged debauchery, like no one has a care in the world.

—I found it, Gigolo says.

—Yeah, I heard … but how d'you go about finding a house?

—Couple of the homies and me came across it while scouting to do some B-and-Es. The joint had a pile of mail at the front door and I had a peek and some of em dated back more than a year, so I tried the door, and it opened right up. It looked like everyone just got up and bailed … plates on the table, fossilised food, wine glasses with moss sprouting out. The fridge had living shit in it.

—Sounds pretty sinister. Electricity and all? I say.

—Nah. I got it put on, in the principal of my old high school's name, the fucker.

Much laughter then from those listening in.

6

Gigolo and I go stealing. Clothes, cologne, watches, shoes, jewellery, sunglasses, cassettes. We walk into David Jones, on a school day, dressed like rich-kid tourists, reeking of hundred-dollar perfume, wearing designer shorts and sandals, five watches on each arm. We carry empty David Jones bags and we walk around, shopping casually, filling the bags with desired booty. Then we walk out like we belong there. I did research, spent hours poring over books on human psychology and body language, learning how to lie. I teach Gigolo these things and in return he teaches me how to graffiti, proper style, how to breakdance, and how to break and enter.

We murder a lot of schools together. In the dead of night, while the baby-boomers dream of financial security, we meet up in backstreets, armed with Nikko pens and spray cans. Over the fence, to work. The next day everyone in the southern hemisphere talks about catching the little bastards responsible. What a feeling – a large crowd baying for your blood. The cops come to school. Newspaper reporters. Every kid's parents try to get out of them the names of the evil vandals. For several months we go by the school again and watch the newly hired guards do their rounds with dogs. We have to wait out the budget. Before long, because they get no results, the guards disappear, and we go murder the place again.

—

In school one morning in Year Ten the first bell rings and the teacher hasn't shown. I feel pretty mopey because I haven't seen Billie-Jean for an entire year. The temperature hovers around a billion degrees and the whole class sits in pools of sweat. The chairs, moulded out of this shit-brown plastic, stick right to your arse. The fans buzz and the blades creak. At any point one of the rickety blades could come off and decapitate some poor kid, hopefully not me. Soon I hear someone running and assume the teacher will rush in all flustered and sick-looking from the heat. Instead a kid speeds past.

As he runs by, he grabs a schoolbag out of the row along the wall outside the door and hurls it through the open window. The bag smashes this chick right in the face, breaking her glasses. She starts up howling and bleeding all over her legal-studies textbook. I think some glass got in her eyes. The teacher arrives in time to see the aftermath. A couple of kids point the finger at me!

The teacher puts me in a half-nelson and marches me to the principal's office. I plead my innocence to the deputy principal, Mrs Hudson, who has hated me since my first day in Year Eight. She doesn't give two farts for my story and goes right ahead and calls my father, which gets me angry because I've kept my nose clean for so long. I don't deserve to take the rap for something I didn't even have the pleasure of doing. I shake, feeling a madman fit coming on. She manifests a cane and holds it in both fists, bending it while she screams at me:

—Violent worthless delinquent!

—Fucken plebeian moll!

She clutches at her heart like it stopped, and her toucan nose has a bead of sweat on it that trembles like a fly on a banana. Arctic cold now, she picks up the phone and calls the school nurse. A knock at the door and the nurse comes in. I hate this person. She talks to you like at toilet training, in a high-pitched ga-ga-goo voice. Hudson and the nurse huddle over in the corner of the office, whispering and glancing at me. The nurse takes me into the sickbay, directs me to sit down on this vomity-looking couch and starts asking me questions from a sheet of paper. She holds a red pen between her fingers and taps at the page.

—Do you feel depressed? she asks in her patronising baby voice.

—Yeah.

—Do you feel as though, sometimes, the world works against you?

—All the time.

—Do you experience despair? She scribbles on the paper.

—I will never surrender.

—Do you think about taking your own life? Scribbling, again.

—I read a lot of books by people who committed suicide.

She stops scribbling and looks up from the page.

—Like who?

—Plath, Hemingway, Pavese, Crane, Chandler, Woolf and Berryman.

—Hemingway? You read Hemingway? She ruffles through a file on her desk: You read Hemingway and Plath … at fourteen. That, what you said before: never surrender. Did Hemingway say that?

—No … I read it in *Memoirs of a Revolutionary* by Victor Serge. I shrug, distracted by a thread sticking out of a cushion.

—Who?

—The Russian anarchist.

—Ahh. She snorts: Mrs Hudson said you have issues with authority … Do you have issues with authority, Brentley?

—Authorities in what?

She glares at me:

—Authority! Police, priests, doctors, teachers, parents, adults.

—Who gave them authority?

—They have authority by precedence of age, and the law … You will do better in this world if you obey authority, keep your head down and pull your weight.

—The nail that sticks out gets hammered down, I mumble.

—Exactly!

—Well, fuck that.

She shoots a look at me and sniffs, either a suppressed laugh or something up her nose.

—Mrs Hudson thinks you may have a psychological issue. Will I find drugs in your bag, Brentley? She gives me this look like she wants to put me over her knee and burp me.

I have a brief moment of panic, not because of drugs, but because I have a sketchbook with all my Mr Risk practice tags in there. The game will end if I get linked to Mr Risk. I'll get executed. Not three weeks ago we murdered the school. The place still stinks of fresh government-issue whitewash.

By now I've picked the thread out of the cushion. The more I yank at it, the longer it grows. She grabs the cushion off the couch but I don't let go of the thread and the whole damn front comes off, spilling millions of feathers and mank-looking shit all over the grey linoleum.

—You know what, she says, derision curling the corners of her mouth: I think I will make you an appointment to see the Ward 10B psychiatrists. She stands up and towers over me, then scuttles out of the room, leaving me sitting on the vomity couch like an eagle in a budgie cage. I feel panicked because recently Ward 10B received a lot of bad publicity in the newspaper. A crap-tonne of psychiatric ex-patients started a lawsuit for mistreatment and abuse against the hospital.

I watch the clock. Two hours pass. I fidget and sweat, despite the administration block air-conditioning. I convince myself they'll give me a lobotomy. Then, like in a cartoon, a light bulb comes on in my head. This voice, deep like a grandfather, says: *What can they do? In the worst possible scenario, son, kill you. I doubt they'll kill you.* So I grab my schoolbag and leave, walk right out of there, out to the bike racks, unlock my bike and ride away. Headphones on, Duran Duran blaring 'The Wild Boys', feeling calm.

I go and ride my bike around Willows shoppingtown, jump bins until a guard comes and starts closing the roller doors in front of the stores and shouts *piss off.* That guard sums up this whole city. It crawls with arseholes who think themselves important. No one stops here, not even Captain Cook in 1770; he sailed right by, naming things from his ship. He named Cleveland Bay and Magnetic Island. Legend has it that the strange rocks of Magnetic Island sent Cook's compass into a frenzy, hence its name.

The teachers at school say this city hopped during World War Two. Fifty thousand troops and fighter pilots swarmed all over the place, staging battles out on the reef. A poster in that damn sickroom explained the Japanese tried to bomb Townsville, but they missed their target and blew up a palm tree. I'd miss the city too, if I blinked. When you look for the place on a map, your eyes skip right over it, gravitate instead a few hundred kilometres north to Cairns, or a thousand ks south to Brisbane, or out to the islands off the coast.

I get home and find Dad sitting on the front porch. He says:

—Next year, boy, you go to another school. These coming holidays, everywhere I go, you go.

—Good, I retort: Send me to Pimlico, or Ignatius Park. All my friends go to those schools. Kirwan sucks.

He shakes his head. Goes inside.

In the Townsville city mall the council installed a public chess set, with pieces the size of a toddler. All around the chessboard, under the shade of a walkway that leads to the second floor of cafes and bookshops, we sit on the large benches that double-serve as lock-away cabinets for the chess pieces when the city shuts down for the evening. Most of the posse posture and hang about, hustling, comparing weapons and sketches of graffiti tags. A couple of us play chess. I do quite well, considering I've never studied it. I can't remember learning to play. I beat a lot of people – everyone my own age, a couple of older men and a few German backpackers.

Maz turns up with his new brother, Reuben. Reuben looks pretty wild. He has a Mohawk haircut, both ears pierced and a ring in his nostril, and he wears spiky wristbands. I like him right away, and equally as fast he kicks my arse at chess. Reuben outplays everyone. By and by he gets bored and starts to hustle these shady-looking travellers who sit about in the mall drinking out of wine casks. He bets fifty bucks he can get them in checkmate within ten moves. He pockets their fifty bucks. I tell him I can read people and they look like roving serial killers, or worse: wharfies! He says:

—I consider myself a lover, not a fighter … but I'll stab any cunt who picks me. He spits on the ground in their direction as they huddle together, plotting his murder.

To dispel the situation we both walk off to the tobacconist to get some smokes. Reuben smokes Gudang Garam cigarettes, from Indonesia. The cloves laced with the tobacco crack and pop. Reuben has no problem buying smokes because he looks a lot older than I do. Street wisdom shines from his eyes when he talks. And can he talk! He reckons he studies game theory as a philosophy, a way of living. He says all human interactions conform to rules of games, which, in turn, mankind invented to make sense of reality. He talks for an hour about how our systems of living need subverting. About then I notice the way he walks, tilted back on his heels, in a kind of shuffle. You only notice after a while because of his charisma, and the fact that he looks exactly like the spaghetti-western actor Terence Hill, including those piercing blue eyes that always look amused. And his clothes. He dresses like a hippy punk, a real stylish character. He sees me notice his strange walk and says:

—I have no toes.

—Fuck. I pause. He keeps walking. I catch up: What happened?

—Burned, brother, right up to my knees … look.

He stops, puts his left hand on my shoulder, stoops over and pulls up a jeans leg. Above the Doc Martens his calf looks like Freddy Krueger.

—Don't ask me how it happened, okay, man.

I've spent the last couple of months of school sitting under Reuben and Maz's house listening to AC/DC blaring on a tinny cassette player and reading Reuben's library. I've heard multiple stories about what happened to Reuben. It hasn't come up again. He spends hours under the house shaving calluses off his scarred feet with a butterfly knife. He massages sorbolene cream into them from an enormous tub. I stop noticing his feet, like you stop noticing someone's huge nose after you've known them for a while. He rolls perpetual joints from a stash of weed he keeps in a hollowed-out dictionary.

We catch a bus into the city and go to Cafe Nova. We play chess and drink coffee and smoke cigarettes and read the magazines they leave on the tables. Gigolo arrives at Reuben's house unannounced – an unusual thing, as Gigolo always plays the host, never the guest. Maz's dad has a three-quarter-size pool table down there in the cool, and a bar fridge and a bunch of couches.

Reuben and Gigolo get along very well. They out-boast each other, talking big numbers of chicks each of them has fucked. I've spent a lot of time studying Gigolo's method with girls. At a dance, or a party, he picks a girl, stares at her until she gets the idea, then he walks up, grabs her and starts kissing. Nine out of ten kiss back, after the initial shock. I put this down to twenty per cent style and eighty per cent celebrity status. I modify it somewhat. Talk to the girl – then I let her notice me get all distracted by her mouth, like I want to kiss her. She either gets all hot and bothered or not. If so, we kiss awhile, then I say *what a shame you have stockings on.* Reuben just goes right ahead with his silver tongue and charms girls out of their panties. He dead-serious tells them how attractive he finds them. Right in front of their boyfriends, too. Sure enough, at a party or whatever, the chick'll rubberneck Reuben all evening. As I said earlier, the dude has handsome on his side. The boy can fight, too, and his swagger subtly points this out to potential aggressors.

When Reuben came around to my house, my mother took one look and instantly despised him, forbade me to keep his company. She now acts all interested in my whereabouts. Before I met Reuben, darkness could easily have fallen before I got home from school and she wouldn't question me. Now I keep getting the *why so late, boy? What mischief will we hear about from your teachers next, son? Why do you stink of cigarettes, boy?* If I simply say I stopped to talk with Reuben, she hits the roof and screams that she forbids me to associate with that criminal. She reckons Dad made enquiries at work and found out he means nothing but bad news.

—A no-hoper crim, says Mum and folds her arms.

I know the truth of it, though. Reuben smiles with his eyes. You don't need to see his mouth. That disarms people. Everybody knows Aussies swear. No one swears more than Aussies. And no Aussie swears more than Reuben. Every adult instantly despises him.

Mum hates him even more since I let him pierce my ears. Reuben has both of his ears pierced, unlike other boys, who only pierce their left.

Reuben pierced both of mine, like real punks wear them. Mum offers to pay me if I take out the sleepers. She also offers to pay me to quit smoking.

The school holidays have arrived and I've lost my freedom. I have to hang with my father. He has this notion that he'll keep his eye on me the whole time. I figure he must have his bullshit hat on because he can't take me to work at the police station. But on the first morning of the holidays he says he's changed to the graveyard shift! I have to hang out with him all day, mowing the lawn a hundred times and fixing whipper-snippers and crap in his shed.

At 8 pm we get into his police cruiser and go on patrol. If you've ever ridden in a police car, you'll know how they smell. Police cars smell like the system, and nightmare factories. Cop cars don't have carpet, only industrial vinyl, which gives off a petrochemical perfume that creeps up your nose and deep into your clothes. I have some fun, though, riding around in Dad's patrol car. He lets me cuff myself when he busts kids who've snuck out to vandalise stuff or fuck in supermarket car parks. When he piles them into the back, they see me already in there, handcuffed. I look pretty bad.

Tonight I outdid myself. I rubbed the label off a whiteboard marker with sandpaper in my dad's shed. The whiteboard marker wipes right off the vinyl-clad seats. At a corner store my dad whoop-whoops a couple of kids from the housing estate throwing up tags on the phone box. They get in, swallowing hard, and see me, hands in lap, cuffed. After a while I produce the marker and tag the back of the driver's seat. My real tag too, *MR RISK*, because by now everyone knows my tag. Damn well never seen more-impressed kids.

Most of the time, though, I get bored as a worm. My dad and his partner, this fake jerk named Baz, talk in cop code or something, muffled, ignoring me.

Tonight, a horrible motorbike accident on an overpass. You can see where the two dudes hit the guardrail. I sit in the car, staring at a helmet lying on the road. I gaze at it for about twenty minutes before noticing this *Day of the Triffids*–type stuff bleeding on the white lines of the road. Well … you get the picture. Dude's head came right off. My dad spent most of the night there on the rail overpass and he forgot about me, sitting in the front seat, blue and red flashing on my paper face.

We've driven carousel style around this city for five nights and over the radio a voice requests we return to the station. Palm Island needs cops in a hurry. A dispute has come to blows. For one glorious moment I smell freedom, my dad's long arm letting go for the rest of the holidays. Nope. He tells me to pack enough undies for a week and off we go to the docks.

On board the police boat. Seasick. I throw up the Big Rooster I had for lunch a month ago. Trying to read the last letter I received from Billie-Jean. You shouldn't read on choppy seas. We only have to sail about sixty ks north-west of Townsville, but it'll take easily a week to get out there with waves this big. The police boat lurches so the propeller comes out of the water. I hear Palm Island has nothing to do with paradise. For about a hundred years the government banished people out there: Aboriginals they considered troublesome, people of mixed blood.

After a couple of hours the water calms down and turns cornflower blue, as clear as Billie-Jean's eyes. The sun comes out, revealing little islands with no trees on them. Then we sail through an oil-rainbow and a haul of dead fish. The hull of the boat hits something and I rush over to have a look. A dead white goat swirls in the slip, one horn above the water like a cynical fin.

Palm Island looks like a ghetto built on a rubbish dump sticking out of a cesspit. Everything smashed and neglected in this world has come here to die. I lag to have a smoke. I pull out my pack and about a dozen Aboriginal girls materialise.

—Gis a durrie, cuz. Carn, bro, a few say in unison.

I offer my packet and it empties instantly.

—We don't see many white-boys here, cuz, says a thread-of-cotton girl with a serious bruise under her left eye.

I manage to smile and then she says:

—Wanna scrape, white-boy? Garn … gis a scrape.

The girls titter and giggle. I feel pretty glad my dad and the other cops ahead on the boardwalk wait for me to catch up.

I step over two dead dogs on the road outside the general store. Kids clop by on horses without saddles and kick cans in the street. I ask one of the cops what the girl meant by *scrape* and he laughs and reckons I made a good impression. Inside the general store the cashier sits in a cage with everything you can carry away without assistance. I ask for St Moritz but they don't have St Moritz, only Longbeach menthol, and I hate Longbeach menthol. I settle for a twenty-pack and the dude says:

—Six bucks, cuz.

—Fucken six bucks! You only pay two dollars ten for a pack of thirties back on the mainland.

The cashier goes to put the pack back on the shelf but I slap down six bucks.

I leave the store and get in a police Land Rover with the others. We drive up a potted road past buildings which look like someone fought a war in them. The walls have random bricks missing or disintegrating, every space murdered with terrible graffiti. The police have a compound on a hill surrounded by thirty-foot-high fences with the tops leaning out and coiled with razor wire.

I have to stay here all day, in this cop fortress. A cop named Gary shows me his video collection. Dude must have some cash, owning a video machine. After they leave, it takes me about thirty seconds to find his porn collection. I watch a couple of *Color Climax* videos. They star a dude named Long John Holmes, who has a monster cock. He looks bored most of the time. I can't concentrate due to the noise from the pub down on the beach. I go out on the balcony to have a look but can't see much on account of the palms. I go back in and watch some more porn but feel paranoid because they could come back any second and it'll take me at least five minutes to get the videos back in the box and arranged how I found them under the bottom drawer in his bedroom. So I stash away the porn and go back to the balcony and smoke about ninety cigarettes before the Land Rover returns.

The pub rocks all night, top-forty shit from the jukebox filling the air along with animal sounds, gunshots, screams and police cars roaring around. As our side of the planet turns back towards the sun, the pub still rages on. After hearing Billy Ocean sing 'When the Going Gets Tough' for the five thousandth time, I jump at the opportunity to have a look around the island.

I truly wish I hadn't. The rainforest has me in awe but I see extended families living in garden sheds, the kind you find in the suburbs for storing lawnmowers and pushbikes. Scattered through the trees, the corrugated metal gleams. When I get back down into the town, a riot has started at the pub because they've sold out of alcohol and a bunch of locals have made threats about burning the place down. I've spent all day worrying that I haven't got a letter from Billie-Jean for several months. I write to her even though I risk crossing letters. When you cross letters, shit can get confusing.

Back in Townsville. A week remains of the school holidays. I check on my bike and have a smoke and notice new green and gold school uniforms hanging on the line. They have *Thuringowa High* written in a circle with a green jumping kangaroo in the centre. I go inside, furious because this new school will have every pleb from the nearby housing estate in it. My damn parents and their obsession with convenience have again reduced my social status.

7

The first day of school, 1987. Reuben and I walk together. I piggyback him half the way. We stop about a dozen times so he can toke on the joint he has that won't stay lit. He swears weed fixes his pain. He says a few days without weed and he catches fire inside. Then his lighter craps out. To make it worse it starts to rain. We arrive stoned as gargoyles, about twenty minutes late, and get sentenced to detention in the library. We sit. Presently I notice a face peering in with hands cupped up to the glass, trying to see through the tint. My heart drops clear down to my Vision Street Wear sneakers. Muddy! Muddy, the half-Aboriginal kid, who looks like an anorexic leather jacket dragged through broken windscreens and thorny interpersonal relationships. He sees us both notice him and mouths *Fucken faggots*. I knew that every kid on the Thuringowa side of the tracks would end up at this new school.

At first break we come out of the library to find the entire school around our bags. Muddy stands over Reuben all filled up like a toad. I warned Reuben the notorious Muddy would pick a fight with him as soon as their paths crossed. Reuben shrugged it off. After all, he spent five years leading a gang on the streets of Sydney. Muddy steps forward and hisses:

—C'mon, faggot new kid with ya poofter hair and ya faggot wristbands … Wotchya gonna do, cunt? Fucken slap me with ya fucken limp wrist, faggot? I'll fuck up ya gaylord pretty-boy faggot face, faggot. And he takes an awkward swing at Reuben.

With all the grace of Nureyev, Reuben sidesteps the punch and produces his butterfly knife, demonstrating some impressive handling skills.

—He has a knife! about two hundred kids yell in unison.

—Welllll, faggot cunt … Fucken tough cunt … Gonna fucken stab me, cunt. Go on then, ya cunt. DO IT!

He throws a straight left arm into Reuben's face, but, as he does, Reuben pulls his chin down and the fist connects with his forehead. Muddy's knuckles crack and he screams. Then, in that instant, Reuben drops to one knee and drives the knife into Muddy's ribs. A dull THUNK cuts through the stunned silence of the crowd. Everyone gasps. Muddy steps back and looks down at his Sweathog t-shirt. A tiny drop of blood appears. Then, like when you drip ink onto blotting paper, the blood spot swells to the size of a dinner plate. He lifts his shirt, pales. A spray of blood arcs from below his left nipple and disappears into the dust left by five hundred kids running away as fast as possible.

From the opposite direction come the teachers, sprinting with ashen concern. The principal arrives first. Muddy rolls in the dirt, screaming he doesn't want to die. Reuben sits cross-legged, watching. I stand there, not sure what to do. I don't know why I didn't run. The principal bellows:

—WHAT THE HELL HAPPENED?

Sirens closing in.

The cops take Reuben aside and pretty soon they handcuff him. He does the perp-walk past all the shocked staff and assorted teachers. One of the cops says as they pass:

—We intend to charge you with assault with a deadly weapon … and, mate, if I can determine any premeditation in my investigation of this matter, attempted murder.

I get marched into the school office too. I watch Reuben from across the room, his face unmoved. A cop asks me what happened. I say:

—Muddy always picks fights, and Reuben carries a knife because of his feet.

The cop has no idea what I mean, so he ignores me.

—Muddy's beaten me up at least a dozen times!

I show the cop a scar above my left eye, which I did not get from Muddy, but it adds effect. Then the bell rings and they let me go. At the front gates the entire school waits for me. Muddy's little brother launches out of the crowd and punches me in the face.

—Ya gave that cunt a knife to try and kill me big brother, ya faggot! he screams at me as I roll in the gravel. A couple of stinky sneakered feet kick me in the ribs.

—I didn't give him the knife! I say, trying to rise.

—Ya did, cunt. Ya threatened to stab Robbo, with the same fucken knife, ya poofter.

I did in fact threaten to stab Robbo, a nondescript slinky waste of space three years ago, in Year Eight. He punched me as the starter gun fired for a fifty-metre freestyle race. I could have drowned. But I never pulled a knife on him.

Despite the obvious trauma in my countenance – the fat lip, a black eye and the way I favour my ribs – I hope my parents will remain none the wiser about the day's events. But as I drag myself through the front door and throw myself on the couch, my mother's face betrays otherwise. She looks vindicated. She claims she had a mother's intuition all along. Reuben comes from the Devil. Again she expressly forbids me to *ever spend another second in the company of that delinquent.* She doesn't notice my beaten face.

—

A cop car outside our house. It doesn't park where Dad parks. Two policemen knock on the front door and serve me a summons, to appear as witness for the prosecution against Reuben. How did I end up a witness for the prosecution, considering the rumours that infect school that I gave the knife to the dude who almost killed Muddy? The court date looms only a couple of months away. Now my parents *and* the police expressly forbid I seek Reuben's company. I just want to write poems and have sex. A poem for each girl.

8

Two tramp preachers come to stay. They get my room, because it has two single beds. Both of them go by the name of Bruce: Bruce the Elder and Bruce the Younger. This first Bruce, the year I fucked Billie-Jean, promised my dad he'd put the fear of God in me. The same creep I saw in Greenvale watching a boy in the shower. The smile of the Devil, he said about me. I hate this man. But my hatred for him soon pales, eclipsed by my hatred for Bruce the Younger. They put their bibles on my desk and hang their suits in my wardrobe.

After dinner they crowd around the sink, helping to wash the dishes, with their fake sincerity and pious conversation. I slip out and climb up on the roof of the garden shed, to exhale in the breeze. The two Bruces know I smoke. Bruce the Younger, a balding thirty-something who owns an awesome pushbike, encourages me to take rides with him along the river. *To increase your fitness*, he says, flicking his blonde comb-over as he flexes his biceps while changing a tyre. He favours ten-speed bikes, racing style, with thin tyres. I like BMX bikes. If I bunny-hop a gutter on a ten-speed, the rims buckle.

His electric typewriter with disposable ribbons piques my interest. Despite its name, my Remington Noiseless 8 typewriter, which I got from a second-hand store, makes me pretty unpopular with my family, and the neighbours. If I sit in my room hammering out a poem past midnight, people three houses away scream for me to shut the fuck up.

Bruce loans me his typewriter when he realises I favour intellect-based machines. I can sit out in the lounge room and write all night, with only a dull clack which disturbs no one. He says:

—When the ribbon runs out, simply throw the cartridge away! He hands me a packet of spare ribbon cartridges.

I love the writing of William Burroughs. He used what they call an aleatory literary technique. He'd get a sheet of typed-up writing and cut it into strips. Then, relying only on chance, he'd rearrange the words into an entirely new text. When you use an electric typewriter with disposable ribbons, the words appear on the ribbon in a continuous stream, no spaces. I go through a couple of the ribbons typing up poems from my notebook. Then I break open the cartridges and cut the plastic ribbons into ten-centimetre strips. I arrange the ribbons into an A4-size block on the carpet and hope for some genius sentences.

I notice a couple of times that Bruce the Younger smells like my Yves Saint Laurent signature scent, not his regular Old Spice, which means the bastard has gone through my cupboards. He comes into the bathroom while I shower, saying he needs to comb his hair, that *his* room has no mirror. I get ready to punch his face if he peeks around the curtain. He strikes masculine poses and acts all manly, flexes in the mirror, grabs at his balls. I tell Mum I feel pretty uncomfortable. She says Workers have right of way in our house. They speak for the Lord.

Feral alights from his bike in front of my house and says:

—Don't let Bruce the Younger take you camping, even if your mother makes you.

—Why? I ask.

—Trust me, he says and rides away.

Tonight I sneak out later than usual for a cigarette and climb the shed.

A sliver of light like Sauron's eye shines across the lawn. The Bruces haven't shut my bedroom curtains properly. I adjust my position and expect to catch sight of a couple of old dudes with skin like curdled milk on their knees praying. Instead, Bruce the Younger, indeed on his knees, has Bruce the Elder's cock in his mouth. I shake my head in disbelief. My cigarette drops from between my lips, down into Mum's roses. I shut my eyes, open and refocus in time to see the Elder's sperm hitting the Younger's glasses.

—Mum, I say, at breakfast: Last night I saw the two Bruces sucking cock.

Her wedding ring leaves a tear-shaped mark under my eye.

I seek refuge at Feral's house. We sit in the backyard, trying to sneak a cigarette. I say:

—I saw the two Bruces sucking cock.

Feral looks nervous. His mother comes into the garden with a jug of Coke. She chirps at me while looking at him:

—Have you gone camping with young Bruce yet? Joe went last weekend and had a fantastic time … Didn't you, Joe?

He looks interested in something on the ground, ears like sunsets. His mum puts the jug down on the garden table and disappears among the plants.

—What the fuck happened, Feral? I ask, concerned.

—Nothing, man, nothing! Why would anything fucken happen? Fuck. We camped, swam, rode bikes. He talked God at me the whole weekend. He lights a cigarette, sucks half of it down in one drag. Pales.

—I reckon that sick fuck likes boys. Even younger than us, I say.

—Naaaw … doubt it … ya BS-ing me … You reckon ya saw em sucking cock? How d'ya make the leap from him blowing the dong to him liking young boys?

—He put the make on me a couple of times … Real subtle, but unless you have the brain of a fucken plebeian, you get the picture. I saw the Elder dump his load on the Younger's glasses, and the creep licked them clean … No way I would bullshit you about it. My fucken mother won't believe me … Slapped me right in the face when I told her what I saw. I'll have to run away. I mean … man … I feel like I've lost trust in my own family.

When I get home, intending to pack some bags and bail, my mother sits waiting for me on the porch. Straight up she rips into me, demands to know why I'd say such evil things about the tramp preachers. I shove past and kick open my bedroom door, not giving a single damn if they sit in there with God himself. I have the room to myself. I storm about, gathering up my prized possessions: books, pens, knives and letters from Billie-Jean. I shove Bruce the Younger's typewriter across my desk to get my pencil tin, and then I see it. On the ribbon in the typewriter, this sentence:

> Iwanttogiveyouabirthdaypresent.Howoldnow?8,right?Ilovehowyoulove itwhenIcuminyourmouth

I eject the cartridge and smash it on the carpet with a wooden horse-head bookend. I reel out the sentence, revealing more pornographic musings:

> well,nexttimeIwillshowyouwhatitfeelsliketotakeitinthearse.Theenclosed photosofmycockshowhowexcitedIgetwhenIthinkofallthetimeswegot nudetogether.

I go to the kitchen, where my mother has pulled up a chair and strains on tippy toes, trying to get down the Discipline Stick from the crockery cupboard. I read. Her shock turns to disgust as I drone on and on, wheeling out the filth on the ribbon cog. She puts up her hand and I stop. She looks drunk, or sick. She leaves the kitchen. I follow, taunting her:

—Do you believe me now then?

She storms into my room and starts tearing Bruce the Younger's cupboard apart. She pulls out a grey vinyl briefcase, tries the clasps. Locked.

—Mum … I can pick that lock.

But she ignores me, smashes it on the windowsill, the end of the bed, the doorframe. It bursts open the same time the handle comes off. An arc of photographs, glossy magazines and letters fan across the room.

—I knew … I felt it … something not right about him! she says to herself.

—Both of em, Mum. I saw the Elder getting his c— Well, what I told you I saw. But, as I say this, Mum's already made it halfway down the hallway, looking ready to kill Bruce the Younger. She grabs the telephone.

Hands shaking, she dials while standing there snatching horrified glances at the polaroids of little boys on the kitchen bench.

—Sue? Her voice quakes.

Sue, a fellow Friendly, and, as far as I know, Mum's only actual friend.

—Sue, can you come over? … I … I can't explain. No, no one hurt. Just come over, please.

—Mum, both the Bruces have some explaining to do, I say while she paces up and down in the lounge room: I saw the Elder perving through the window at a boy way back in Greenvale! The Younger comes into the bathroom when I shower. I think he raped Joe.

She keeps pacing, looking out the curtains. Sue's car roars up the gravel driveway.

—Go to your room and wait, she says, hand on the doorknob.

Mum and Sue murmur in the kitchen. I hear Sue say:

—I knew it, but I didn't have the gumption to raise my suspicions.

The screen door at the front of the house slams and I hear Bruce the Elder say:

—Evening!

An audible silence. Crows on the clothes line out back. Mum, voice shaking:

—Bruce … do you know about this?

Silence. A television somewhere.

I can't resist the scene any longer so I go down the hall to the kitchen. Mum holds a fistful of the polaroids and she waves them like a schoolmistress waving a secret note in the face of a student. The Elder's face freezes, his eyes terrified.

—What? Disgusting! Where did you get those? He turns his back on us, opens the fridge. Mum swoops around and gets right up under his chin, tense as a prize-fighter. Sue also closes in. I stand in the kitchen doorway.

—He had them in his briefcase. Bruce. Do you know about this?

—Um … I suspected, but … I never … dreamed … I never imagined …

—MUM! I shout: I know he knows! I saw him getting his cock sucked!

Mum's wedding ring splits my lip.

9

I leave home. I go to the house that Gigolo found on Love Lane. Gigolo lives somewhere else now and Reuben has already moved in. His dad and his new mum kicked him out the week of the stabbing. A naked girl lies sleeping on the floor and Reuben has passed out on the couch, also naked. I shove his shoulder to wake him up. He hugs me. The girl goes right on sleeping as I fill him in on all the stuff that's gone down in the past few weeks. He doesn't look surprised when I tell him I have to act as witness for the prosecution. He reckons this plays to our advantage; we can collaborate on our stories. I muse that the cops must have newt brains; they haven't figured out our association. I tell him about the tramp preachers and how my parents didn't report them to the cops. This makes him disgusted.

—Your parents didn't believe you? Sent you right out into the ever-welcoming arms of the street, brother. There you will learn truth … capital T, Truth, about weapons and predators and living by your wits. I'll go right over to your place now, brother, with that cricket bat over there, and I'll turn those tramp preachers' skulls to red mist on their pillows, if you want me to.

He has actual hatred manifested in his eyes, sneering his mouth.

—

The cops come and take me to court. I feel pretty glum, having to testify against my best friend.

We arrive at the courthouse in the city. The cops escort me up a flight of stone steps. We walk by a brass statue of Justice holding up the scales, blindfolded, upon which a billion pigeons have shat.

—Blind Justice. How can she examine the evidence? How does Justice know the scales balance if she can't see the scales? I say to the cops.

They look at me. Both roll their eyes, laugh. Inside, the public prosecutor says to me:

—Tell me your statement.

—No fucken way. I already told the principal, the cops at the school, the cops at the cop station, my parents, my parents again, and you, four times. If you want to hear the story again, refer a couple of chapters back.

—You'll have to tell it again on the witness stand, before the judge. If you fuck it up, or change it, you'll make me look like a dickhead, mate, says the barrister.

—We wouldn't want that, I intone.

I find the whole thing a relief actually – and not only because of the air-conditioning. Reuben looks real smart in a suit. He cut his hair, removed his piercings and dug out his walking stick, which he rarely uses, on account of his general pride. Muddy has done nothing to improve his appearance. His hair looks even greasier. He has a packet of cigs wrapped up in his t-shirt sleeve so it sits atop his shoulder, like regalia on the shoulder of the Bogan General.

The day drags on. They won't let me sit in on the proceedings until after I've appeared. Finally they break for lunch. Reuben walks down the corridor towards me with his lawyer and winks. Muddy comes out with a bunch of Aboriginal people and cops, bringing with them the perfume of a cold library, walnut desks with vinyl tops, linseed and biro ink. Muddy wanders up to me where I sit waiting in the hall outside the courtroom.

—Wanna go play spacies down at Crime Zone? We got two hours for lunchbreak … fucken ace.

He means this place by the city mall called Time Zone, which buzzes with the opera of a thousand pinball machines. Bored kids spend countless Friday and Saturday nights stealing people's milk change from front steps and meeting up at Crime Zone. It stays open twenty-four hours, the only place in the city that never closes. But I kind of fall into a bit of shock right there. Muddy acts like an old mate, with no bad blood! He has that way about him. Last year all us Year Ten kids went on a biology camp. The first day of the camp, sitting out there in the mangroves, I got on with sketching a big old crab that busied itself dragging a bit of seaweed into a hole, when Muddy walked up and punched me in the face, knocked me out. Then he helped me up and tried to wipe the blood off my acid-free drawing notebook, but it soaked right in there. All the while surveying his handiwork with a damaged look in his eyes, he said:

—No one else'll pick on ya this camp … okay, mate. And he walked away.

I compose myself, stammer something and walk awkwardly out of the court building. I feel like an ibis who's had one of its legs cut off with secateurs, half-proud that I walk beside the most deranged and famously bad kid in the whole city, but hobbled with fear that a mega-beating will rain down on me at any moment. We walk in silence out into the ringing heat, down the hill into the city mall. Then Muddy says:

—Ya mate, deadly cunt, ay … Fucken near killed me, the cunt, eh. Fucken … doctor … fucken … said, couple more millimetres and the blade woulda cut me heart clean in fucken half, ay.

—Fuck, *really*? I offer.

—Yeah. I'll get him yet, he says, lighting a Winnie Red.

I let him beat me at *Double Dragon* multiple times, but I get bored and beat him a couple of times in a row. Expecting at any minute a fist that doesn't come puts me in a stressed state and I sweat a lot. We drink a couple of Cokes and smoke his Winfield Reds. Presently we run out of twenty-cent coins. Usually when this happens I head off and jammy a Telecom phone box for change. To do this you need a simple butter knife. Not one of those old-fashioned ones with the faux bone handle and the flimsy blade, but a sturdy stainless-steel butter knife with a good handle. You jam the knife into the coin slot and, with your fist bunched over the handle, you hit it with your other fist, like a flesh hammer. Coins come bursting out of the return slot like a poker machine. I don't know how it works and I don't care. I learned this from Gigolo, who has it down to an art.

Countless nights I've snuck out with a butter knife and a football sock and hit half a dozen phone boxes on my way to having an adventure. Most of the cash goes on *Double Dragon*, *Galaga*, peppermint Aero bars, soft drink and smokes. Arcade machines give you three lives for twenty cents. A one-litre bottle of Coke costs eighty cents, and you can get twenty back if you don't end up smashing the bottle.

So I open my mouth to suggest we do some phone boxes, but Muddy walks over to a group of young kids, obviously wagging school, all striking tough poses and smoking all wrong, crowded around a seat console playing *Moon Patrol*.

—Oi, cunts! hisses Muddy: Give us ya fucken money now, ya fucken little cunts. He randomly throws his fist into a kid's face and knocks him back into his mates.

I make it to the door and up the street before Muddy comes flying out, a look of sick glee on his face, hauling a load of change in his t-shirt bunched up to his chest. The coins bounce and jangle and fall out the sides, clanging on the pavement as he runs. Muddy buys more Winnie Reds and two Cokes. He drinks them both.

We make it back to the court and into the fantastic air-conditioning. Before I know it, my turn has arrived. I walk down the rows of people sitting in silence in the courtroom and it feels like church – priests up the front, except they have stupid wigs and black robes, like a satanic mass. I feel a little worried. I get up and position myself in the box. The marshal comes over, clutching a bible.

—Do you swear to tell the truth, the whole truth and nothing but the truth, so help you God?

—Yeah.

—I *do*! humphs the judge.

—I … I do.

The defence sizes me up, a gaunt-looking bloke with an Adam's apple like he swallowed a gavel. His grey suit has yellow sweat patches under the arms. A pen leaked in the breast pocket once, a long time ago. What hair I imagine remains on his balding scalp under his lawyer wig he has bunched up into a grey mangy-looking pigtail. It lies like a deceased mouse across the collar at the back of his neck. I want to say I think his wig looks totally homosexual, but I refrain. He circles in, cheap stink, hands shaking.

—Who owns the knife with which the defendant stabbed the boy known colloquially as Muddy?

—Reuben owns the knife.

—I have heard otherwise … that in fact the knife belonged to another boy from Thuringowa State High School.

—Nope.

The judge clears his throat, which sounds like someone smothering a budgie in their armpit.

—I will establish, your honour, ladies and gentlemen of the jury, my learned friends, the knife in exhibit A belongs to no other than the witness who now sits before us! He spins dramatically around as he addresses each group, and now he looks all sick and woozy. He takes a breath, exhales through his nose. I can see thick shiny hairs waggle like silver anemones in the salty caves of his nostrils.

—Nope, I say: Reuben had the knife when I met him. He uses it to shave the calluses off his feet.

We've arranged all of this, Reuben and I. Reuben, the game-theory expert, has determined that naturally the defence will try to prove he doesn't own the knife. I'd implicate that he does own the knife, but for legitimate reasons. Following this Reuben meant to get his feet out to show the jury why he carries a knife, to shave the painful calluses that build up, because he wants to walk, like everyone else. But none of this eventuates, because when Muddy climbs into the stand and the Crown prosecutor asks him what he likes to do on weekends, trying to establish the countenance of a regular young man, Muddy says:

—I go down the … fucken … skating rink, ay, mate, and beat up young kids for change to play … fucken … spacies and buy smokes.

The Crown prosecutor, trying his damnedest to convict Reuben of the attempted murder of the dickhead in the box, fails to disguise the mortified look on his face. The crowd starts up mumbling. The lawyer turns around and shrugs to his learned friends at the prosecution's table. The judge starts banging his gavel, looking all bullish and explosion-faced.

—Order! he screams over the murmurs.

The defence calls me to the witness box again. Reuben's lawyer reminds me of my oath and asks:

—Have you ever had a fight with Muddy?

—Yeah, a few hundred, I mumble, looking at Muddy squirming over at the Crown's corner. The Crown lawyer has his mouth right up to Muddy's ear and I can see the anger writhing around in his face.

—Excuse me … Can you repeat that?

—I've had a couple hundred fistfights with Muddy, at least.

—A couple hundred?

—Yeah … at least. He put me in hospital once … Well, my parents had to take me to the hospital. He punched me so hard in the guts I couldn't piss … sorry, urinate, right for a month. And once, at a biology camp, he split my lip so bad I thought I'd have a deformation for the rest of my life.

—Ya fucken dead, cunt! Muddy yells from the prosecution's corner.

10

—Let's get the fuck outta here, Reuben says, stuffing a duffel bag.

I gather up my notebooks, a few pairs of jeans, a spare pair of bootlaces for my Doc Martens, my Sid Vicious tee, a bottle of Yves Saint Laurent signature cologne and a bunch of raggy-looking letters from Billie-Jean I can't bear to part with. I stuff it all into my antique canvas mailbag and we cut out, up the street, as night sets in like the curtain of a final act. As we stand beside the train tracks in the West End of Townsville, we realise we don't have a dollar between us. That, mixed with the weed and adrenalin from knowing that Muddy wants to kill us, makes us both sick with paranoia. The first freight train that comes along, we'll jump right on, but then I remember Reuben can't run.

I suggest maybe we hitch the thirteen hundred ks south to Brisbane, instead of trying to jump a train north to Cairns. Reuben agrees. We set to walking south out of the city, plotting ways to get cash, reminiscing about the court appearance, making plans, deciding on a destination, keeping one eye out for Muddy and his gang.

We've spent a week getting nowhere. Both so hungry we begin to hallucinate. Reuben's run out of weed; every hour that passes sees him all the more antsy.

—Fucken DTs! he says over and over as he shuffles up and down in the dirt in front of me, where I sit trying to write everything down into my notebook.

No one wants to pick up two chain-smoking skinny punks wearing torn jeans, Doc Martens and Sex Pistols t-shirts, two lost apostles of freedom, holding a sign that says *Now or Bust*. A couple of cars pull over and we huddle up to the window to get some of the air-conditioning that pours out into the mercurial heat, straining to hear a few riffs of music to counteract the ringing in our ears from the cicadas in the gum trees. Each time, the driver takes one look at Reuben and assumes he escaped from an asylum. His stunning blue eyes, when his pupils disappear into tiny pieces of nothing, look too far spaced apart. When this happens, his silver tongue gets stuck like he ate a bottle of clag. The driver of this car assumes the same, hits the accelerator and showers us in gravel and dust that reeks of sump oil, diesel and eucalyptus. A box of fishing tackle dislodges from the roof rack. It explodes on the bitumen and the lead sinkers melt into the road.

We've happened on a phone box, by itself, out in the middle of nowhere, between nowhere towns. I go through my mailbag, hoping I have a butter knife to jammy out some coins, but I don't have a butter knife. Neither does Reuben.

—We don't need fucken shrapnel. We need a fucken bunch of real cash! he snaps.

—Sometimes you can get a hundred bucks out of a phone box, I say into the glare and the shrieks.

—Only a dickhead would think that you'll get more than five bucks out of a phone box by the highway in the middle of fucken nowhere. He spits and it sizzles on the road.

We argue and he gets all aggressive and I hate him a little. Then a couple of hours pass and I feel like I could drink diesel out of the road dust, and I say *sorry* and he says *groovy*. Out of desperation I ring home, reverse charges, hoping my father will agree to at least talk, or maybe even put some cash into my bank account.

—Dad? I say as the phone clicks up.

—Mate! We've worried ourselves sick! You okay?

—Yeah, alive.

—Have you come back?

—Not yet.

Silence.

—Standing in a phone box out on the Bruce Highway, near a place called Gumlu.

—About an hour or so south of here, Dad says, mirth rising in his voice.

Silence.

—Um … yeah.

—But you left a week ago!

—Yeah.

Silence.

Fits of laughter from Dad.

—Fuck you, Dad … Muddy wants to kill us; we had to get away.

—Yeah, but, mate, why has it taken you a week to get a hundred and forty clicks?

—Reuben can't walk, Dad, and I've piggybacked him this far and I feel fucked and I haven't eaten in a week and no cunt will pick us up. I cry. Looking around I see that Reuben stands a safe distance off, kicking at the side of the road. I sob, audibly.

—You with Reuben, huh?

—Yeah.

—I'll come and get you.

—What about Reuben?

—I'll come and get *you*.

—I can't come back, Dad. Muddy threatened to kill me.

—Muddy got busted stealing money from a Telecom phone box. This'll see him in prison, mate; that problem has gone. Just lie low for a while, come home.

—I won't come back to the meetings, and if a single tramp preacher comes near me, I'll—

—Bruce the Younger got sent overseas by the Head Workers.

—What? He should get locked up!

—We'll talk about it when I come get you.

I agree, hang up and walk over to where Reuben busies himself kicking the living shit out of the lip where the asphalt curls over onto the dirt on the roadside.

—Ya goin home, right? he mutters at me, flicking a cigarette butt into the blistering wind.

—Man …

—You do what ya gotta do. Groovy … no problem. Don't fucken worry about me.

—I do worry about you, brother. I feel *real* bad that my olds hate you so much. If I had my way, we'd both go back, eat till we vomit, have showers, ya know. I just dunno if I can go on another day without …

But then I realise how it sounds, and I open my mouth to say *fuck it – let's keep going* as a car swerves off the road and skids to a halt. The Sex Pistols' 'Anarchy in the UK' blares out the windows of a beaten Holden Kingswood with shiny mag wheels and doors either blue with rust or rust with blue. A skinhead sticks his head out the front passenger side and says:

—Both ya cunts wanna lift? Sorry, fuckers, we only got space for one … ay.

Reuben doesn't look at me, spies the back driver's side seat has a vacancy, checks for traffic, walks around and climbs in, still not looking at me. The car roars off, backfiring in a black cloud.

About an hour later Dad pretends to not see me on the highway and drives on. Then, about five minutes later, he pulls up coming the other way, winds down his window and says:

—Need a lift, mate?

We sit in silence for about half an hour before Dad starts on about maybe going back to Kirwan High.

—After all, he says: the bullies have all gone to Thuringowa. He says *bullies* real patronising, like I'd cried in the sandpit. He grins awhile, which pisses me off.

We roll up the gravel driveway and I see Mum looking out through a gap in the curtains. I go into the house purposefully not looking at where

I saw her standing and straight to my bedroom. I sleep for two days in my filthy clothes. The first thing I realise as I awake, Dad never said a thing about why he didn't report the tramp preacher to the cops! Perhaps another form of justice awaits him. Maybe Dad didn't want to talk about it. I don't think I want to talk about it either.

Part Three
Aftermath

I give the name violence to a boldness lying idle and enamoured of danger.
Jean Genet

1

December 1987. On the Greyhound, en route to Brisbane and Billie-Jean. Sitting at the front above the steps, on the highway somewhere south of Rockhampton, the rain belting down in the dark, cars screaming right at us out of the howling black. The driver hunches forward, jaw of stone. I feel alone among the mumbling and snoring of the other passengers behind me. Put on my headphones: Floyd's 'Comfortably Numb'. Trying to picture Billie-Jean in her bed in Brisbane, her breasts, her lips in the moonlight by a Cadillac on a grassy knoll.

The rain clears around dawn and I stare out the window, hardly blinking. Reuben might appear out here somewhere, by the side of the road with his thumb out, or at a servo trying to hustle travellers for food and smokes. I don't see him.

I spend four or five hundred kilometres of the trip worrying that Billie-Jean will no longer find me attractive, or that she has an actual boyfriend. Not that I can claim sainthood. Since Billie-Jean I've had sex with at least a dozen girls, I figure. I busy myself trying to remember them in chronological order, writing a list in my journal, but I keep getting stuck because I don't know some of their names. Reuben says you should never kiss and tell, though he tells all the time. Reuben also says that oral sex counts on his tally sheet. I growled out a chick who lives across the road the week before I slept with Billie-Jean, and before that I growled out three of my sister's friends when they came to stay.

I listen to Echo & the Bunnymen on my Walkman, rewinding 'Bring On the Dancing Horses' over and over, while I spend the next six hours drilling into my memories, trying to complete my list:

Kim
Claudia
?
?
Billie-Jean
Sophie
Marcella
? (Marcella's sister)
Kim number 2
Marnie
Josephine
Nicole
? (Nicole's friend)
Narrelle
Michelle
Cindy

Sixteen girls! I feel kind of ashamed but a bit proud. Should I hang my head and sigh or shout with joy and punch the sky? I ponder this for a while. Dawn strobes through the trees as the bus passes factory outlets and freeway overpasses. My batteries run flat.

The bus wheezes into Roma Street Station and all the broken-looking travellers get out like Jonahs from the belly of a silver whale. I notice Billie-Jean's mother first, in front of her daughter, holding her back. Billie-Jean peers over her shoulder with a big beautiful smile on her perfect face. Billie's mum has a space helmet of silver hair piled up on her head, lacquered like a Caravaggio masterpiece. Part of me knows that my parents and Billie-Jean's mother plotted this whole trip to try to get me back to the fold of Friendlies, but I don't care. Won't work on me. Billie-Jean's mother has a rank high up the food chain of religious freaks who belong to this cult. I guess she feels pretty confident about her evangelical skills if she thinks she can convince me to believe in crazy.

I kiss Billie-Jean on the cheek, real polite like, but, unseen to her mother, I poke her cheek with my tongue. Chicks love that shit. I also notice she now has rather large breasts! We ride in silence for a while in her mum's Peugeot back to her house in the suburb of Nundah on the city's north side. Billie has three sisters and a brother. Her mum leads me up the stairs to her brother's room, which has two single beds in it. I feel pretty shy right about now. Her mum has a real intimidating stare and one of those letter-slot judgemental mouths. She points at a towel on the foot of the bed over by the window and grunts:

—That … ugh … perfume. You should have a shower, Brentley.

—Cologne, I say: Yves Saint Laurent, signature … You don't like it?

She sniffs through one nostril and her horizontal mouth goes about forty-five degrees east. Her tongue sticks out like a pink telegram as she crosses her arms. I wonder how Billie turned out so beautiful. She leaves. I scope out the room.

The possessions of a downtrodden and restricted kid. Including two bibles. Kids who still dig sandpits shouldn't have bibles. The kid doesn't have anything to nick the batteries out of. The room has an air-conditioner and a fancy remote control, with double-As. I nick those, stick them in my Walkman, get my cigarettes and INXS's *Kick* cassette from my duffel bag and go out on the balcony to have a look. I check out which way the wind blows, light up a cigarette, pop my headphones on and hit play. 'Devil Inside'. I drum on the railing, head banging, lost in the music, and a hand comes down on my shoulder. I spin on my heel and exhale smoke right into Billie-Jean's mother's face. She snatches the phones off my head and spits:

—Really into it, huh? The Devil's got you, boy.

I stammer through dinner, anxious to get some time alone with Billie-Jean. Her old man asks me a bunch of boring questions about school and my plans for the future. He doesn't say much else, just hunches like a vulture over the head of the table. Her siblings stare at me.

Then I have to act all polite and amiable as the whole family crowd around the sink doing the dishes. Soon her parents say we all have to go to bed – at eight fucken pm? Billie gives a little sad pout and dutifully heads off up the stairs with her sisters. I go up to her brother's room and sneak a smoke out on the balcony. I sit in bed reading Byron for a while. I must have drifted off, because, as I awake to Billie-Jean shaking my shoulder, the light still burns overhead.

—Let's sneak out. We'll go to Macca's, she whispers with a sweet breath.

It takes me a couple of seconds to adjust but I heartily agree and get out of bed, still fully dressed. The clock in the hall reads 12.30 am. She expertly, silently, opens the front door of the house, despite the large deadlocks, which I tell her I find an admirable skill. We walk up the huge busy Sandgate Road and across a rail bridge, talking the whole way. I fill her in about Reuben and Muddy and the stabbing and the court case, and then we sit in McDonald's drinking Coke and smoking cigarettes. I tell her about the posse and Gigolo's house on Love Lane and all about Bruce the Younger. I skip the bits about the girls and the stealing and I get up to the part about watching Reuben roar off in a Kingswood with a group of skinheads when the manager of McDonald's politely requests we buy more burgers or leave. We walk back up the road hand in hand as the first train trembles underneath. We kiss each other near to death in the hallway before going to our separate rooms.

At breakfast Billie says she will take me into the city. I feel pretty excited, and I busy myself getting dressed for an hour until Billie comes in and catches me in the bathroom stealing her mother's hairspray. She doesn't say anything and helps me tease my hair up more at the back where I can't see it properly in the mirror. I've got on black jeans, tucked into my twelve-hole black Doc Martens, a James Dean t-shirt and a black duffel coat with *Punk* and *Anarchy* pins down the lapels. A small silver pistol that works as a lighter hangs from a keychain on my studded belt.

Billie says she wants to see *The Lost Boys*, a film about vampires, but her mother reckons vampires sleep with Satan, so we keep the cinema plan quiet. About then her little brother happens by the bathroom and informs me in this sweet-innocent-kid kind of way that only girls use hairspray. Billie says:

—Fuck off, ya little arsehole!

He scurries off to dob on us. We hightail it out of the house, back up Sandgate Road to the train station, and as we get down the stairs a train pulls up. We get right on and Billie tells me we will get off at Fortitude Valley. I go on about what Fortitude means, particularly in tarot cards.

In the Valley she takes me up into McWhirters shopping centre and shows me where she smokes after school on this covered overpass that crosses Wickham Street. We sit awhile, watching the cars below, reading the street press piled along the window ledge, smoking cigarettes.

Pretty soon Billie-Jean leads me to the subway to catch a train into central Brisbane, to go see *The Lost Boys*. All these bummed-out scabby-looking tramps sit around in the subway, clinking bottles on their rotten teeth, walking back and forth along the concourse looking for cigarette butts people have stomped out as they board the train. It only takes about five minutes to get to Central Station. We go down the escalators and cross a little park into the city mall.

—

Billie-Jean sits by my side in the cool dark of the cinema. I should feel elated, but I don't. And I don't know why. I guess I built her up in my mind, as a goddess. Now I dunno. She seems more interested in the experience than the person she has it with. Her hand in mine should give me a buzz, but I only get static. My mind wanders like this all through *The Lost Boys*, despite the fact I really dig vampire films and develop an instant crush on Jami Gertz. I can't suspend my disbelief. All the acting feels stilted, the actors like Mr Potato Head, the director shifting around their facial expressions. Before I know it, the end credits roll. We wait there until the credits finish and everyone else has left the theatre. We sit in silence until the overhead lights come on full strength and a bunch of people come in to pick up empty popcorn buckets and choc-top wrappers. Billie leans in and whispers:

—Let's go fuck.

This picks me up a bit. I look at Billie under the cinema lights and the way her breath pushes her breasts against her Madonna t-shirt, and my cock throbs.

—Okay, I say, managing to suppress the tremble in my voice.

We go back out into the Queen Street Mall and sit on a circular bench. We smoke a couple of cigarettes. Then Billie rises and says:

—Wait here.

I watch her walk off. She goes into a chemist. Then she comes out, says:

—Let's go.

Leading me through the crowd. On Elizabeth Street we wait near a bus stop. We ride the bus to New Farm and get off on the corner of Harcourt and Brunswick streets. We walk by all these artist and hippy types.

—I'd like to live in New Farm one day, I say.

We get to a street that runs right by the Brisbane River. It has rows of old Queenslander-style houses. Billie leads me up the steps of one with *Back Packers Hostel* on a sign hanging above the gate. *Vacancy*, it reads underneath. We go into a musty-smelling foyer that looks like someone set up an office in a lounge room. A dreadlocked old bloke huffs up out of an overstuffed couch and says:

—Yeah.

—We have a stopover for a few hours, on our way to Melbourne, Billie says.

—Yeah.

—Can we get a room for a couple of hours? We could use some sleep.

He looks us both up and down.

—No bags?

—Left them in a locker at Roma Street.

—Two hours?

—Max.

—Ten bucks, drawls the dreaded man, and yanks a key off a board on the wall behind him.

He watches us creak up the stairs and huffs back to the arms of his couch. Billie-Jean has done this before; I just know it. We have sex for about an hour, using three of the condoms Billie stole from the chemist in the mall.

We do this the rest of the week. Only we don't go to the cinema, or the city. We get off the train at Brunswick Street Station in Fortitude Valley, walk down into New Farm, pick a random backpackers' and fuck like Adam and Eve, like all human life depends on it. We use all twenty condoms in the box.

On my last night at Billie-Jean's, around midnight, she creeps into her brother's room. She gingerly slides open the glass door onto the balcony and beckons me to follow. I get up off the guest bed and of course the damn thing creaks like a freight train on a collapsing bridge. Her bloody little brother jolts open his eyes. I figure I don't care if he sees me going out on the balcony, so I pop a cigarette in my mouth and give him a good stare right back. So what if the little shit tells his mum he saw me smoking; my parents already gave up trying to make me quit. *No smoking at Billie-Jean's parents' house, okay!* Mum said as she waved me off on the bus.

We kiss out here on the balcony and I finger her awhile. I love how a girl's scent lingers for hours, like a fragrant cloying mist. We make plans for our last day together.

—Let's hang out in the Botanic Gardens, she says.

We set out early the next morning and catch the train into Central Station. I have my duffel bag and my old postman's satchel with my journals and pens and everything in it. I put my bags in a locker in the subway. Tonight I have to meet with my aunty at some train station out in the deep suburbs. She takes religious fervour to a whole new dimension. Her voice has the timbre of a church organ. Repression has taken such a grip on her soul that her insides have twisted up like a pretzel. My uncle, this old coot, reminds me of an Enid Blyton character. He wears one of those tweed hats and a matching jacket with the fucken vinyl elbows. He smells like camphor and lavender and my aunty's hairspray. All those religious zealots use so much hairspray they caused the hole in the ozone layer.

We slow-walk through the city. The Brisbane mall looms fifty times bigger than in Townsville. The Townsville mall feels abandoned, like a theme park after dark. The first time I walked through Queen Street, I'd just turned thirteen. I'd only had sex with Billie-Jean once. I dreamed of seeing her again after saying goodbye to her at that religious fruit-cake Convention. Now, three years later … this other idea, one I've had to work hard at suppressing, bursts out of my chest like an alien. For years I've pondered how precocious Billie-Jean acted that night, on a blanket beside her dad's purple Cadillac. I wanted to believe that all city girls did it like her. But no girl I've come across since acted like that, in towns or in huge cities, throwing caution to the wind and initiating *actual* sex. And that story about her friend getting pregnant from her dad … I kind of knew, back then even … I shake my head, try to dislodge the thought. Billie-Jean gives me this strange look, says:

—What ya thinkin about?

—Nothin.

—You look … I dunno, worried?

—Sad … You know, our last day, and all.

—Oh.

Silence.

—How many letters do you reckon we've written each other?

—Couple thousand, she says, laughing.

I try to do the maths in my head. At least one letter a week, fifty-two weeks in a year, three years …

—One hundred and fifty-six, she says, way too fast.

—I suck at maths. They actually put me in this special education class at high school.

—What?

—Yeah. All the other kids had actual mental and physical disabilities … in wheelchairs, and shit.

—I wouldn't tell too many people that story, she says as we pass a war-veteran-looking dude playing a saxophone.

We watch him tear it up for a while. His moustache has white bits on the droopy ends, like he dipped it in a cappuccino. Billie flips a fifty-cent coin into his hat. As we walk away, the music sounds sadder.

We get to the Botanic Gardens and sit on a grass slope with hundreds of little white flowers. Beyond shines the Brisbane River. A path down to the water. We watch the boats, share a cigarette, neither of us wanting to talk first. Billie sighs:

—I don't know if I love you anymore … I can't decide. And she turns her mouth down into a literal sad clown face.

I wait for a couple of seconds, to see if her words will hit my heart like an anti-aircraft shell. Nothing happens.

—I know how you feel, I say.

—What?

—I know how you feel.

—So, you don't love me anymore?

I look into her huge blue eyes. She seems hurt.

—I dunno. Like you, sometimes I think I do, but … yeah, like you, uncertain, I guess.

—I've had other boyfriends … since you.

I feel paranoid for a second that she read my journal, the half-remembered names of all the girls I wrote down on the bus coming to see her. I light another cigarette.

—Same, I say.

—How many girls have you had sex with?

—Er … a few, I lie. Even a few sounds too many, in answer to a question like that.

—I've fucked about thirty guys.

—Thirty! I do my best not to inhale my whole cigarette. I want to look like I don't care. Jealousy dragged me down just then, like a rip in a wild ocean, caught me by surprise. I don't know whether I feel envious or sick, or what.

—How does that make you feel? Billie asks.

—I don't trust Love anymore. Everyone wants her … I don't want her. I push her away so when she leaves I will not miss her. I want to harden my armour against Love … against loss, this stupid human condition which drives me to seek out things which hurt me. Why should I fight? Just look at Cupid: he has a weapon and a benevolent smile. So yeah … I feel ambivalent … Good for you, you've fucked thirty dudes … Live fast, die young.

—Ambi … what?

—Ambivalent: I dunno whether to vomit or laugh.

—You talk weird. Why would you laugh?

—I dunno. Shock?

—You calling me a slut?

—No! Well … no.

—Well fuck you, she says, standing, blue eyes ferocious.

I don't stand. She walks away, towards the path and the river beyond. I sit there, looking at her silhouette against the sky and the buildings across the water. I think for a moment about asking if her dad molested her, to see how she reacts. But this would only hurt her, whether it happened or not. I realise I've picked one of those little white flowers and I've actually started plucking the petals, saying, *she loves me … she loves me not.*

Totally disgusted with myself I dig around in my pockets for my cigarettes, only I've put them in Billie's bag. The story of my life: always yearning for something slightly beyond my reach. I feel like a young Werther in a capitalist hell, or a frozen Han Solo watching Jabba the Hutt fucking my true love with his hideous tongue. Werther had the guts to shoot himself in the head. I took the journey instead. What would I write in my suicide note? I get up, feeling all wooden and creaky, and walk over to where Billie-Jean stands, pretending to watch the water-birds and the boats.

—Sorry, I say, putting my arm around her.

She doesn't pull away, but she also doesn't answer.

Before you know it, 3 pm has come around and I have to go and catch a train to meet my aunt. We walk in silence back through the city and we stand around by the ramp into Central Station, sort of scuffing about and taking interest in anything distracting. The whole city teems past us. She breaks first, says:

—I'll come down to the platform with you.

She gives me this huge hug and we stand there holding each other for a while. The train roars in. We kiss. I get aboard and turn to wave.

—I just realised … I really do love you, she says over the hiss of the automatic doors.

2

No sooner do I get off the bus in Townsville and into my parents' car than I feel a mixture of defeat and elation that I've had sex twenty times in the last week but I might never see Billie-Jean again. Then my old man starts on me. *What will you do now?* he asks a dozen times before I've even rolled down my window. He thinks I should return to Thuringowa High for Year Twelve, which starts in two weeks, despite the stabbing. *Thuringowa has a new principal now*, he says.

I want to put high school behind me, way behind me, so I busy myself trying to find a job. I get the newspaper off the front lawn at dawn every morning and make sure the old man sees me poring over it when he rises. If, for some reason – like an all-night jaunt – I haven't woken before Dad, he comes into my room, like the first rays that ache through the curtains, and kicks my bed, throws the newspaper at me and tells me to put a pot of coffee on and get cracking looking for a job. I pretend to look mighty interested in the employment section until he roars off on his motorbike. When he returns, I, having spent the whole day writing or hanging at my friend Maz's house smoking, do my best to avoid him until dinner.

—

No job offers have come in the mail. The house phone hasn't rung. School starts next week. Dad takes me down to Thuringowa High and introduces me to the new headmaster.

—You can take him from here, he says to Mr Hargreave.

Mr Hargreave shoots Dad a concerned look. We go into his office and I throw myself into a chair.

—Tell me about yourself, he says, appraising my dishevelled countenance.

—Um.

—What plans do you have? What do you want to do when you finish school?

—I thought I'd finished school.

He shakes his head.

—Do you like girls?

—What? For a second he morphs into a Bruce, semen on his glasses. I feel sick.

—If I let you come back here, you have to make me a promise, he says, tapping a pen on his desk, trying to peer into my soul.

I don't reply.

—Promise me you'll concentrate on your studies and that you'll leave the girls alone.

—Sounds like two promises.

—What?

—Nothing.

He taps his pen harder on the desk, and the lid flies off and hits the window. Beyond the glass the gardener on a ride-on mower makes his way around the school oval. I pashed girls on that oval. I got legless drunk out there on the grass. I sat with my graffiti posse there, waiting for the security guard to leave so we could murder the school.

—Tell me your plans. After school, what do you want to do?

—What I already do: write.

—What … for a newspaper, or novels, or … what?

—Poetry.

—No poet has made a living from poetry since Byron.

—Byron didn't make a cent from poetry.

—What?

—He refused money for his poetry. Sullied the purity of his verse, he reckoned.

—I didn't know that.

—Well now you do, I say, too sarcastically.

He humphs out of his desk chair, goes across to the window and kind of grunts over and picks up the blue pen lid from the carpet.

—That flippancy will get you nowhere. You know that, right? he says as he straightens himself up, puffing like he's run a triathlon, not walked three steps across the room: You have to make a living somehow. This world can get nasty. He plops back down in his desk chair and the vinyl makes a hissing sound.

—Fuck the world.

—What!

—I said: Fuck. The. World.

—I know what you said ... Don't speak to me like that!

—Or what, Mr Hargreave? Or, what?

—What makes you so angry? He takes off his glasses and peers down his nose at them. He gathers up the front of his sweaty-looking shirt and rubs them vigorously. Probably wiping off the semen.

I think about my rage for a while. I have anger boiling inside me. Sometimes I look in the mirror and imagine the boys who used to beat me. Imagine fighting back, a dead disinterested look in my eyes. I smash their skulls and pull out their brains while they still breathe. I fantasise about eviscerating them, their agony as I kill them. Those boys bashing me didn't make me angry, though wishing I could kill them sure lets off steam. I stare at Mr Hargreave and imagine a couple of expert karate chops and straight knuckle punches to his throat.

What *has* made me this angry? This whole damn world feels inverse and upside down. People who don't deserve what they have have everything. Everything that tastes good ... bad for you; tastes bad ... good for you. Money. Don't get me started about money. What a whore. It doesn't care who holds it; it doesn't care what you do with it. It'll happily fund a charity for crippled kids or the terrorist organisation that crippled the kids in the first place. I've never had money. I don't have anything. I always end up at the back of class, invisible. I spent years thinking I'd learned some neat magic trick, to make myself invisible. I have to face the truth, though. No one notices me because I don't matter. Not even my dad notices me. I ask him a serious question and he starts up with some fucken anecdote, or shows me a cartoon in the newspaper. Dad gets angry about money a lot – you hardly see him angry, but money does it every time. In the grand scheme of things I rate pretty damn low. Just a grain of sand between the toes of someone great, a bubble in a king's champagne, a suckerfish on a shark's belly, a fawn in a lion's jaws. I've had enough of nothing.

—Brentley?

I snap back. Mr Hargreave has his glasses on crooked. A mutant eyebrow arcs down. The drone of the ride-on mower makes me drowsy. A lone crow gives a lazy hot caw from the cricket pitch.

—What do you think, then? he asks, impatiently now.

—Okay, Mr Hargreave … You know what? Fuck you and fuck this school.

—Hem, he grunts.

I rise and he also rises, the vinyl whistling under him. He leads me out through the school and all the classrooms full of kids. They stare like a carnival has arrived. He stops abruptly at the quadrangle where Reuben stabbed Muddy. It has grass now and they've planted hedges to break up the space. He watches me looking around.

—Don't ever come back here, mate, he says, pointing at the gate.

3

So I return to Kirwan High for 1988 – at least in theory. Dad insists on dropping me at school and I dutifully walk in and right out the back gate. I go to Fulton's house. I like Fulton's parents. We can smoke right along with them. His whole family emigrated from New Zealand a couple of years ago. Fulton only stayed in school for about six months and then dropped out to work at Coles. My dad calls him The Sheep, not only because of his origins but also because he has a portly appearance and a head of hair like wool. It has this greasy look about it too, like the dude's scalp produces lanolin. Fulton's mother shares my fascination with tarot cards. I love sitting on their lounge-room floor with her, smoking cigarettes and reading fortunes.

—

Kirwan High called my dad and told him of my zero attendance status. Now Dad keeps me at home, poring over the job ads and cold-calling people for work. Salvation will only come if I get a job. The phone rings in the house. A German dude invites me to his bakery to interview me for the role of apprentice baker. I tell Dad. Dad shrugs and doesn't even look up from his James Bond novel.

Mum drives me a few suburbs north to Mount Louisa. The boss looks like an anorexic fascist. When he stalks around his giant bakery-kitchen-factory-thing, he has a gait that must've resulted from a motorcycle accident or a stint in the Hitler Youth. For some reason, he cuts me off before I can answer his rapid-fire questions. He tells my mum I have the job and to make sure I get here at zero-three-hundred on the dot.

—Zis iz hart verk … Does zeus haz ze gumptionz fir zis hart verk? he shouts at me.

I hate people who use the word gumption. My dedicated parents take turns driving me to work at three in the morning, Monday to Friday. We have only one car: a poo-brown Commodore station wagon. Dad says bronze, but no.

My day starts with firing up the ovens. Then I have to follow precise instructions and dump half a tonne of mince and chopped-up mushrooms and onion and filler-grunge stuff into a huge pot that has wheels and a petrol pump kind of thing sticking out the side. As soon as the ovens get hot and the pie-mix starts cooking, the nausea comes on. Every day this happens. Then I spend an hour lining up pie tins in a precise symmetry. If I get it wrong, the Nazi says I have to pay for all the pies I've fucked up. All the while the bakers mix dough in machines and stand over in the corner watching me do all the work. They roll out the dough and I press it into the tins. Then I drag the huge cooking pot on wheels up and down, pumping a splurt of mince into each tin.

I do this for six months, getting more tired and angry as the weeks roll by. Incrementally the Nazi adds more work to my duties. Originally I'd start at three and get home around midday – that stretches out to 1 pm, and a couple of times even 2 pm. Other dudes say *think of the overtime you'll get*. An extra hour, when you begin at three, for twelve lousy bucks doesn't incentivise me. I have huge dark circles under my eyes. I find myself yelling all the time.

One morning the boss screams more than usual. He throws an old dried-out ball of dough at one of his apprentices and it clocks him right under the eye – opens him up, too. The apprentice staggers around wailing and sheeting blood, which turns pale pink as it hits the flour-covered floor. Blood rain in moon dust. The Nazi yells at us, standing there gawping, to get our arses back to work *or I'll fire ze lot ov youz.*

He tells me, when the sun passes midday and I go to clock out, that I've fallen down on my duties.

—Huh? My cigarette drooping in my lips.

—Zeus haz nit scrabbed ze potz! he bellows at me.

I've never had to scrub the pots in the last six months. Another dude clocks in every day as we all leave.

—I don't …

—SCRAB ZE FARKUN POTZ!

—Fuck you, you Nazi cunt! I scream back.

Uh-oh.

He comes at me in a stride, left arm out shoulder height, elbow bent like in a parade, and he gets me in a headlock somehow. His forearms hard and cold as steel rails on a staircase. He drags me out of the kitchen and into the cafe. We burst out behind the counter and scare the shit out of the chicks. The customers recoil in horror as the door bangs open. He drags me behind the glass cases full of pies and sausage rolls and croissants and custard slices and lamingtons and gingerbread men. We knock over a wire bread stand with a crash. A bunch of families sitting around tables up in the window scream and trip over each other. He goosesteps me through the crowd, kicks open the door and throws me out into the street. The door slams behind me.

The rest of 1988 sees me back on Fulton's couch and reading fortunes. I have a great future just waiting to happen to me.

The first few months of the new year don't seem like the future yet. Rejected job applications pile up on my desk. Dad suggests I join him on a canoe trip he organised for a local Adventurers' club, down the Burdekin River, from Greenvale to Charters Towers. He gets out these huge maps of Australia and lays them across Mum's precious lace tablecloth, and then, when she shoos us out of the living room, we lay them out on the carpet in the lounge. We pore over them, trying to work out from the scale how many kilometres the river flows between departure and destination. It gets difficult because the river doglegs and turns back on itself in a couple of places, passes between hills and through valleys.

—I reckon it'll take about five or six days, Dad says. Then he rubs his chin and looks at me with a hint of disappointment, like he does a lot lately.

Sometimes I feel pity for my parents – not often, but sometimes – sorry they have a child like me. I said to my mother once during an argument that I'll never forgive her for getting me circumcised, that my recalcitrant attitude results from her karma. I can't wear the blame for her wanting to bring a child into the world, because she wanted a baby, without consulting me. Of course she doesn't know what the word karma means, or recalcitrant. She accused me of swearing at her, in Latin or something.

The prospect of returning to Greenvale for this canoe trip, the first visit since I left a few days short of twelve years old, fails to stimulate me much, but to keep the old man happy, and to take a break from the daily routine of hunting for work, I agree to go.

As soon as he starts looking pleased, I ask if I can take a friend. I owe Fulton a favour. I've smoked about two hundred packets of his cigarettes, because I have no money. Fulton hasn't seen any more of Australia than the drive from the airport and the pushbike ride to school and Coles. I've entertained him countless times with tales of my wild boyhood in Greenvale. I invite him; he gets excited.

—

The more I think about it, the more this canoe trip down the Burdekin River sounds cool. It'll do me good to get out from under the wires of the city and de-static my brain. Fulton has worked himself up about poisonous snakes and spiders and shit in the Australian outback. I explain that they sense people's fear – if you don't even think about them, they'll not bother you at all. Then I throw some stuff in there about karma. If you don't have bad karma, then the snakes'll leave you alone. Fulton doesn't buy this, however, and mouths off at me that snakes don't give a flying fuck if you have a clear conscience. He might have it right, but

I prefer to believe in karma. Worst thing that ever happened to me in the bush, that fucken yowie near scared me to literal death. I better not tell him the yowie story. At least until we get out there, in the middle of nowhere, in the dark, as the fire dies and the dingoes circle in.

Fulton spends the night before we leave at my house, and we spend most of it fussing about with our canoe and duffel bags. He smokes a whole packet of cigarettes in about two hours, and paces nervously around the backyard. I fill up the canoe with water on the lawn, to see if any leaks out. It all seems pretty shipshape.

We get out on the highway at dawn, after stopping by the TAFE College to pick up the Adventurers. Most of them look about thirty, apart from a couple of older women and one real old dude who acts all sprightly but you can tell it exhausts him. Out of earshot I exclaim to Dad that the old dude looks like he might drop dead at the first hint of exertion, but Dad reckons the dude just looks old because of his alcoholism. Besides, he won't join us on the water. He will drive the bus back from the river to the end of our journey at Charters Towers.

Dad has rented a bus that fits all thirteen people on board, and he has a huge trailer hooked up with six canoes and about eight hundred pieces of luggage strapped to the sides. Fulton and I don't talk much – not that we could above the excited clamour of the tourists. The landscape starts looking all too familiar to me after a couple of hours. The eucalypts crowd in over the single-lane highway. The insect-screech rips through your head.

About four hours later we pull in to the servo at Greenvale to fuel up the bus. Then we roll into the town and all pile out for a counter lunch at the Three Rivers Hotel. When we've finished our schnitzels and chips, my old man says we have about half an hour, so I rush Fulton out of the pub and up the street towards the old police station and the house I grew up in.

The nickel mine has since closed down and the town looks dead – everything brown and crinkled, the chain mail fences all rusted and sagged in, signs creaking in the stifling wind. The supermarket has an *open* sign, but as we approach we see through the glass that only a couple of shelves in the cavernous space have anything on them. An ancient bored woman sucks on a cigarette in the doorway. I expect the old familiar welcome blast of the air-conditioning in the supermarket mall but it feels even hotter in here. The Fish-n-Chip Shoppe now offers only a black shape in the wall with dust and cobwebs up against the door. The mall smells like fetid cooking oil and stale potatoes. A sign leans up against the window. *Out of Business*, it reads.

We cut out the back and through the car park to the old school oval and the tennis courts. Now only a brown circle welcomes us. Someone has bulldozed the courts. We walk across the oval, growing taller with the billion prickles that attack our sneakers. We stand out on the old cricket pitch in the middle of the oval and I scuff around in the oiled dirt, surveying the horizon. The whole place has died. A crow crows from atop one of the lighting towers, which sags dangerously. We go through the gates, which hang off their hinges, and up the path towards the school. A tramp has fallen asleep on a bench in the shade underneath the building. Everything has shrunk. I feel sure it used to take at least five minutes to walk from the oval, but now we cover the ground in about twenty steps.

The quiet blankets us. Fulton shudders, though the temperature has reached about a thousand degrees. This place once teemed with kids, green everywhere. Even the sky in my memories looked brighter. I rub the dirt off a window and peer into the classroom I spent seven years of my life plotting to escape. The room now looks about the size of a broom closet.

—See that aluminium siding there? I say to Fulton, who joins me at the window: I kicked it all the time, by my desk right there, and one day it sprung up and this teacher tripped over it. She broke her arm!

—Brutal, says Fulton, out of the corner of his mouth, sucks on a cigarette.

We wander past the quadrangle, where all the picnic tables have yellow umbrellas blown off them, the concrete mouldy from the rain and the heat. We go out through the front gates to my old house, which sits right outside the school. Obviously the new cop lives there. The grass shimmers all fresh and green, and we can see clothes on the line down the side. We get around to the parallel street and a shiny grey police-issue Toyota sits at the front of the police station. We cut across the park where years ago I sliced my toe on a piece of glass and had all those memories about circumcision. Back up the street we pass the swimming pool. The bushes and trees which obscured the pool beyond the fence have all wilted and died. The pool has no water in it but a shirtless man fusses about over by the diving blocks, doing something with the tiles.

—What a fucken dump! says Fulton, kicking a crumpled Coke can.

—Yeah, I offer to the murder of crows watching us from the lifeless electrical wires.

The tourists fidget in the bus, waiting for us. Frowns and grumbles as we board.

—Get me outta here, I say to Dad as he adjusts the driver's seat.

The bus pulls out of the town and across the bridge over Redbank Creek towards the cattle station Lucky Downs, which nestles right up against the Burdekin River. Dad estimates it'll take us five days to row all the way down the Burdekin to Charters Towers, where the three-hundred-year-old alcoholic will meet us with the bus. So we get to the spot where we will set off and start unloading the bus and getting the canoes off the trailer. The bus roars off in the dust, the old bony fellow perched up there in the seat like a skeleton in a chariot. A couple of the keener dudes get in their canoe and shove off, despite my dad's massive talk about all sticking together for safety, blah blah blah.

—

We slink along the river. The water doesn't have any rapids for the first part, so Fulton and I get out in the middle in our canoe and kick back, saying stuff like *this feels like real living* and *fuck city life*, generally talking shit. We smoke and yawn and laugh at a couple of the dudes who ram into a sandbar and get stuck there as we all drift down the river in front of them. Only occasionally do we have to get busy with the oars to navigate a bend in the river or a tree leaning out over the water. Fulton fusses about, trying to drag his knapsack from the bow of the canoe, complaining about hunger every ten damn minutes.

By and by Dad shouts back that we should break for lunch. We careen over to a sand island in the middle of the river. We break for about an hour and then prepare to get further downstream and set up camp before night sets in. Everyone pushes off. Fulton and I hang back to finish our cigarettes. We get in, last on the water. About fifty metres down the river the dudes in front of us shout back:

—*Look out for the log!*

—What log? I yell across the water, as Fulton says:

—Oh shit!

I look over his shoulder and see a limb sticking out of the water at a forty-five-degree angle from the depths. Only a small white crest reveals it. Fulton furiously paddles right as I madly paddle left. We approach the broken bough sideways, about midway on the canoe. This doesn't feel good. The current slams us into it and it cracks right through the fibreglass. The strength of the river breaks the canoe in half, and we go under. I get my head above water and look back upstream as Fulton surfaces screaming. All of our supplies – our cigarettes and our food for the five days – vanish. Half the canoe bobs up. We drag ourselves out of the river and onto the sand, in shock. We see my dad paddling hard against the current, back to where we sit on the riverbank.

—Mates! Dad says, stepping out of his canoe, his travelling companion smirking at us from behind him: This ends your trip!

Feeling shocked as I do, I haven't thought about that. A thousand kilometres from anywhere – how the fuck will we get back? Only room for two in each canoe. I shake my head, trying to get the water out of my ears instead of answering. Fulton looks ready to burst into tears.

—Mate, says my dad, looking back down the river as a faint shout of *should we wait* comes with the breeze over the water. Canoes like chaotic flies in the distance: Mate, he says again: about ten to fifteen ks through those trees you'll find Greenvale Station … Keep the river behind you, walk in a straight line. Tell them your name, what happened and ask for a lift to Lucky Downs.

—But …

—No, listen to me, boy. When you get to Lucky Downs, call your mother. You'll have to stay there until I get down to the bottom of the river. We'll work out how to get you back to Townsville after that, okay?

And then he gets back in the canoe and pushes off.

—But … I yell after him.

—What? he yells back, cupping his ear.

I turn to Fulton. He sits there like a drowned lamb. The arid landscape closes in.

—Welcome to Australia, I say, trying to force a grin.

Nothing then. The river sliding by, bird calls, the fucken cicadas. We might die out here. Will notifying Fulton of this possibility goad him into action or freeze him with terror?

—Right then! I say, clapping three times.

Fulton squeals as I clap.

—Christ! I shout: Stop acting like a poof!

—We might die out here! he moans at me.

—Nah, I say: I grew up in this shit. Drink up, and let's go.

Fulton drags himself on his bum over to the river's edge and gingerly cups some water in his hand. Sniffs at it, takes a sip and screws up his nose.

—Dude, I say, gesturing at the river: water doesn't come any fresher than this, for fuck's sake.

He gulps down water like he has crawled out of a desert.

—Don't fucken gulp it, sip it … But don't take for fucken ever. The dark will come in a few hours and we gotta walk for at least that many.

I can't wait until it dawns on Fulton that all our cigarettes drowned. No one I know smokes more cigarettes than he does.

This bush terrifies me. I feel one hundred per cent certain yowies live here. You get immersed in thickets of ghost-gum saplings, kilometres of them all crammed together like brigades on parade. Your eyes play tricks on you: flashes of light alternate with different densities of foliage. Sometimes you swear you see something dart between the trees and you feel smaller and more scared than a newborn. Your hands swell up from the heat and feel all stiff. We walk like this, single file through the bush, me in front, Fulton puffing behind. My old man said ten or fifteen kilometres, which I consider a pretty shithouse estimate.

After forever my eyes get dry and burny from looking out for yowies, snakes, spiders, surprise ravines, goannas and emus, in that order of concern. Although getting your face torn off by an emu should rate second after the yowies taking out your guts. If I see an emu, I'll use this technique an old-timer taught me. If it looks like it wants to tear you a new arsehole, you pick up the biggest stick you can find and hold it above your head, so you look ten feet tall to the emu. It'll back away, apparently.

Soon the shadows lengthen, the light gets red through the thickets and the cicadas shred the air.

—Fuck, I say.

—What?

—The darkness comes.

—Do ya *hafta* say it like that, ya cunt? splutters Fulton.

I laugh, but it feels forced. I swallow. Even though the cicadas shriek like stepped-on guinea pigs, the bush closes in still and eldritch. Fulton hears me swallow. He looks concerned now.

—I need a smoke, he says.

—Uh-oh, I reply.

—What? says Fulton.

I hold my hands up, framing where we stand, in the middle of fucken nowhere.

—Oh, man, says Fulton, realising we have no cigarettes.

We walk in silence through the trees. As I worry we'll have to spend the night out here, I spot a gleam through the scrub. We push on. An old corrugated-iron drover's shed stands in a clearing, ghost gums and paperbarks towering above. The iron has rusted and creaks in the breeze.

—A shed, out here? Fulton says.

—A drover's shed … cattle musterer's camp … It'll have beds and shit. Hopefully no snakes! Might even find tinned food and water.

I creep up to the shed. I don't know why I creep, but I do, and I peer through a split in the iron. My eyes adjust to the darkness and I see a body lying on a bed chained to one of the walls! I completely freak out. This rush of adrenalin, like someone strapped a rocket to my arse, has me flailing about like a madman. I turn on my heel and run headlong into Fulton, who, seeing the fear in my eyes, screams, *Fuuuuuuuck … hellllllp!* and bolts as fast as his fat little legs will take him. We get about a hundred metres through the trees, crashing through bushes, when we hear a man's voice shout:

—Oi, oi, boys!

I turn and see a bent-over farmer standing in the doorway of the shed, laughing his heart out, rubbing his back. I return to the shed, ears burning. Fulton lags behind.

—Old man Davidson, says the farmer, and he juts out a gnarly beaten-up-looking hand.

We shake and I say:

—Brentley, and Fulton.

—Hey! The old Greenvale cop's son?

—Yes!

—Fuck, mate. You've grown, sport!

—Um … thanks.

—Got any cigarettes? pipes in Fulton.

The old farmer fishes a crumpled bag of Drum tobacco from his baggy jeans pocket. He has those old-man hips which disturb me. Old people's hips get higher and more bony or something as they age.

—What you boys doing out here? he asks, watching Fulton trying to roll a cigarette. His faded blue farmer eyes twinkle in the late-afternoon light.

—We started out on a canoe trip, I say: twelve of us, my old man leading, and we wrecked on a bough sticking out of the water. We lost all our supplies. The old man told us to find you and ask for help getting to Lucky Downs.

—Pretty lucky blokes, I reckon, he grunts: You can die out here in a matter of hours. If the snakes didn't get ya, the yowies woulda.

Fulton's eyes widen.

Davidson leads us a couple hundred metres through the trees and we climb into a Nissan four by four. Pretty soon we get out of the scrub and roar along a dirt road towards the highway. About half an hour later he drops us at the gates of Lucky Downs homestead and we walk over the cattle grid to the farmhouse.

The night has fully crept in now. No lights on in the house as we approach. I hammer on the front door. The whole property has an eerie darkness. I try the door and it opens right up, and we stumble about trying to find the light switch, but then I remember this house runs on generator power. Fulton finds the kitchen and opens the fridge. A gust of cold air blows out but no light comes on.

—Must run on gas? I say.

—Huh? Fulton says, cramming a chicken leg into his mouth.

We fumble around in the dark and go out onto the veranda at the back of the house. The veranda must measure at least a hundred metres, and, unlike the whole damn town, which feels smaller now I've grown, it still looks as huge as it did all those years ago. We sit out there with the moon as our only light until at some point I doze off on one of the big couches, listening to Fulton complain about wanting a cigarette.

A dream of Billie-Jean. She runs from me and screams in terror. I keep chasing her, pleading, *please listen to me, please* – but I can only roar, and this frustrates me, so I bellow louder. I chase her across a rapidly flowing wider-than-the-world river, and she falls in and drowns. I kneel on the bank as the vast body of water speeds away my doomed Ophelia, to the estuaries and the mangroves and the ocean beyond. I stand to roar again and throw myself into the depths, to go with her to a cold dark death. Then I see myself reflected in the water. Nine feet tall, covered in orange gory hair and uglier than Sin herself. I stand there, a weeping yowie.

I awake with a start, unsure of my bearings. Dawn galahs, a splatter against evening's retreating skirts, a single frosted wing arcing in the morningblue. Jasmine on the trellis. A curlew down there on the lawn putting on a show in the dew, like a pastoral Othello.

Fulton has his mouth hanging open, with this sinusy-sounding snore gurgling out. I go along the veranda and into the kitchen, where I spy a telephone. I call my mother. She doesn't sound amused as I tell her the story.

—Lucky you didn't die! she says in her early-morning voice.

—Yeah, lucky.

I stand, looking out the window. The house has a grass airstrip at the front, and a clattering of black cockatoos lift off, screeching like a fighter jet. Mum says down the line:

—Go into the office and see if you can find any cash. Write a note and tell them what happened and that you borrowed money. Get back into town and see if you and Fulton can catch a bus to Townsville.

I hang up the phone and go down the hall, back out on the veranda, past Fulton, who still snores all sinusy-sounding, and try the door of the office. It has a sign on it that reads *Office* in Old-West-style writing. Thankfully it opens right up. The desk has a chaos of papers on it, along with bitten-looking pens and rubber bands and an antique-looking black telephone. I rifle through the drawers and find a tin with *Petty Cash* written on it in black Nikko. I count a thousand bucks in there, in fifties and twenties. I take sixty bucks and write a note telling the whole story in as few words as possible, before signing off with: *I borrowed forty bucks – best, Brentley.*

I go back to the kitchen and stick the note on the refrigerator at eye level, under a horseshoe-shaped magnet. On top of the fridge I spy a pack of Marlboro cigarettes. Over by the stove next to the coffee pot I find some matches. I linger a bit, trying to decide if I want coffee. I do. I hunt around and find a tin that has *Coffee* written on it in green enamel. I put a couple of scoops in and turn on the gas. Milk in the fridge, fresh from the cow too, I bet.

I sit out on the veranda sipping coffee and blowing smoke rings at Fulton until his nose twitches and he springs awake. He snatches the pack of Marlboro out of my hand and has one lit and half-smoked before I stop laughing. We walk around the farm, hoping we'll run into someone who can drive us into town. No one – not in the sheds, nor in the huge workshop. We go down to the orchard where years ago Albatross lived with his family in a shed among the mandarin and tamarind trees. Seasons of fallen leaves buckle the roof. The bus Trossy used to sleep in has gone. We peer into the shed. Only cold shadows and the scuffing sounds of rats on the beams. Around the front of the farm we find a Toyota Land

Cruiser. I clamber in. Sure enough, the keys dangle from the ignition.

—Let's drive into town and get the fuck outta here, I say to Fulton, the first thing either of us has said in an hour.

—You don't have your licence! he protests when the engine comes alive: We can't steal this truck, man!

I sit ignoring him, with the engine idling, to see where the needle of the petrol indicator stops.

—Half-full … awesome. Let's bail, man!

Fulton shrugs and jumps in the passenger seat.

—I didn't know you could drive stick! he says as I shift into second.

—My old man taught me to drive one of these exact trucks, years ago when I lived out here, in case he got fucked up out in the bush and I had to drive for help.

—Man, cool, says Fulton as we clang over the cattle grid onto the dirt road.

At the Shell on the edge of Greenvale I go in to talk to the man behind the counter. I explain the whole story to him. My parents and the family from Lucky Downs go way back and I will leave the Toyota with him and catch a bus to Townsville. I've left a note at the homestead which explains everything. The counter dude laughs at me and says we'll have to wait an eternity for a bus out here. He goes on to say we have a snowman's chance in Hades of getting a truck to take us, too, because since the mine shut down hardly any rigs come through here.

—You'll die of old age waitin out there, city kid, he says.

I do this kind of mental shrug as the wind, stenched with hot diesel and sump oil, blasts my face.

Fulton has never hitched in his life. We stand in the dirt outside the Shell and watch road trains roar by like machines of the apocalypse in clouds of red and ochre dust. None of them even glance at us standing out here, by the lonely servo on the highway to nowhere.

—One of the trucks'll pass through Townsville for sure, dude, I say: Someone has to stop to fuel up or piss or something.

A few hours pass. By now Fulton stands on a hill of cigarette butts.

—Gonna go and buy cigs, he grunts.

I join him, for a fresh Coke and some air-conditioning. As we come out of the store, a double-decker triple-trailer Mack truck hisses up to the diesel bowser. A hundred cattle kick the sides. This scaly little dude jumps out and lands on Fulton, all distracted skinning his fresh pack.

—Gotta spare durrie? he says, picking up his cap from when Fulton's flailing arm knocked it off.

Fulton gives him a cigarette. I wander over.

—Hey, mate, you passing through Townsville, by any chance?

—You boys need a lift?

—Would appreciate it.

Fulton nods his frizzy head.

We cram into the sleeping box behind the driver and get under way. The passenger seat has a huge cassette player on it and the dude keeps flipping U2's new tape over and over. He munches on a burned roadside burger and drives with two fingers as he wipes at his mouth with the back of his hand. A slice of beetroot drops out of the burger onto his lap. He spends a good thirty seconds fussing around with his shorts, ignoring the road.

—How many cattle in back? I shout over 'Angel of Harlem'.

—Dunno, mate, he yells: We measure shit in tonnes. This whole rig, head of cattle included, tops out at one-eighty tonne!

His face reflected in the windscreen looks proud. I look at the speedometer: a hundred and eighty tonnes travelling at a hundred and twenty kilometres an hour. I light another cigarette from the butt of my last. The mattress in here feels damp and the sleeping bag looks stiff. I chain-smoke to cover the sweat stench. Fulton also chain-smokes and dry retches occasionally. We listen to U2's *Rattle and Hum* all the way back from Greenvale.

—I'd love to go see them in Brisbane in October, Fulton says as we pass the *Welcome to Townsville, Capital of North Queensland* sign.

I've seen that sign a thousand times in the last few years. I think of my last trip to Brisbane and the sad-face Billie-Jean gave as I pulled out of the train station. Now, a year and a half later, not a single letter. Chicks confuse their animal passions for romantic notions. I've travelled the thirteen hundred ks between Townsville and Brisbane so many times I don't know if I can do it again. Do I like U2 enough? Will I see Billie-Jean again if I do go? Maybe I'll just go anyway and not look for Billie-Jean. I might run right into her. I wonder how many people live in Brisbane? At least a million, probably more. What chance do I have of bumping into her?

—Sounds like a good idea, I say.

—Huh?

—U2 … Let's do it.

—Fuck, dude, I said that twenty minutes ago. I reckon the tickets'll cost.

—How much, ya reckon?

—Dunno … At least sixty bucks?

—So we have five months to get enough cash to get to Brisbane and buy U2 tickets.

—What about accommodation? Fulton says.

—What about it? I say: You worry about your destination when you get there.

—What about planning it before we go? Sounds smarter to me!

—Doesn't sound like much of an adventure.

—I doubt my parents will let me go if we don't have someplace to stay.

Both the truck driver and I laugh at Fulton.

The truck driver drops us at a Shell on the outskirts of Townsville. I call home. My mother and both my sisters laugh pretty hard at me lasting only one day on the river before we crashed our canoe. I refuse to talk to them – until the old man gets home and relays the rest of his adventure.

4

I run into Maz on the street and he tells me that Reuben travelled with the skinheads clear down to Melbourne but had to come back because the DSS cancelled his dole cheque. He has a room at a flophouse in the city, opposite the cinemas. I knock on a dozen doors before Reuben opens up. He looks leaner and more hungry than he did when he sped off.

I go with him to reapply for his dole cheque. He stands there arguing with the chick behind the counter. A woman brushes by and sticks a card up on the job board with a thumbtack:

> Wanted: House Keepers
> The Four Seasons Floating Hotel
> Apply at Counter

I take the card before she turns away from the board. I fill out a bunch of papers. The Floating Hotel opened a year or so ago. Basically they anchored a pontoon out in the John Brewer Reef and built a hotel on it. Well, actually, they built the hotel in Singapore – I remember reading it in the newspaper. They shipped it to Australia. Five storeys high, with genius engineering. Permanently anchored at one end, but they can lift anchor at the other, so if a cyclone hits it out there in the open ocean, the hotel can rotate three-sixty degrees with the wind and the tide and not capsize.

The place gets mentioned in the news all the time. Environmentalists went mental when someone leaked that getting the hotel into the reef lagoon required the cropping of coral bommies. Then the four-hundred-passenger catamaran they intended to ferry guests out there with caught fire, on her maiden voyage too! Then, before the hotel even opened, a cyclone smashed it. I think the tennis-court pontoon sank, or something. The bloke who built it also built an artificial island, not far from the hotel, called Fantasy Island. The whole thing went down in another cyclone. Lots of cyclones and storms out there in the middle of the ocean. Then, to top everything off, some divers found an old navy ammunition dump from World War Two sunk out there, about five ks from the hotel. Also, police, or customs, or something like that, keep raiding the place for drugs. A five-storey Ritz floating seventy kilometres out in the ocean: it sounds so close yet so far away, like science fiction.

Dad looks real surprised when I land a job on the Floating Hotel. He says he hasn't abandoned all hope for my future now. I will live there on a seven-day rotating shift.

I fly in a helicopter for the first time, getting taken out to the reef. I fucken hate helicopters. Rich power-tripping bastards fly helicopters. Oh, look at me, in my fucken helicopter, flying up here above all you plebeians.

It takes about an hour up here in the heliosphere, coptering across the ocean. In the deep of the Coral Sea we see a shoal of sharks. Then the water fades to a calm blue shallow lagoon, an oasis in the sea, oceanic beasts circling its edges. Bellies of coral push out of the depths and then the hotel comes into view. It looks like a ship below us at first, but as the helicopter drops altitude and we hover barely above the water, the feat of engineering looms on the horizon of nowhere. It resembles a ship that has flipped over, a five-storey keel jutting into the sky. People on the tennis-court pontoon playing a game. The sun gleams off sunbathers stretched out on the three-sixty-degree deck. We pass over, people on the roof looking up. The roof has rows of huts on it, clothes on lines. Behind the hotel we drop down to a helipad floating in liquid sky. Hundreds of schools of fish flash in the blue.

I don't get much chance to write here on the Floating Hotel. Twelve-hour shifts: 06.00–18.00. I feel exhausted but have struck it rich. I pay a small percentage of my wage for board and food. I get three meals a day, canteen style, huge meals, all you can eat. I end up with eight hundred bucks, for seven days' work! I have to look after an entire floor of the hotel. It has thirty-five twin-share rooms and five doubles. The place hops with activity, always helicopters and catamarans coming in, private yachts sometimes. Hundreds of business guests and tourists. The majority of guests come here for corporate stuff, outside of regular holidays, which see the place fill up with mostly curious Aussies. The corporates come from Japan. No better tippers exist than the Japanese. Every morning under every pillow I find a packet of Japanese Mild Seven cigarettes and a five-dollar note. On top of that, the amount of stuff guests leave behind when they go astounds me. It makes it bearable that, for twelve hours a day, seven days a week, I change come-covered sheets and scrub shit out of toilets.

My locker in our room teems with half-drunk bottles of every alcohol imaginable, hundreds of packets of cigarettes, and a wad of five-dollar bills thick as Arnold Schwarzenegger's forearm. I have to share with three other dudes. The room has two double-decker beds, a locker each, and a door off the back that leads to a narrow shower with a toilet. We live on the roof I saw with the clothes on the lines when I first flew over in the helicopter. I share with a dude named Sam – a tall dude, basketball tall – a guy named Ben, who amuses himself by keeping an album full of photos of turds in toilet bowls, and an older South Sea islander bloke named Phil. Phil smokes a fuckload of weed, all day, all night. Walking into our room will get you high.

We all work under this neurotic fascist named Patti. Patti keeps a collection of amusing things left behind by guests. Like this huge black rubber dildo she claims a couple in their seventies left in a bedside drawer.

That makes her bearable. I find it hard to put up with this older Italian woman named Maria, my one-up – she screams in my face if I use the pink fucken spray instead of the purple fucken spray.

Some days, if the hotel has few guests or I finish my rooms extra quick, I have to polish the mirrors on the ceiling of the main foyer. I use this thing that looks like a Muppet head on a long stick. I stand up on the first floor, leaning out over the reception desk, rubbing the mirrors. This extremely cute blonde named Cali works at the reception desk.

When I return for my seven days off, and I get my land legs back, I look up Reuben and shout him to a good time.

—Let me get this straight: you get paid, free cigarettes, free piss, wads of tips and you work with hot chicks? Reuben intones as I give him a handful of fives from my massive roll.

—Yeah.

—Groovy.

—I spend my days up to my elbows in shit, though ... but if I get drunk before breakfast, the days roll by.

—You have any of those bottles of Sambuca you mentioned?

—Nah. Security checks our bags as we leave. Can't take alcohol off the hotel. Something to do with customs.

—I heard the place has gone bankrupt?

The hotel has a bar, down in the boiler room. It has portholes like an imaginary submarine, because real submarines don't have portholes. I go every night. Most people who work there either forget I haven't yet turned eighteen, or they don't care. Staff drinks cost one dollar. I drink hundreds of vodka and oranges. So much that it comes out of my pores the next morning. Cali hangs out in the boiler room too, but I find her so damn attractive I can't bring myself to try to chat her up.

I swear I don't know how it happened. I come to, I mean, sort of fade back, right in the middle of having sex! I don't remember getting back to my room or getting undressed and making out. Now, Cali, moaning. I decide not to think about it, at least for now, because the hot blonde notices me getting all thoughtful. One moment, thrusting like a possessed animal, now the human's come back in and ruined everything. We lie there, spent, and I get up and flick my zippo so I don't stumble over anything, and – damn it to hell – my roommates start clapping. I assumed Cali and I had the room, so I stand there, naked, condom still on. Three dudes cheering.

—

The weeks pass like the tides that lift the hotel. No sooner do I get my land legs back than I find myself boarding the catamaran back out to work. Cali scares me sometimes. She has it in her mind that we'll end up getting married. I don't know how this happened. Perhaps when, at a party recently, she told me all her friends think of me as a *keeper*, I shouldn't have raised my glass and said *to the future then*. I should have said *until someone sexier comes along*. I have feelings for her, and all, but every time I go out with Reuben, we pick up chicks and I don't feel guilty.

As everything does, everything changes. This new manager has come to live on board the hotel. They call him a manager but I know what administrators do. He calls a staff meeting. The whole hotel sits there as the new manager tells us the place has gone bust. The tourists stopped coming when the novelty wore off. He says to expect a massive last few weeks on the hotel, because as soon as they announce to the press they've sold the hotel to a Japanese company, all the tourists will come rushing to get a look before it leaves. The thing that sucks: my shift finishes three days before the hotel closes. I will miss the closing party.

—

The night of the closing party, in the city with Reuben, figuring I'll have a good time anyway, despite my paranoia that Cali, who has the right shift and therefore can attend the party, has said some other dude's name a bit too frequently lately. Jacques – this French bastard whom all the girls love – has a reputation for sleeping with the female guests, and I heard a rumour he gets paid for that.

I see this chick, and wow. Sitting there at The Terrace nightclub, down on the water, watching the volary of women – they all dress so similar, dance the same. Shuffle shuffle shuffle, lift left heel, little backward kick. Clop clop clop. I can hear their high heels on the tiled dance floor over the music. Then, this crazy little chick dancing like a pop star. She sure doesn't look over eighteen. She has black teased-up hair, sixties eye make-up and a tiny black dress with circles cut out of the sides – paired with Doc Martens boots! Girls in this town have never heard of Sinéad O'Connor. They definitely wouldn't dress like her if they did. I wonder where she comes from? Melbourne, Sydney. I haven't seen chicks this cool in Brisbane. I bet she comes from Europe, Paris even. I figure I have nothing to lose so I slaunt right up and say hi.

I find her incredibly engaging. I can't remember what I say, but I learn she has recently arrived in this backwash from Perth. I can't remember her name because, damn it, too much whisky.

—

So the hotel has closed. I spend the weekend hanging out at this resort where Cali works now. We've started going out and getting drunk a lot. She works at the Lakes Holiday Park all day and I don't have a job, so I hang out with Reuben in the city, playing chess mainly. Now and again Gigolo comes along. I think he's fallen down on his game. He doesn't come across so suave and stylish anymore. Running with this posse of real pretenders, who all think they come out of the Bronx, Gigolo has started taking bigger risks. He tags right where he sits, air smelling of spray-paint, like he wants to attract the cops. I haven't tagged anything since high school finished.

Anyway, I go to the bank in the city mall and I have only a couple hundred bucks left in my account. All those months' work, getting a good wage, and I don't have a thing to show for it. I may as well spend the two hundred bucks and show Cali a good time. So I rent a room at the Sheraton casino on the breakwater and book a table for two in the restaurant. We get drunk, have sex countless times, gamble in the casino and get room service. Our suite has these king-looking fluffy bathrobes with the casino logo. We steal them. Cali says *I'll put these in my glory box, for when we get married*, as she spirits them away. She scares me.

I found out from this punk at the chess set in the city you can make okay money picking vegetables. About a hundred and twenty ks south of Townsville you'll find hundreds of farms, run by Italians mainly. You can take your pick. They put you up and pay twenty bucks a day. I tell my old man at dinner and he reckons he'll join me. Dad's left the police force now; done his twenty years, he said. Typical baby boomer: he waited until I'd finished school to hand in his badge. As luck would have it, on 1 October he has to drive to Brisbane for a bunch of job interviews! I reckon we'll travel down with the old man, chip in for a caravan park with him, go and explore the city for a day or two and buy U2 tickets for the concert on the 4th. Perfect. I inform Fulton of the brilliant plan.

Not much happens on the farm in Gumlu. This grizzled old Italian farmer with skin like droopy tanned leather darts around us like a prize-fighter when my dad, Fulton and I arrive and ask for work. He says we can weed his eggplant plantations in the afternoon and pick rock melons in the early dawn. *A hard day's work for a good day's pay, I always say*, he drawls with the air of a backyard Aristotle. Broods of peasant-looking women sit under the eaves of a huge tractor shed, sipping from flasks, digging around in sandwich bags, eyeballing us. We have to stay in a beat-to-shit caravan at the back of the tractor shed. The only good news, the punk at the chess set in Townsville got it wrong. The farmer says he'll pay Fulton and me eight bucks an hour and my old man twelve bucks an hour. We go to get our bags and stuff from the car, but the bastard says, *No, no, do that later, after a hard day's work.*

The whole experience goes from terrible to catastrophic. My ingrown toenail that I developed the first time I went hitchhiking with Reuben becomes infected from standing in mud. Every ten minutes I end up with a gnarly-looking spider or some damn stingy thing in my clothes. The seriously dehydrated beef-jerky bastard of a farmer comes out into the eggplants at least a thousand times a day and shouts his proletariat mantra at us from the back of his truck.

About a dozen Italian women work in the field next to us, picking zucchinis. Most of the time they stand about laughing and nattering and smoking cigarettes. Then, when they see the dust trail of the farmer coming, they work harder than anyone on earth. The farmer climbs up on his truck, wearing football shorts without underwear, and his balls – like an old leather wallet – hang down damn near his knees.

We do this for two months, five days a week. We drive the hour back to Townsville on Friday afternoon, and back down here on Sunday afternoon. At this rate of pay I figure we could easily get the worst seats in the house at the U2 concert.

We have to rush in from the fields when thunderstorms roll in from the ocean. The fucken fauna-infested caravan leaks when it rains and everything inside floats in an inch of water. I lose a journal, two years' worth of poems and fragments and scribbles and crap. The only thing in there I will miss: an impressive sketch of Billie-Jean, naked on an overstuffed lumpy bed in a backpackers' hostel in Brisbane. I captured the curve of her thigh and the cigarette smoke curling up in the late-afternoon New Farm light perfectly. I used a stubby carpenter's pencil I found in the Fortitude Valley subway. My waterlogged journal swells up like a dead possum in the sun. The good thing about this, I guess: my old man seems pretty relaxed the whole time. He doesn't give me grief about smoking, or anything.

Today we unceremoniously quit our jobs. Fulton and I feel pretty excited about going to Brisbane to see U2. We spent the months in the fields picking weeds and trying to out-sing each other, mostly U2 songs. I like 'Angel of Harlem'. If you want to know the truth of it, though, I have an awful singing voice. When God asked *Awesome voice?*, I thought he said *I have no choice*, and I told him to go fuck himself.

I suspect Dad has some new tactic in his arsenal against me. He seems way too tolerant lately. He stayed cool the whole time on the farm and now he even says Fulton and I can smoke in the car as we drive to Brisbane. Out of respect, we hang our arms so far out into the hundred and twenty kilometre per hour wind that the glow goes out. He tells us to not do that in case we spark a bush fire. It hasn't rained here in a decade, and he says this like only an ex-cop can. So we end up only smoking when we stop for lunch or to piss or whatever, even though he seemed the coolest father around by saying we could smoke in the goddamn car. We don't want to bear the responsibility of burning down hundreds of farms and maybe even killing people. Clever.

The ever-evolving factories and freeway billboards on the outskirts of Brisbane flicker in. The trees get sparse. We pull in to a caravan park, close as Dad can find to the Boondall entertainment centre, where U2 will blow us away in a few days' time. Fulton and I feel pretty cashed up. I have five hundred bucks and Fulton has six hundred and fifty, because his parents don't make him pay rent. We want to explore the city right away, but the old man's cool sheen wears off at that point and he makes us stay, because the sun has already started setting. I think Dad fears for Fulton's safety, not mine. Fulton and I bum around the park all night, walk by the caravans scoping for cute chicks. We play some ping-pong in the recreation room, until the manager of the park, who lives right there in a room in the next building, comes and shoos us out.

We get out of the caravan park early as Dad has his job interviews. He drops Fulton and me at the train and we get tickets for Central Station, only we get on the wrong train. I don't realise for a few stops until I notice out the window the city disappearing behind us. We get off, Fulton losing his confidence in me with every moment that passes. We wait for a train that goes in the right direction. We make it to Central Station, passing through Fortitude Valley. I want to get off there but I figure it makes more sense to get off there on the way back, to save cash on train tickets. Fulton wants to go to McDonald's. We sit eating cheeseburgers, watching the pretty girls going by, smoke a couple dozen cigarettes and drink about forty Cokes each. Then, as we get up to go to the ticket place, I can't believe who comes along, hands dug down in his pockets, all dressed in denim, some gang-looking patches on his jacket, hair in a greased quiff.

—Harley! I shout across the concourse, scaring Fulton and a group of shoppers walking by.

Harley lowers his Ray-Bans, and crinkles that infamous scar he has right between his eyes. We go to shake hands. It ends up in one of those bro-hugs that result in you slapping each other's back. I introduce Fulton, and Harley flops down and lights a cigarette with a cool-looking zippo. Harley looks at Fulton with those frozen eyes, like an arctic wolf sizing up prey. He has a vicious beauty. His fighting prowess saved my balls the first day I met him. Many, many times he saved me getting beaten to death at school. He studied Rhee Tae Kwon Do back then. He had a black belt with three dans. I might have said that wrong. A three-dan black belt? Something like that anyway. Harley dedicated himself to martial arts – and wow, can he fight.

Harley's decided to come with us to see U2, so we go and buy tickets. The ticket chick tells us the 4th has sold out and so has the 3rd. So we can only get tickets for tonight. She offers us three seats in a row, which amazes us, but when she shows us the seating map, they obviously suck. They look down at the back left of the stage. I say to the chick, *Can you do better?* And she laughs at me. Harley laughs at me too, saying at all the concerts he goes to in this place you get a good view from wherever you sit.

We buy them, not exactly spoiled for choice. I know, though, that U2 has a wall of Marshall speakers twelve feet high, and from the angle of our seats we won't see the band. I complain like this for a bit until Harley gets bored and starts giving Fulton shit about his Kiwi accent. We amuse ourselves giving Fulton shit for a while. We head back to McDonald's and grab a table on the concourse.

Harley has a wad of cash, rolled up gangster style with a big red rubber band around it.

—Where'd ya steal that from? I stub out my cigarette.

Fulton looks concerned again. Poor Fulton, fresh from Sheep Island. The whole of New Zealand has fewer people than Sydney.

—Me job, sneers Harley.

—Yeah?

—Dealin.

—Yeah? What?

—Weed.

—You have weed!

Harley gestures for me to drop the volume.

—Sorry, man.

—Yeah, I always have weed.

And then, in total contradiction to looking paranoid about talking too loud, he pulls out a tobacco tin full of weed and rolls up three huge joints, right there. Not with any subtlety either. He spends some time toasting the cigarette with his zippo to make the tobacco fall out easier, crumbling up the buds on the table, rolling slowly.

—Fuck, I haven't had a smoke since I last saw my friend Reuben. I don't think you met him; you left before he showed up.

Harley carries on crumbling weed on the laminated table at McDonald's in the middle of the busy concourse.

—Nah, didn't meet him.

—Lives on weed ... Actually lives on it.

We walk around the Queen Street Mall all day, try to sneak into a few pubs but get refused service every time. As the clock in King George Square chimes six, Harley says he'll pay for us to get a cab from the city out to the concert.

In the taxi Harley starts on about how his father hates U2 because he served twenty years in the British Army.

—Besides, Harley says, ashing his cigarette out the window: I prefer the support, BB King, anyway.

Harley has the cab driver drop us outside the gates of the entertainment centre. We stand out here blatantly smoking the joints Harley rolled for us, in front of all the traffic pulling in to the car park. Fulton takes a bum-puff and gets all ashen-looking. Harley and I share Fulton's joint, and then we walk down the road to see U2.

We get through the gates and into the building. Fulton and I look as stoned as garden gnomes. Harley has an extra lilt in his swagger. The ticket dude snatches our stubs and completely ignores me when I ask if I can keep mine for a souvenir. How else will I remember 1989? As suspected, our seats have a crap view. We sit down just as the crowd leaps up, cheering, and BB King ambles onstage.

The audience fidget and look around, but BB King blows my mind. The dude has the bluesiest voice possible. Even though I only see a glimpse of him when he turns to acknowledge us plebs, simply the way he holds his guitar has me mesmerised. Then an interval, and loads of people get up to head out to the bar. Harley reckons we should kick back and have a cigarette right here. He pulls out a hipflask of Jack Daniel's. By the time the crowd starts milling back in, I feel pretty toasted. Stoned and drunk.

Then Bono hurtles out of the wings on the haunting organ riff of 'Where the Streets Have No Name'. The crowd goes fucken wild. My ears crackle from the screams and the whoops. The guitar picks up. Then, as the drums roll, the lights burst on and we see the band has snuck onto the stage. Bono starts singing, and fuck me if the whole place doesn't explode into absolute rapture. Where the streets have no fucken names … fuck yeah. As Bono croons the lyric about love turning to rust, I realise I haven't thought about Billie-Jean at all since I got to Brisbane. Wow. She *loves* U2. It wouldn't surprise me to see her here; it really wouldn't. I haven't thought about Cali, either. I do find myself thinking about that crazy little chick I saw at The Terrace. Weird. I wish I could remember her name.

Feeling pretty fucked up, I sit down. But then the riff to 'I Will Follow' starts and it picks me right back up. I leap to my feet – fuck greening out and missing U2! That signature riff. You can only appreciate it at a trillion decibels. It cuts right through me. And Bono standing there crooning in his whisky-smooth voice, dressed in his tasselled leather jacket and huge boots. What a fucken rock star.

They play a bunch of medley-type stuff and unfortunately one of the medleys has 'With or Without You' in it. I've cried myself to sleep listening to that song. And then, when you think it couldn't get any better, BB King comes ambling out again and he and Bono sing 'Angel of Harlem'. Total fanatical behaviour ensues. Then they sing 'When Love Comes to Town' and the place gets screamed down. Fuck I feel wasted. I hold myself up against the chair in front. Then the King and Bono sing 'Love Rescue Me'. Everyone pulls out their cigarette lighters and waves flames above their heads. I can't help but attempt to sing along.

U2 leave the stage and come back on a few times, the crowd stomping, screaming *more, more, more*, louder and louder. They play 'All I Want Is You'. I don't know if I like it. It seems a poor attempt to imitate the awesomeness of 'With or Without You'.

Harley suggests we get the hell out of there before the crowd bedlams. I've kind of had enough anyway, three encores and all. So Fulton and Harley and I get up and hightail it into the cool Brisbane night. My ears clang like a school bell. We stand around shouting our reviews, smoking cigarettes. Fulton, thoroughly rooted, now looks wispy, for a fat kid.

—I wanna go back to the caravan park, Fulton says, yawning.

—Come out to my house in Ormeau Town to smoke more weed and drink tequila.

—I dunno, Harley. Ormeau Town sounds kind of far away, I reply.

—Yeah, about halfway to the Gold Coast, Harley says, with a shrug: We'll jump on a train, get a cab up into the hills and get fucked up.

—What about your parents?

His dad doesn't fuck around. He clipped me on the ear on more than one occasion.

—They won't fucken hear us, man.

He says this like I should somehow know his parents won't hear us, and then it dawns on him:

—Ah, my parents built a fucken huge house up in the Ormeau foothills, right near this place called Old Ormeau Town. My dad has pots of money.

When he says *pots* of money, his British heritage shines through. Fulton hadn't realised until now that Harley comes from Pom land. He suddenly blurts:

—Ya fucken Pom, and throws a drunken mock punch.

Harley instantly drops Fulton to the ground and gets a knee on his throat.

—Fuck, dude! I shout.

Two security guards lingering near the gate, waiting for us to cause trouble, come rushing over. Harley gets off Fulton's chest. Fulton lies in the car park gravel and broken taillights blubbering like a two-year-old who's skinned his knees. I don't know about Fulton. Harley and I look mega rad, like proper Greasers right out of *The Outsiders*. Fulton doesn't look right. His Doc Martens shine, he doesn't lace his boots properly, his leather jacket looks like something a mobster wears to a wedding. Also, he looks young for his age, because of his puffy cheeks.

I feel bad I haven't warned Fulton about Harley. I didn't get a chance, though, since Fulton and I ran into him in the city earlier today. He'd long gone when Fulton arrived at school. Harley's violence started in infancy. It only took one kid on his very first day of primary school to ask if he'd had a dick chopped off his scarred forehead for Harley to start studying martial arts. It takes nothing to set him off. The slightest breeze of aggression and you'll find yourself drinking steak dinners with a straw threaded through your wired-up jaw.

Dusting himself off, Fulton says he'll get his own cab back to the caravan park. I say to tell Dad I've run into my old school mate and I'll come back in the morning. I know my dad will have some sort of conniption, but what does he expect letting me out alone in a big city? Fulton speeds off in a taxi.

5

Harley and I walk for about an hour, until we find a train station. Onboard, Harley finds a seat and kicks back, his legs stretched out, taking up at least three standing spaces. People keep tripping over his eighteen-hole Doc Martens. Full and rowdy, the train trundles to the Valley, where a rough prison-escapee-looking dude boards. He has spider-web tattoos on his elbows and one of those teardrops inked on his face. I read somewhere that a teardrop on your face means you've killed someone. The prison-escapee dude stumbles his way down the aisle and trips right over Harley's boots. Harley must have dozed off behind his Ray-Bans or something, because it takes him a second to react. He sits up and lowers his sunglasses, and the rough dude taps him right on the forehead scar and blurts in a whisky mist of spittle:

—Ya get a cock chopped off, ya cunt?

Harley punches him so hard and fast the dude vomits as he doubles over. As he splurts foamy-looking shit everywhere, Harley stands and smashes the dude's face right on his kneecap. The dude lies there, unconscious, in a pool of vomit and blood.

No one stops us getting off in the city. We walk down the ramp, where not too long ago I stood in uncomfortable silence with Billie-Jean. Instinctively, I look for her face in the crowd. A pretty girl catches my gaze and smiles at me. I say out loud, *Billie who?* The city pumps at night. Cars tooting horns, a thousand different tunes tumbling out of cafes and pubs, dudes busking, drumming, playing guitar. We soak it all up. After a while Harley says:

—Fuck it, man, let's just get a cab. I reckon a hundred bucks will cover it. He pulls out his huge roll of cash to check if he has a hundred bucks. He easily has a thousand bucks there.

Harley wins the understatement of the year award for saying his parents built a huge house. This place resembles the Lodge mansion from *Archie* comics – an *actual* mansion, built right back into an excavated cliff. Rain sheets down as we alight from the cab. Inside his home's cavernous interior Harley says *Let's go down to my level.* He doesn't have a bedroom; he has a level. And on it he has a bar and a full-size pool table.

About halfway through a bottle of Monte Alban Mezcal and about a quarter ounce of weed, I swear the worm comes alive. We run out of smokes. Harley suggests we go buy a pack from the servo down by the freeway. We drag ourselves away from MTV as 'Orange Crush' by R.E.M. starts playing and float down the hall to the front doors of the house. Harley pushes me out and tells me to wait down by the gates. He dead-bolts the door behind me. The rain has cleared. I stagger down to the gates and hang out in the cool hinterland night, digging the view across the range with a perfect full moon rubbing its Buddha-belly up against the mountains.

A crunch of tyres on gravel reveals Harley slowly rolling from the shadows in a blue Porsche Carrera, the kind without the air-scoop on the back. I jump in and we spirit down the hill. Harley fires up the engine.

—Dad'll never know, he says: We'll just go get some smokes. Too far to walk.

We pass million-dollar dream homes with boats in the driveways and manicured lawns with lit decorative fountains out the front. We roll through streets that have no name, barren cul-de-sacs not on the map yet, new housing estates, gated communities that have broken away like little feudal kingdoms.

We pull in to a Caltex and park near a dumpster. Harley leaps out through the window. I follow. We swagger in through the diner and buy a packet of cigarettes and a bottle of Coke. We linger in the air-conditioning, then head out the electric door back into the humid night and the smell of spilled oil, petrol and ozone from rain in the pine forests by the freeway. Between the Porsche and the dumpster rumbles an early-model Chrysler Charger, all scraped up and beaten to hell. A skinny kid, younger than us, with scars worse than Harley's, leans on his elbow out the driver's window. Above the V8 rumble he drawls in a thick south-eastern accent:

—Hey, ya rich faggots wanna drag? He makes this disgusting sucking-back-snot sound and spits at the Porsche.

Harley laughs, and then stops abruptly, madman style:

—You look damaged enough, cunt.

The boy slides out of his window like a bogan Starsky, wiping blonde matted cobwebs from his eyes. He looks older in the neon, late puberty or fifty, I can't tell. He takes off his denim jacket with a badly drawn scorpion on the back, revealing an Iron Maiden t-shirt with both armsayes cut out. He drops a cigarette butt and scrubs it out under his thong.

The dark shapes behind the tinted windows of the Charger rearrange themselves and, as the chopstick-thin driver barks *Wanna go then, ya filthy fucken poofter*, five other boys and two girls, all wearing jackets with the same badly drawn scorpion, emerge from the car. Harley's eyes light up. He reaches into the Porsche and the hood pops. His hand comes back in view, holding an aluminium baseball bat with a black rubber grip. The girls get back in the Charger. The ratty, drunk, cobweb-headed man-kid steps forward, his shoulder coiling for a punch. He swings his arm in a giant arc. Harley drops down, dodges the fist and expertly ends him in the stomach with the bat. The man-kid falls up against his car, attempts to stand, but falls again, coughing blood on the passenger window. The girls inside scream. The five other scorpions scuttle away towards the servo.

—Get in the car, man! Harley yells.

We both scramble in and he opens it up. The tyres squeal on the asphalt. A hundred faces press against the glass of the diner. Vacant tourist faces glued like travel stickers on the back window of a caravan.

—

We roar through the dark. The light of the dashboard glows orange on Harley's corrugated face, his jaw set hard and unforgiving like the freeway beneath the tyres. The headlights reflect off road signs and flame up his glacial eyes. Moths explode on the windshield like thrown mulberries.

—I love speed! Harley shouts: Yeah, baby! and he punches the roof of the car.

I pretend to hunt through my pockets for a lighter, cast a furtive glance at the speedometer. The needle hovers just below a hundred and thirty kilometres per hour. I hunker down in the racing seat, clutch the belt across my chest, light a cigarette and muse on German engineering. I wind down the window and flick my cigarette butt out into the wind as the Charger comes up beside us like a rusted rocket on mag wheels. The front-seat passenger throws a beer bottle and it smashes on the driver's door of the Porsche. A blush of rage plays across Harley's face. His eyes drink up the road, fierce determination wrinkling the scar on his forehead. He stomps harder on the accelerator. The Charger cyclones beside us, inching slowly forward. Bogans hang from the windows hurling abuse. The Chrysler leaps in front, cuts dangerously close. Heart pounding. Harley eases back on the gas, and then the driver in front slams on his brakes.

Slow motion. The windscreen implodes. My head snaps forward with tremendous force. As I recoil, my knees smash into the dashboard, or the dashboard smashes into my knees. The freeze-frame spectacle of the front end of a Porsche crumpling like a broken slinky. Pale opera. A nebula of blue paint and sparks. Chorus of a compacting fuselage. Ecstatic song of metal bending in unplanned directions. The engine block of the Carrera drops down and shrieks as it bites into the asphalt. The steering column spears forward and Harley's forehead hits the wheel. Blood sheets from a gash on his hairline. Steam from the destroyed radiator clears and the back wheels of the Charger, which now rest on the roof of the Porsche, grind to a halt. A brake pad falls down onto the remains of our hood. Moans and metallic creaks and the hiss of a punctured tyre. Someone scrambling in broken glass. Horrified silence on the edges.

A vision. Curtains stirring in a breeze, a wind chime tinkling. Reaching out for the curtains. Tiny hands.

Standing off the freeway on a rise, looking down at the melancholy wrecks, I watch Harley and the other driver stumble about, taking swings at each other. Screams and shouts for help from the Charger. I can't move; my legs feel numb and my neck aches. The chorus from a hymn the cult nailed in my mind plays, complete with organ accompaniment, clear as if I sat in a church tent, with a thousand lost souls singing out of tune for salvation:

Tell me the story of Jesus …

I hear myself praying:

—Lord … God, can you hear me?

Clearer than ever I see.

—First let me apologise for telling you to go fuck yourself because I have a shit singing voice. I didn't mean it.

Stay, let me weep while you whisper …

A girl falls out the door of the Charger, her arm bent all the wrong way. Several cars on the freeway slow for the spectacle.

—Lord … I don't know how I survived. No man alive knows more repentance.

Love paid the ransom for me …

Part Four
North of Vortex

Everything remains unsettled forever, depend on it.
Henry Miller

1

Spent the last month recovering, lying around reading Dante's *Inferno*. Damn my neck hurts. My mother begrudgingly lets Reuben come to visit. I tell him about the car crash and that I now believe in miracles.

—Did you find God on the highway? he says in an over-the-top patronising voice: A hundred and thirty ks when you hit the Charger. No one could survive that.

I let it go. He won't let it go. He wants to know what the doctor said. I didn't go to the doctor. My dad doesn't know about it. Reuben says he can hook me up with a crooked quack who'll prescribe me the good stuff without needing parental consent.

Cali comes by and takes me out. I don't have much spirit for socialising. She kind of drags me around to parties and to the movies.

I try to avoid noticing the charms of beautiful women, but for some reason they get right in my line of sight.

Adrift on the ocean of life, gybing with the wind.

Another year begins. Rains come with Cyclone Ivor.

The election. Bob Hawke wins again. I didn't vote.

Standing in a window at Sebastian's place and looking out at the ocean, I've decided nothing matters. Sibby strips for a living at a pub named Miner's Right. They have a ladies' night there. Sibby says it gets rowdy and a few times a pissed chick has near torn his cock off. Reuben met him a while back, at Cafe Nova. I think he has a thing for Reuben. Far as I know, Reuben doesn't have a gender preference; he just likes sex.

Last night, out with Sibby and Reuben, I pointed out the little chick I see everywhere. She butterflied around the room, because she knows everyone now. I tell Reuben I have a thing for her and he glides right on over and starts working his silver tongue. He starts up buying her drinks and then dancing with her, and before you know it they hide over in the corner, pashing. I watch in disgust as they leave.

Sibby and I stagger out at last drinks and clamber up the thousand stairs to his top-floor apartment. I've had about enough of this town, the mangroves and the mosquitoes, box jellyfish and dead brine on the wind.

Dawn now, the fourth I've seen without sleep. My ears still ringing from the club. Here comes Reuben shuffling up from the beach. I don't see the little chick with him. He looks pretty pleased with himself. He comes up the path five floors below. I imagine dropping a piano or something on him. I look around the room. After a while he slaunts through the door and spies me looking out the window. Sebastian has this huge apartment right opposite the beach. The windows go from about waist height up ten feet above you.

—You right? Flops down on the sofa.

—Hello.

—You pissed at me?

—Did you fuck her?

—We made love. He sniffs his fingers.

—Did you get her name?

—Candy! She moved here from Perth recently. Lives with her sisters on Redpath Street. I walked her home. She has this fucken giant Doberman.

I turn and look at him finally. Handsome prick sure got lucky in the genetic lottery. Tight black jeans, a shirt and vest buttoned up, and his hair shaved back and sides, long on top and Brylcreemed. He has a fat filterless French cigarette. Sitting there he looks like a handsome bastard from a 1920s gangster film, even in this shitty morning light. He has this fantastic reckless charisma, with the perfect amount of facial scars. My hair sucks, wispy and sticking up like static.

—You know what! Reuben joins me at the window, looking out at Magnetic Island: I wouldn't mind living over on the island for a while, score with some backpackers ... You know about German backpacker chicks, yeah?

—I know that backpacker chicks like to get their kit off. I spent months over at Rocky Bay, the nudist beach, wagging school.

—We should go over there and fuck like tomorrow might never come. He exhales in this authoritarian way he has, which makes him sound wise, like he's said something of great importance.

—Yeah ... I have fuck-all cash, though, since the hotel closed.

Reuben offers me a French cigarette, Gitanes. We smoke in silence.

—We need cash. Let's rob a few cab drivers. He exhales in his fascist way again and flicks his butt out the window. He takes the cig he always has behind his ear and lights it. It burns a little odd from the Brylcreem.

—You find a pushbike, right, and let down a tyre, flag a cab, and when you get to your phoney destination you ask for help getting the bike out of the boot. Then, when he gets out, you grab the money tray, or whatever.

—I want to go on a road trip. I really do. I light my cigarette.

Reuben puts his hand on my shoulder and I shrug it off.

—Still angry about Candy? He puts his hand back on my shoulder.

—No.

—Brother, sorry, but in love and war, I have no morals.

—May the best man win, huh? Dragging heavy on my cigarette.

—Nah, fuck that ... forget Candy. Let's go to the island.

—Dunno. Cali might get pissed.

—You still seeing her? I don't want her to come. We'll clean up on chicks over there. You don't want her hanging around.

—But we need cash.

—We'll go to Nelly Bay. I met this professional vagabond who reckons that you book in there, pay a few days, then extend your stay. They start you a tab to pay when you leave … only you don't pay. You piss off in the middle of the night.

—Nelly Bay, huh? I think he might actually have a good idea here and my heart lightens.

—Yeah.

—You know what? Let's fucken do it!

—Great! We'll stay free, fuck hot tourists, get drunk, smoke weed … live a little. Let's go!

—Now?

—Yeah. After we go by the safe house where I left my stuff.

—Okay. I left my bag at Cali's house … Fuck. She'll think I cheated on her or something. I didn't go back there last night like I promised.

—Man, you get all hung up on chicks. Do you need to buy tampons?

—Funny.

Just then someone shouts *Oi, arsehole* from outside the window. We both lean out for a look. A dude a couple of floors down stands on a balcony, shaking his fist up at us.

—Ya fucken chuck any more cigarette butts down here I'll smash ya fucken heads in, cunts!

Looks a rough bloke, too, kind of scraggy and tatted like a bikie. I duck my head back in but Reuben grabs a little cactus in a glass bowl from the windowsill and pegs it down at the upturned face. We slam the door leaving Sebastian's place. He's slept through the whole last hour as we've talked shit and made plans and probably killed someone with a flowerpot.

We go to Cali's place first. I leave Reuben to hang out on the driveway and climb in her window. She sniffs the air around me and insists on having morning sex. She wants to cuddle awhile after we both come. She dozes off again. Then a ruckus from outside disturbs half the suburb. We look out. Her old man went out in his jocks to water the yard and found Reuben hanging around. He stands there waving a rake and shouting at Reuben to get off his property. I tell Cali about our island trip, kiss her goodbye, jump out her window and run past her shocked old man to catch up with Reuben. We split up the street, laughing at the spectacle of a furry beach ball in Y-fronts.

We have a way to walk, through the suburbs and parks, to where Reuben stashed his worldly possessions at a state-run halfway house for wayward youth. Reuben only walks a few hundred metres before his feet act up. I haven't slept in four days, have a raging hangover and feel half-starved. I can't piggyback him for more than twenty metres before we have to sit down and rest. Sitting there at a bus stop, sharing his last Gitane with me, Reuben says:

—Have you ever wanted to kill someone?

—Not really … A few people I'd like to scar for life.

—You should never say you want to kill someone unless you mean it … and even then, you shouldn't say it. You should just do it.

I glance up to see if he has a smile on his face. He doesn't. The Saturday-morning traffic rumbles around us.

—I wanna kill one of my stepfathers. Blow his head off with a shotgun. He flicks his cigarette lighter like a trigger.

—What'd ya stepfather do, the fucker, to make you wanna kill him? … Or shouldn't I ask?

—He raped me.

I don't know what to say, so I don't say anything.

—He crushed my balls, destroyed my left.

I audibly choke. Still can't find any words. A bus hisses to a stop and the doors open. The driver looks at us sitting on the bus-stop bench in the side mirror. We don't get up, though I'd sure like to get on the bus and away from Reuben's story. He sort of curls up, like an apostlebird dying in a gutter.

—He then held me over a stove and dipped my feet into a pot of boiling potatoes … He lives in Cairns now. I found out recently.

The bus doors slam shut and it roars off. Reuben looks at me, sitting here, feeling sick:

—C'mon, brother! He slaps me on the back: Let's get the fuck outta here. The island awaits!

We amble down the path a bit. I still don't have any idea how to react to what happened to him. I want to change the conversation but I don't want to seem like I don't care. We come across a welcome distraction in the form of an old beat-up suitcase leaning against a fence. It has a red sock sticking out of the zip. It looks like an exhausted square brown-vinyl dog.

—Perfect! Reuben grabs the suitcase. He opens it up and it has some old-person clothes and a couple of paperback books by Stephen King in there. *The Dark Half* looks like a swollen bruise.

—Let's find a cab, he says, zipping the case back up.

He stands out on the kerb, waving down taxis. A couple pass by, and then one pulls up with a massively obese man sweating in the driver's seat. Reuben leans in the window:

—We need to get to West End. Can you help us put my suitcase in the boot?

The cabbie grumbles and fumbles around and the boot pops and he heaves out of his collapsed seat and grabs the suitcase and throws it in with zero ceremony. I go to throw my duffel bag in there but Reuben kicks my foot. Reuben gets in the front and the driver squeezes himself in and groans like he climbed Everest.

—Havin a good day, mate? Reuben says to the stinking rhino of a driver.

—Yeah.

—Drivin all night?

—Yeah. Busy as fuck, too. Where you boys comin from: clubs?

—Good! Busy night, huh? Lotsa cash. Yeah, a couple of clubs, a few parties … My girlfriend threw me out this morning because I came home reeking of pussy. Reuben slaps the dude on the shoulder.

The cabbie lets out this blokey kind of laugh. Reuben charms him like this as we head into the deep suburbs, looks over his shoulder and winks at me in the back. The fake pine-needle-fresh smell taxis stink of gets right up my nose.

West End in Townsville you could compare to the Bronx, I guess, without high-rises. Recently a tourist had a puncture here and some Aboriginal kids smashed the dude's face in with his tyre-iron. It has share houses and safe houses and halfway houses and cheap motels and illegal brothels and bikie gang headquarters. All the shops have roller doors and caged windows. Shifty characters stand around on the street corners with hands in pockets. Graffiti murders everything with a flat surface. I see my tag more times than I remember tagging it.

Reuben directs the driver to pull over somewhere deep inside West End. The driver hauls himself out to get the suitcase from the boot. I get out, but Reuben lingers in there a second. Next thing I know, Reuben yells *Run!* and the cabbie slams down the boot to see Reuben sprinting up the street on his heels, clutching a cash box. I bolt and jump right over a wood panel fence. Figuring the fat bastard won't follow me, I peer over and see the driver trying to force himself back into his cab to make chase. No sign of Reuben. I sneak through some yards and over the fences of some factories and circle back around to see if I can spy him.

Nope. Nowhere. Gone.

I find him as the sun starts bleeding out, after wandering around West End all day trying to not get stabbed. He sits on the fence outside a huge derelict house. The whole place looks deceased, a heckle of crows calling from the vacant lot next door, busted umbrellas and junk along the bottom of the fences. A few kids hunch like victims on the sagged veranda. Reuben has his army duffel and a pile of books on the fence beside him. Everything he owns in the world he has in that bag, and probably half of it he acquired only recently.

—What took ya so long, brother?

—You didn't give me the address.

He offers me a smoke from a fresh packet.

—Cabbie had three hundred bucks, man! Let's get a ferry over to the island tonight. The cops'll have our description by now. We should lie low.

We cut out of West End and into the city and stop by a dealer's place to score an ounce of weed. Reuben reckons if we split the bag into twenty-dollar deals, we can triple our money. He borrows a roll of aluminium foil and sits there while I make small talk with the dealer, who I think shot up heroin not long before we arrived. The couch has absorbed him and he keeps missing his mouth with his cigarette. Reuben hums in the kitchen, splitting up our ounce into one-gram foils.

We make it down into the city and onto a ferry and we sit out on the bow and spark up a joint. Soon I feel pretty good. We disembark at the main ferry terminal on the island, at Picnic Bay. We walk off the jetty and through the little township and find a shop on the beach so we can buy cigarettes. We catch a bus around to Nelly Bay. I feel exhausted, awake for four days straight.

The chick at the backpackers' hostel doesn't ask to see ID or anything, just gives us a key to a bungalow and disappears. The bungalows have two double-decker beds. They don't have showers or cupboards, only a square of carpet and two chairs. I expect to find some dudes already in there but we have the place to ourselves.

—

So I spend a month partying so hard I don't get a chance to write anything down. We drink Cinzano, smoke a fuckload of weed and veg out on the beach all day. We share our bungalow with two British dudes. The Poms have a huge clippie bag of this new drug they smuggled over from London. *X* they call it, short for *ecstasy*.

—No one back in London can get enough of this shit, mate! They call it the Second Summer of Love over there … Acid-house music, mate … Dancing to those mad beats on X with a fit bird shaking her buttocks, bruvver … Bliss has arrived, here on earth … Take some.

I don't dig it much, makes me anxious. I play with the hair on my arm for about six hours one night. Then I see a possum and get all serious about trying to give it a rub, but those varmints will take your face off and piss in the wounds for good measure. Reuben gobbles down handfuls of ecstasy, swaps some of our weed for the pills.

I can't remember the British dudes' names, on account of perpetual intoxication. I want to see Candy. Reuben has forgotten she exists. I try to talk him into going over to the mainland and hitting the clubs, because I hope to see her, but he reckons the cops will still have our *wanted dead or alive* posters in their cruisers. I don't get lucky at all the whole time.

Reuben sleeps with parades of backpackers, but he has his heart in it.

I have a fantastic tan.

2

We packed up our stuff this morning, left it in the bungalow and hung out on the beach all day. As night tripped over the kerb of the ocean, we returned, grabbed our bags and caught a bus to the ferry. No one chased us or anything. Six weeks of free accommodation – what a bargain. At midnight we boarded this Greyhound bus to Cairns. The green electric clock above the driver says 3.43 am.

Rumbling to Cairns. We roll through banana plantations and sugar-cane farms and fig trees on the beach in Cardwell. The rainforest fans up the ranges in a mist. After staring into space through rain-streaked glass, I get out my journal and write down some of the Magnetic Island adventures. Reuben watches me, scribbling away under the reading bulb. He grows curious when I get a flow on, don't stop writing for half an hour or so. Leans in.

—Writin an epic?

—A novel.

—What about?

—A true story about smut and crime and poetry and life. About running from Love.

—Groovy … You writing me in?

—Nope.

—You gonna do anything pretentious with your grammar?

—What do you mean?

—Ya know. Pretentious. He shrugs down in his seat: Like fucken Joyce … I can barely read that shit. He breaks the rules of written language … like, imagine if a guitarist said, *Nah, fuck using established musical notes, don't fucken expect me to tune my instrument.*

—I might try something like that. Have you heard that album *Psychocandy* by The Mary Chain? They don't even know how to play guitar.

—Yeah, they bend the rules. I don't mind writers who *bend* the rules.

Reuben goes through his jacket and produces a decayed soft-looking copy of Céline's *Journey to the End of the Night*:

—Listen to this, man … just listen to this, my favourite passage from my favourite book in the world: *In the corners of all parks there lie forgotten any number of little coffins garlanded with dreams, thickets charged with promises, handkerchiefs full of everything. All a big joke.*

—Wow! Can I borrow that?

—No. Never leaves my person, bro.

Strange, I've never seen him with it before. That doesn't surprise me, though; he has all sorts of shit secreted away in his hustler's jacket. Reuben slumps right down in his shoulders then. He has on a pork-pie hat that he can't quite get over his eyes, but he tries to anyway. I drift off somewhere and dream of the Aboriginals standing on the beach in 1770, watching the British ships gliding like Irukandji up the coast. *Terra nullius*, ownership by occupation, to the victor the spoils. I write:

Australia, land of brazen scum.
Come one, come all and get a sunburned bum.

I chuckle out loud.

—You laughing at yourself again, man? Reuben tries to get deeper into his seat.

—Yeah.

Shakes his head, stretches out.

—

Australia. Most times I hate this island. I've spent ages figuring out ways to get deported. I wouldn't mind if they sent me back to Denmark or Prussia – or Wales or Scotland or France, or wherever the hell my ancestors hail from. My nana, my dad's mum, she told me her ancestors originally came from Palestine, before they emigrated to Wales and eventually on to Australia. Grandma, my mother's mother, told me her family emigrated from Prussia. Once she said she had relatives on her side who broke off from a band of Latvian gypsies. I don't know where to find my history. Does Prussia even exist anymore? I don't think it does.

I find it surprising how little I think of my family history. I guess that happens to most Australians. We've had to build our own culture. We don't have a single lineage to guide us in our infancy. The British came here two hundred and two years ago, and in that time a lot of history can fall off the pier and get swept out to sea.

Dark outside. Late June moonfruit oozing nightnectar in a blue garden. Dawn will break soon, like an egg on the edge of night. The bus slows as we cross Mulgrave River. We'll pass through the township of Gordonvale soon. I've travelled this road a thousand times, felt it beneath my boots, marvelled at the way it simultaneously offers promise and dread, demonic one moment, an angel the next.

I wonder what happened to Albatross and Uncle Parky? I called Uncle Parky *sir* sometimes – he never seemed to mind. You would too, because he commands respect without asking for it. You'd really like him. We should all call the Aboriginals *sir* and *miss*; they deserve it more than the fools we call teachers at school. The first people here, like Parky, they deserve reverence, not some fops from England. He taught me some real knowledge. How to quieten my mind, to let in the dreaming. How to see in the dark. I have nothing but respect for Aboriginals anyway. I've sat around in parks and on beaches with those dreaming souls. They have a fucken grand old time, mostly. Sure, I mean, when I visited Palm Island I had the shit scared out of me by the unhinged drinking and the violence which holds its hand. The cop stories of generational rape and incest haunt me, but the same shit goes down inside the walls of castles. Look at the whites with their royal fixation. They stand around on their own side of their picket fences saying things like *Oh, the Abos, they don't participate ... if only they'd stop drinking and integrate.* You see the irony, people talking about integration over fences.

A crunch of gears there as the bus navigates a bend. We've left the coast now. Mountains on either side. Rainforest reaching up. If I ever get off this island, I'll miss the various perfumes the most. The eucalypt soprano drops in, riding on the cicada screech, then the contralto of rotting mangoes, which grabs onto the skirts of the toad croak ... then comes the baritone of molasses on the smoke from sugar mills. Above all of this, in the crescendos, the tenor, the stench of death, roadkill rotting on bitumen. It tremors in from the edges on the cry of crows.

The bus rolls into Cairns with dawn. We wander down the beach and find a cafe and sit drinking coffee and smoking cigarettes. Reuben says he has a granny we can stay with, but we have to kill a few hours before we go to her house.

Like Townsville, they built Cairns on cleared-out mangroves. Both cities stink like swamps. Cairns has a lot more tourists than Townsville, though, so the scent of coconut oil pervades. We go into a pawnshop and I hock my Walkman, buy a bottle of Jack Daniel's, a carton of Marlboro and pay for a cab.

I shouldn't have smoked that joint on the beach before we came to Reuben's grandma's house. A vertical rain coming down as I stand at the bottom of the stairs and Reuben bangs on the door. I feel north of the vortex now, like an astronaut circling a black hole. His granny's house sighs under the weight of mango-tree leaves choking the gutters. It looks unkempt, like a web when the spider's left. The house creaks and the door swings open. An ancient lady in a wheelchair has this look on her face like when you fake feeling pleased to see someone. Reuben has a stilted conversation with her and she rolls down the hall in front of us and shows us the room where we can stay. It has a double bed. I don't know how I feel about sharing a bed with Reuben, but we both flake out on there anyway, exhausted.

The next morning I find Reuben at the kitchen table. He sits there in a singlet, smoking and reading the newspaper. His grandma busily rolls about the kitchen, cooking toast and eggs. She asks about forty times how long we'll stay. Reuben shows me an advertisement in the paper. The Cairns Show has jobs available. After we eat eggs and drink coffee and smoke about fifty cigarettes, we cut out to the showground. Reuben's grandma lives quite close.

The place has a million trucks zooming around and thousands of show rides half-constructed. You can walk through the gates for free today … tomorrow it'll cost at least ten bucks. Forklifts whiz by and brakes screech all over the place. People shuffle past with boxes of clown heads and teddy bears. Sledgehammers, shouts and that beep you hear when a truck reverses. We walk beyond skeletons of roller-coasters and gravitrons and men fixing dodgem cars.

We stop outside a huge dome tent going up with a sign leaning on the front of a ticket booth: *3D Cinema Experience*. Reuben goes right over to the dude who looks like he owns the thing and strikes up a conversation. I shuffle around until I notice a trailer coming up the dusty road, consisting of a big cage with a trillion coloured balls in it. This withered-looking generic alco bloke alights from the truck and nods at me. He runs one of those kids' rides that has all those obstacles in it, like rolling barrel hallways and nets to climb and a huge pit full of balls for them to wade through. When they get to the top of the ride, it has a spiral slippery slide to get back down to the ground.

—Ya lookin for a job, kid?

—Yeah.

—I need someone to sit up top there by the slippery slide and make sure kids don't kill emselves on the way down.

—I can do that!

—Can you work the whole five days: 9 am to 10 pm?

—Yeah!

—We can do it two ways. I can do up this form – he waves a form in my face – which means ya'll pay tax, or I can pay you cash in hand, off the books, like.

—I need as much cash as I can get.

—Start tomorrow, 9 am sharp. Now piss off, I have shit to do.

I meet Reuben coming back up the road. He landed a job selling tickets at the 3D cinema. He starts tomorrow too. We figure this means we can go into the city and get drunk with the last of our cash. Soon we'll have a payday. We make it into Cairns city and find somewhere to play pool and drink beer. We run out of cash in the late afternoon and get ready to leave when a group of American chicks come pouring into the bar. A couple wander over and ask us if we've finished with the pool table.

Right away Reuben starts up the silver tongue. They pour us beers from their jugs and challenge us to a game of pool. When our turn to pay comes, Reuben says we have to split for a while to go to the bank. We walk up and down the main street looking for unlocked cars. Reuben slips into a Mercedes-Benz and goes through the glove box, pocketing change. We have about fifty bucks. We get back to the bar and the American chicks in time to find them leaving. We act all disappointed and they invite us back to their hostel.

We sit in their room in a cloud of weed smoke and cheap alcohol, and Reuben starts making out with a stunning brunette. A couple of the chicks leave about then but one asks me to go for a swim with her. We get out to the pool as dawn reverses the shadows and she strips off and jumps right in, naked as Eve herself.

—Fuck! she squeals: Freezing my tits off!

She swims over to the edge and offers me one of her nipples. She has silky skin like a seal. I suck her erect nipples and breasts for a bit and then I go for her pussy and she purrs for a second and spreads her legs, but then breaks away, kicking off from the side of the pool with a huge splash, soaking me.

—Fucking hammering! she says, looking wasted.

—Speaking of fucking, let's go to your room and get warm. I stand there dripping, shivering, looking hopeful, I guess.

She laughs and says:

—Dude, that only happens in books.

—

We make it to the showground right on 9 am. The carnie glares at me as I clamber up the ladder, obviously smashed. I spend the whole day catching kids trying to kill themselves on the slippery slide. The thing drops three floors down in a tight spiral. It has a bar across where the kid sits. I pull a lever, the bar lifts and the kid drops screaming out of sight. A few of them take to swinging on the bar before they sit down. They hang out above the crowd of hot-dog-munching fairy-floss-eating showground patrons below. I save about fifty kids from grievous bodily harm or certain death on the first day. Other kids get bogged in the pit of coloured balls, sucked down screaming as others come out of the rotating barrel hallway and jump on top of them. By 10 pm I feel pretty fucked up. I find Reuben coming out of the 3D cinema looking like I feel.

—Let's hit some clubs. I nicked a kid's wallet today. Little cunt had a hundred bucks in there! Fucken rich kids, man … I fucken hate rich kids. Disgust lurks furtive in his soul.

The next three days look like someone photocopied the first day. Saving kids' lives, sitting at the top of the show ride watching everyone having fun. I have one more day of this until a pay cheque. I haven't eaten since breakfast at Reuben's grandma's.

We get off work and make our way back to her house. Reuben seems oddly quiet. We walk along a path beside a park and two young kids stop us and ask to bum a cigarette. Reuben grabs the older one by the throat and screams in his face *GIVE ME YOUR FUCKEN MONEY, YOU LITTLE CUNT!* The kids empty their pockets, shaking like kittens that have fallen into a fishpond. The little fuckers had a hundred and eighty bucks between them! I think Reuben might have some real malice building up in his heart.

Anyway, fuck sleep when we have a hundred and eighty bucks. Reuben has a go at the cab driver, who says, jovial:

—Where ya headed?

—Take us the long way and ya'll get yaself stabbed, cunt.

—Settle down, mate! The cab driver sounds serious.

—Just drive, cunt, Reuben barks.

—Bad day then, feller?

—Just fucken drive, mate. Don't fucken bother with ya small-talk shit.

—I need a destination, or I can refuse your fare. He slows, like he intends to pull over and kick us out.

—Mate … drop us off at the clubs, will ya? I say, defusing the situation.

We get out of the cab in the city and wander around the nightclub district, looking for pretty girls. Outside this place called Gilligan's Bar we spot the two British dudes from Nelly Bay who gave us the ecstasy pills. We get in and drink about two hundred pots of beer each.

The Poms tell us about this chick named Alexandra they met while snorkelling. She arrives and blows both Reuben and me away. A total honey: long sun-kissed tresses, goddess features, perky tits and amazing arse. Alexandra and Reuben flirt right away, but then, when I get left alone with her for a minute, she leans in:

—I wanna do something outrageous tonight, something I've never done. How amazing … ecstasy … wow. Have you tried those tablets the Poms have?

—Yeah. What you thinking? Late-night beach capers?

—Where do you and Reuben live?

—A short cab ride. We have some weed.

—Let's go! She leans on me.

I try to sneak her out of there, but Reuben sees us leaving and shuffles over.

—We bailing? Drains his pint.

—Yeah.

—Let's go! Alexandra breathes and leans on Reuben, too.

Reuben starts feeling Alexandra up in the cab and soon they pash like long-lost lovers. The cab driver has his eyes fixed on the rear-vision mirror as her bare breasts escape her singlet. I give up. Maybe I'll get to watch Reuben fuck her anyway.

We have to sneak in so we don't wake Reuben's grandma. Of course the whole damn place creaks and sways as we tiptoe down the hallway. When Alexandra sees the double bed in the room, she looks concerned, but Reuben rolls up a joint and she starts getting all liberal again, lying back on the bed, flashing her underwear, playing with her hair. I lie down beside her and she rolls on top of me and starts kissing me. Reuben sits there watching, rolling joints. After a while she jumps up and says she needs to go to the bathroom. Reuben takes her down the hall. I wait for my erection to subside before I get up and roll myself a joint. I smoke the whole thing and roll another and they still haven't come back from the toilet.

I get up and creep down the hall to find Alexandra on the toilet with Reuben kneeling between her legs, licking her. She holds herself steady with these steel rails bolted to the wall that Grandma uses to hoist herself out of her wheelchair and onto the bowl. I watch for a bit but the whole thing looks disgusting to me – an old lady uses this toilet. I go back to the room. Pretty soon they both come in and Alexandra says, taking off her dress:

—Do you wanna share?

I get behind, licking her as she gives Reuben a blowjob. I start fucking her, and then her hand gropes Reuben's scrotum, recoils.

—Born like that, with only one, Reuben says, and then he moans: Babe, you give great head.

—Pull out before you come! she says over her shoulder.

We fuck all night. Then we lie around smoking. She decides to give us both head again but the sound of a wheelchair rolling down the hall wrecks the scene. Alexandra rises, dresses all erotic in front of us, bends over, teasing us one last time. Then she says:

—Thanks for the great night! and sneaks out of the bedroom. She bumps right into Reuben's grandma, who doesn't sound at all impressed.

3

After slumbering for a while I awake with a jolt, remembering I have to save kids' lives at the show again today. I bail out of there, leaving Reuben still asleep, as he doesn't clock in at the 3D cinema until midday. I run to the showground and through the gate, flashing my staff card. I make it to the ride about twenty minutes late and start to climb up the ladder when the carnie comes out of his ticket booth and says:

—Oi, fucker, what ya doin?

—Sorry, late, I know, scooting up.

—Get off my fucken ride, ya little cunt. He spits and pulls me off the ladder.

—Huh?

—I said, get off my fucken ride, ya cunt! he screams in my face.

—Man …

—I don't know you, mate … Why the fuck ya on me ride?

—You joking?

—FUCK OFF! And he punches me in the mouth.

I get up, spitting blood into the dust. A million people suddenly crowd around. The carnie fakes a move to hit me again and goes back into his ticket booth. The crowd thins out, my swearing drowned by a loudspeaker which screams *Roast beef sammidges – come and get ya roast beef sammidge – free can of drink with every roast beef sammidge.*

I wander around, sucking my fat lip, in shock I guess. The cunt totally ripped me off, tricked me from the beginning with the paying no tax thing if I didn't fill out the form. I have no proof that I've worked there. Trying to figure out what he owes me makes me even more depressed, counting the money I *should* have.

I get up the courage to roll a few kids for cash but, as I pick a target – these two in the crowd wearing three-hundred-dollar Nikes – I find five bucks on the ground. I get three hot dogs in a row and inhale them. Feeling a bit better I figure I'll find some cops and tell them what happened, but as I get out to the gate to where the cops hang around every day, I see Reuben coming in. Bastard looks all refreshed. He has shaved and left some stubble so he looks sophisticated. Before I can open my mouth to tell him why I have blood all over my shirt and now talk with a lisp, he says:

—Fucken Grandma kicked us out. Called my uncle – another cunt I want to kill. Had him come over and watch me pack up our shit and leave. Stood there slapping a shifter in his hand.

—Fuck … What did ya do with our bags?

—Left em under her house. We can go get em when we finish work.

Then he surveys my busted-up countenance. Eyebrows raise.

—He fucken ripped me off. The carnie cunt claimed to not know me.

—Fuck me dead.

—Yeah, man. I argued and the fucker smashed me in the mouth. I pull out my lip to show the huge gash my teeth made.

He looks concerned – Reuben rarely looks concerned.

—Ya know what?

—What?

—The fucker who owns the cinema and the cunt who ripped you off … I bet they have some game going because I didn't fill out those fucken forms either.

—Fuck.

Like every cornered animal Reuben's pupils sharpen, hypodermic and precise. He shuffles off, shouting back:

—Wait for me out front!

I wander across the road to a crowded burger joint on the corner. I stand around by the phone box, looking for someone to bum a cigarette from. Reuben comes out the gates and stands there, waiting for a break in the traffic. He shuffles over, shaking his head.

—Same shit, brother.

—You serious!

—Yup … cunt said he didn't know me when I tried to get in the ticket box. Had some chick in there doing my job already. Told me he'd call the cops if I didn't fuck off.

We sit around the burger joint, both glum as puppets in a tragedy. Reuben has ten bucks left from the wallet he stole yesterday, so he buys us a pack of smokes each. We spend most of the day there, standing around the phone box, not really talking, just trying to figure out what the hell to do next.

—If we get our bags, I can read some tarot down the beach. I crush an empty Coke can under my heel.

—Granny has my cunt uncle fixing her washing machine.

As Reuben says this, lighting a cigarette, the carnie who ripped me off comes out the gates, through the crowd and across the street. He walks right by us and doesn't look at me, or notice my rage building as he approaches. He goes into the burger joint and comes out skinning a pack of cigarettes. Still not looking at me, he goes into the phone box and starts dropping coins in the slot.

—Fuck! That cunt in the phone box …

—What about him? Reuben looks up from the ocean of spit between his boots.

—The fucker who ripped me off!

Without missing a single beat, Reuben stands, shuffles over to one of the tables at the front of the burger joint and grabs a wine bottle filled with iced water. He strides to the phone box, emptying the water from the bottle in front of, maybe, forty people, and bangs on the glass. The carnie looks over his shoulder, pushes out the door of the booth a bit and says:

—Fuck off, ya cunt.

Reuben punches him through the open door and, as the dude crumples down, Reuben belts him in the face with the wine bottle. After a couple of strikes the bottle smashes and the dude's face peels open like an avocado, teeth buckled in and broken, unconscious. The horrified crowd gasp and scatter like a passel of pigeons when you run at them in the city square.

—We should get the fuck outta here, brother, says Reuben as he calmly throws the bloody broken bottle out into the traffic. The carnie crawls from the phone box, groaning, trying to hold his face together. Reuben kicks him hard in the guts and starts running on his heels up the street. I race after him. We run for about a month, not looking back.

We get to this overpass with a ladder down the side and Reuben scoots over the edge. I follow. We huddle up on a ledge beneath until night creeps its feelers around the edges of the concrete. Reuben hasn't said anything for about six hours and then he slaps a freeway moth on the wall beside my head. He has the same flat half-gleam in his eye I've seen in all men who succumb to the burdens of life. Like when he stabbed Muddy. Not an inch of remorse. Only animal satisfaction. Reuben never looks sorry. I've never seen a wild thing look sorry.

I don't have much to say either, not out loud anyway. The malice that curls up in Reuben's heart has darkened since Alexandra noticed his missing testicle.

We make it back to Reuben's grandma's house under cover of darkness. No sooner do we get there than Reuben puts his head on his bag and goes right to sleep in the dirt by her humming washing machine and the rusted-out car she hasn't driven for twenty years.

Sometime during the night, lying in the dirt under the house, I awake to the creak of Reuben's grandma's wheelchair rolling across the floorboards above.

I hear the bathroom door bang open and the grunts of the old lady hauling herself onto her toilet. A loud crash shakes the house! Reuben sits bolt upright, swinging punches, yelling something about a war? It sounds to me like the old lady has taken a fall, so I run up the back steps and go to bang on the door but realise she doesn't know that Reuben and I have come back and fallen asleep under her house. I look through the window and see the toilet door cracked open, with a beam of light spilling out. A leg on the floor. Deliberating what the hell to do, I hear her feebly cry for help.

Reuben comes up the steps behind me, rubbing his eyes, and I tell him his granny has taken a fall. He goes right ahead and shoulders in the back door. As the door breaks, we hear a scream. We rush in and find the poor old dear out cold with her skirt around her neck, spread-eagled on the floor in a pool of piss. She fainted as we burst into the house. One of the steel rails she uses to haul herself onto the toilet has come away from the wall. I really don't want to see an old lady's vagina, but I see it anyway as we struggle to lift her dead weight back into the chair. God has the worst sense of humour.

Anyway, despite both of us feeling pretty good about probably saving the old bird's life, after she makes us cocoa and toast and lets us smoke a couple of cigarettes in her kitchen, she shoos us out as the dawn fingers through the trees. We wander around, feeling pretty lost and hopeless and paranoid, looking out for cops and carnies hell-bent on revenge. We stand by the freeway in belting rain, cars roaring by with warm dry people inside, and I bet none of them have a rumble in their belly like death trying to claw out, either. Carnies learn violence from birth. If the five generations of carnies who share a caravan with the one Reuben beat until he bled clear as a jellyfish catch us, they will kill us.

As I watch Reuben, teeth chattering, trying to light a wet cigarette with a sogged lighter, I see him snap – like one of those proper psychotic breaks you hear about. He has this look in his eyes the same as Terence Hill when he has a bar fight in one of his westerns – he fights mean and dirty. In a scene from my favourite of his films, *God Forgives … I Don't*, his buddy, played by Bud Spencer, has a go at him over some cash they heisted. Spencer dances around, shaping up, all gentlemanly, and Hill slouches there with this calm ferocity in his countenance. As soon as the dancing Spencer gets close enough, Hill jumps up, swings on a tree branch and kicks Bud right in the face with his cowboy boots.

Reuben has this same calm ferocity about him now as he stands here by the road with trucks blasting past and headlights flashing in his frozen eyes. He turns on his heel and starts marching up the side of the freeway. I watch him get a few hundred metres until he disappears in the mist from the car tyres whizzing by. I make chase and catch him pretty quickly on account of his feet giving out as soon as he runs.

—Brother! I shout from behind him.

—Fuck off! he screams, not looking back, but I hear him anyway through the roaring wind and the hissing tyres and the tropical rain belting down heavy as billiards. I catch him and hold him. He shakes with rage. He turns with a demon curling his mouth into a hellish sneer. I make this kind of resigned gesture and back off a bit, dropping my duffel in the mud. He hunches down, sticks his hands in his jeans.

—Man, where …

—To kill my uncle … Don't fucken try to stop me.

—You can't kill him, man.

—Why the fuck not?

—Think of all the cool shit you'll miss out on … all the chicks and weed and living free!

—Don't give a frosty fuck.

I've seen Reuben stab a kid without blinking and smash a dude's face in with a wine bottle. I bet he does have the guts to kill someone, if he hasn't already. Don't ever take a swing at Reuben; you'll get stabbed, or worse. I can't think of anything to say, to try to convince him we should get out of Cairns and never come back, so I slap my heart through my soaked t-shirt and say:

—Sorry, brother, no more for me. Tapping out.

I walk away, not looking back. I refuse to get involved in a murder. I go about a kilometre before I turn around. I can see him way off in the mist, following me, kicking at cans and shit by the freeway. I stop and wait for him to catch up. We walk in silence through a couple of suburbs, slowly, because of his feet. Then I piggyback him and he feeds me cigarettes.

Eventually we pass this Salvation Army place on the edge of an industrial estate. All these down-and-outs and low-lifes have lined up at the door. Right as we pass, the doors swing open and everyone rushes inside. Reuben jumps off my back, joins the line, and I follow him. They have a huge dining hall in there, like an old factory or something. They serve up soup and steamed grunge to the hungry homeless. We gobble down a few bowls of porridge and drain the coffee pot. We sit there out of the rain, soaking up the air of desperation like bread in soup when this Salvos geezer in one of those repressed-looking uniforms comes and sits at our table.

—Welcome. Haven't seen you boys here before, he says in a voice balmy from years of soothing pain.

Reuben doesn't say anything. I shrug.

—You from around here?

—No. Reuben sits up from his slouch: We got stuck.

—Oh?

—Yeah, I say, leaning in: We had jobs at the show … but then on the last day the bosses claimed they didn't know us and refused to pay up.

—Seriously?

—Yeah. Until now we hadn't eaten for days, haven't slept. We don't have any place to go. I say this with the utmost resignation in my voice, at the heavy truth.

—Where you boys from?

—Townsville, we say in unison.

—I can get you boys bus tickets home, if you like. I can even give you a lift to the station.

Waiting for a bus again, the dawn exposing herself like a silver gelatine Man Ray nude descending a sleepless staircase.

I reckon I suffered a bout of narcolepsy or something on the bus back to Townsville. Fitful dreams, like flashing a torch around a cathedral of corpses in grotesque poses. Copulating skeletons. Raped marsupials bleeding on gurneys. Smashed frog. Pickled-looking old-lady vaginas singing Billie Holiday's 'That's Life I Guess'.

We hiss into the bus station in Townsville, again. Reuben and I stand around on the pavement out the front, trying to figure out what to do next. Reuben decides he'll go to a halfway house or something, but it doesn't sound ideal to me. I've had enough of sleeping rough. I call my parents' house reverse charges. It rings out. I search my pockets and my half-dried mud-covered duffel bag for bus fare, in vain. My journal has swollen up like a dead toadfish. The ink of a whole chapter about Reuben's grandma has bled into the paper like her pale grey eyes, fading my memories of her jail-warden-hard face, her hands trembling like a fern near a waterfall.

We sit there for a few hours. I tell Reuben I'll do my best to convince my parents to let him come back and get some sleep in a safe bed. He looks kind of hopeful for a while until my mum finally picks up the phone and the answer comes as a resounding no.

Reuben watches as I drive away with Mum. I see him shuffling there, smoking his cigarette like he always does – without once touching it with his hands. I worry about him; I really do.

4

I lose about ten kilos and feel quite sick for a few days. I drag myself around the house, licking my wounds. My voice doesn't sound right, like rusted parts of something in a glass of lovejuice. My sisters say I look like I escaped from a prisoner-of-war camp and crawled through hell on my face. I don't disagree.

I call Cali's house and her dad answers. I don't feel like getting the speech about how I should treat his daughter like a goddamn princess right now. I say hi and ask if I can speak with Cali. He tells me in a triumphant-sounding voice that Cali went out on a date with Scott. I don't know any dude named Scott so I say *Scott who?* And he says, *No, not Scott, she went out with Scott last weekend. This bloke goes by the name of Adonis. Real good-looking muscly feller.*

I don't really know what to do. I jump on a bus into the city and wander around the nightclub district, wearing a suit. I don't know why I dressed in a suit. I throw my tie in a bin. Weaving in and out of the crowds of August revellers, carried along, lost, not feeling myself. I can't stop thinking about Reuben's grandma and how afraid and ashamed and helpless she looked as we mopped up her piss. Poor old dame left to live out her final years alone while her family rush about doing important chores. Everyone laughing around me now has a similar fate. All the ones who make it to old age, anyway. Jesus Christ.

Poor Reuben has gone through so much physical and mental tragedy.

The look on his face as I drove away from the bus station with my mum, like a puppy about to get adopted from the pound before the kid's father changes his mind and says no. Love runs out of batteries. Everyone who doesn't get killed rots as they live. Buried or locked away and forgotten: I can't figure out the difference. All these pretty girls staggering by: their calves in heels will get flabby before they know it. These tough guys hunching about in their Gold's Gym singlets reduced to one of those withered old dudes you see with walking frames holding up bus queues. I wish I hadn't seen his grandma's vagina. I really do. Maybe Alexandra weakened those handrails by the toilet when she used them like parallel bars as Reuben gave her head.

I watch a dude play guitar for a while. Then, when I turn away from the chords of Guns N' Roses' 'Sweet Child o' Mine', I see Cali and some dude hand in hand walking up the steps of a club called The Bank. I get that kicked-in-the-guts feeling for a minute and smoke my cigarette too fast. I might drown myself tonight; it feels pretty logical. Love, and her other name, Despair … they visit in pairs.

But then along comes the little babe Candy I've dreamed about for countless nights! She has two hot-looking chicks with her. Everyone stares because you can tell they don't hail from these parts. To my surprise she walks right up to me, standing there watching the guitar player strum.

—Looking sharp! She tugs my suit lapel.

The other two chicks look me up and down. One has too much kohl around her eyes.

—Thanks!

—Marie and Blyth. She points at the other chicks: My sisters.

—Plans? I say, acting so fucken cool I feel proud of myself.

—Getting hot dogs, then going home to drink all this wine my dad sent for my birthday. Wanna come?

Fuck yes!

—Sure. I shrug, lighting a cigarette and making the mouth shape you make when you decide you may as well do something as no better options exist right now.

As I climb into a cab with these three hot drunk sisters who dress like gothic fashion models, Cali and her new arsehole come out of The Bank and she sees me. A horrified look on her face. She has no idea I've returned from Cairns, and now this. I notice her abruptly dropping the new dude's hand. Enough to make me smile properly for once.

The sisters have their own place not far away. These girls resemble babushka dolls in reverse order: the youngest the most buxom, the eldest a miniature, perfectly formed specimen of a woman, and the middle a cross between. We get out of the cab. The driver gives me a jealous look and winks. We head through the gate of a big shady old Queenslander and up the path, when there comes a blood-curdling growl followed by the deepest, most vicious barking I've ever heard. They all laugh as I near shit myself.

—Demeter! Candy shouts, and the growling stops.

—We have a Doberman, Demeter … Do you know the name Demeter? Candy fishes around in her handbag, looking for keys.

—Um … Dracula named his ship *Demeter* … but I think it comes from the Greek goddess of harvest?

Candy looks impressed. The growling starts up again, goaded by my stranger's voice.

—Let's see if she likes you. She doesn't like males much, for some reason.

I remember then that Reuben told me about the Doberman; I can't remember how many mornings ago. He got this far, at least.

Inside, Candy's sisters disappear and she takes me into her room and we sit on the floorboards. I nervously fish out a cigarette, trying not to look too interested in her bedroom and all the vampire posters. She has this cool movie poster of the original Dracula, Bela Lugosi, and a huge picture of some black-leather-jacket band called The Sisters of Mercy. I light my cigarette. She rises and opens the French doors onto the veranda.

—You don't smoke?

—Allergic! And she does an adorable little sneeze. She looks so tiny, no more than five feet tall, thin, with curves, though, and really sweet-looking breasts.

—You remind me of Audrey Hepburn … in *Breakfast at Tiffany's*, I say, standing half out the door, exhaling into the sub-tropical darkness.

—Really!

She looks so pleased I worry for a moment I've come home with an underage girl. I pray her height and age have no relation. I've seen her showing a bouncer ID, though.

—Yeah, but you dress more like Audrey in *Roman Holiday* … and you have nicer eyes.

She lunges at me, gives me an impatient borderline-aggressive kiss which takes me by surprise. We fall through the door onto the veranda. To make it worse our teeth clash for a second. Then her sisters come in like wisps. They've changed into nighties and washed off their make-up. They look even prettier. The older-looking of the two, Marie, says sarcastically, seeing us embracing half out the door:

—Have we interrupted something?

—Can I bum a cigarette? Blyth asks as Candy flops back down on her bed.

I get out my pack of cigarettes. As I do, Blyth pushes me back onto the veranda. I light her up and she takes a drag, saying as she exhales:

—You scared yet?

—Scared?

—Most males don't make it this far.

—Why?

—Well, everyone assumes she snuck out of school to go clubbing. She turned twenty-three this year, you know … And the whole goth-punk thing … here, in Townsville.

—Twenty-three!

—Yeah. Also, she has this thing where she thinks … She has body issues.

—What?

About there I smell bullshit, or trouble, or both, and I say, too bluntly:

—You trying to game me for some reason?

She shoots me a quizzical look. I bet I've wandered into a coven of witches or a nocturne of vampires or perhaps a gang of serial killers, or kidney thieves.

—What do you mean?

—Nothing, sorry. I just can't believe ... She doesn't look twenty-three and her beauty stuns me.

—Yeah, but what do you mean by *trying to game you*?

—I've had a crazy time lately – scary crazy. Anyway, why tell me this? You don't even know anything about me. Pretty personal shit about your sister, and all.

—Candy likes you ... a lot.

—Really? We only ever spoke once before tonight.

—Every time we go out, she looks for you. All the other blokes in this town look inbred or something.

—What about my friend Reuben? I thought they made love. I make those annoying quote signs with my fingers people do in motivational speeches when I say *made love*. I don't know why.

—Made love? She laughs: He fingered her on the beach but became aggressive and stuff so she pushed him away ... Nah, they didn't fuck.

The Doberman growls under the house.

—She had sex for the first time only recently. He pretty much raped her, though, and afterwards he tried to convince her to sleep with his roommates.

—What?!

The dog stirs again and you can hear her claws on the concrete under the house. Blyth makes a *keep your voice down* gesture.

—Yeah, trust me, she likes you. I'll let you in on a secret, to help you not fuck up. She whispers now.

—Okay. Why help me, though?

—You could always pass on her and fuck me instead, and she runs a finger down my midriff. I instinctively move to respond but then it occurs to me she might want to see how I react and I'll fail her clever test or something.

—What secret?

—Don't ever call her tiny, or remark on her size, or say stuff like *Oh I could break you* ... She has a thing about her size.

—Okay ... noted, thanks!

Blyth mashes her cigarette out on the balcony rail and slaps me on the arse as she goes back inside. I like her. What a cool chick. I follow. Candy and Marie sit on the floor, reading tarot cards. Now I feel in my element. I entertain them, reading cards until the blood of dawn splashes Bela Lugosi's face and the two sisters go to bed.

Candy and I have strangely familiar sensual sex. Not mad breathless and desperate like recently with Alexandra in Cairns. Candy moves slow and shy and a little wild here and there, but when she comes, she covers her face with a pillow, like real shy girls do. I feel safe with her, a strange, dare I say spiritual connection. We talk awhile, about our lives and stuff, sort of dozing and exploring each other. I tell her some of my adventures. She tells me her mother will get all pissy with her, dating someone younger. She tells me her mother always tries to set her up with older rich men. She tells me she hates her mother. She tells me most men find her too skinny or young-looking, or, because she has A-cup breasts, they don't even notice her.

—

I awake to the sound of a familiar voice. It takes me a second to get my bearings. Candy fades in beside me. I listen to her breathe, stretching, feeling like I've slept better than I have in months. The familiar voice again seeps through the wall. I get up, pull on my jeans and slowly open the door. Gigolo sits in the lounge room with Marie.

—Gigolo!

He looks up and, as he recognises me, a dark expression clouds his face.

—Bro, I've called your house about five thousand times. He sure sounds grave.

—Why?

He stands and says:

—Sorry, Marie, secret men's business. Come outside for a sec, bro.

We move to the backyard and, after the Doberman calms down, he says:

—Bro, bad news, bro … real fucken bad.

—What? Fucken tell me, man. I search his face, guessing the spray-can posse has come to grief, busted after all these years. I feel happy I haven't tagged in ages.

—Reuben … And he chokes up. I've never seen a glimmer of any emotion from Gigolo, so I get real worried now.

—What, bro? Cough it up. Reuben what?

—Bro.

—Fucken what, man? I get a bit angry there, panicky too.

—He came to crash at this place I have a room at.

—Yeah?

—Actin real weird all week. Hardly talked or shit, just read this book on chess moves.

—Yeah.

Impatient, dragging real hard on my cigarette. Some coughing there because I dragged too hard.

—He went to that fucken quack he always goes to … Scored some fucken pills … Hypo … Hyno … Hypno-fucken-something … fucken, some hardcore morphine shit.

—Fuck.

—I dropped a couple with him and we partied a bit. And then … He sobs again and I put my hand on his shoulder.

—Get it out, bro. My voice shakes.

—We ran outta fucken smokes, man. I went to the shops and on my way back ran into some cuzes and I ended up throwing up some pieces before I went back with the cigs.

—Yeah?

—And when I get back to my room, I don't see Reuben anyplace.

—So … maybe he went out, or something?

—No, bro. I found the pill bottle on the table, empty!

—Fuck!

—So I hunt around a bit and I can't find the cunt anywhere, and then … He starts crying now and my heart pounds: I hear this real painful sound come from my cupboard and I fucken rip open the fucken door and find him all fucken blue and not moving, with his eyes open and bleeding.

I feel numb-sick. I collapse on the grass. I think I yell or groan or something, because the Doberman starts trying to get from under the house to tear our throats out.

—Dead? I shout above the dog.

—Dunno, bro. Probably brain fucked if not, though.

—What? You called an ambulance, right?

—Yeah, of course, for fuck's sake! Then I found the nurse who lives in the building. She dragged him out of the cupboard, revived him, I think. They wouldn't let me go in the ambulance, bro … I went to the hospital but no one would tell me shit. He hugs himself, shakes his head, trying to dislodge the memory.

—When did this happen, man?

—Last night … I've just come from the hospital.

—He'll pull through. He has the constitution of a horse.

—I hope so. Gigolo snivels.

—Remember when we dropped those car-sickness tablets?

—Yeah, the Avils.

—Remember, you and I tripped fucken balls, hallucinated so hard … screaming about monsters and shit.

—Yeah.

—Reuben sat there and grinned all night, smoking calmly while we flailed about, fending off dragons. The fucker took forty pills! You and I only had twenty each.

—Yeah, true …

—He'll pull through.

We spend the whole day at the hospital, hanging around outside the intensive-care unit. Reuben doesn't regain consciousness. I detest hospitals. I can smell sickness cloy the air. We go out for a smoke, in a small quadrangle with an evaporated fountain. Hunched-looking people shuffling around in pyjamas. A dude with a drip muttering to himself over by the Coke machine. Broken bodies in wheelchairs.

—This scene disgusts me, I mumble.

—What ya mean, bro? Gigolo paces around the edge.

—I might cut it out of the story.

—You on acid, bro?

—He might die, man. I can't have the anti-hero die so early.

—Anti-hero? Bro, you've lost me, ay.

A doctor comes out to the quadrangle, looks at his clipboard:

—Reuben will live, though he had major organ failure and his lungs collapsed. Because of the way he died sitting up in a cupboard, he cut off his circulation and possibly, but hopefully not, he might lose his legs.

—He died? Gigolo jumps down from the fountain ledge.

—Yeah, mate. The nurse who revived him says she has no idea how long for, though … We worry about that. He scribbles something on his clipboard and leaves.

5

September 1990. I've moved in with Candy. Her sisters don't seem to mind. In fact Blyth keeps making it known her earlier offer still stands. Candy works at the Commonwealth Bank. Both of her sisters still attend school, the rich-kid school. After Candy leaves for work, I go and see Reuben at the hospital. They've kept him there for a month now. The first two weeks he drifted in and out. I sit there reading Kerouac's *On the Road* to his unconscious ears. When he wakes up, he sometimes asks for me.

—Has Brentley visited? he says in a half-dead murmur.

I cry when he does that. I don't see a single member of his family come to visit. This makes me feel like crying also. It makes me think about my family. I *know* they'd come for me. This envelops me in a dark place. When I go there, I cannot withhold my imagination from the abyss. The images come, vivid and sonorous, films on my inner horror channel. Remember, Brentley, harden your armour against Love.

Soon as they let Reuben up, I push him around the hospital grounds in a wheelchair. I bring him things: weed, smokes, books.

When Candy arrives home from work and her sisters home from school, we get drunk and dress to go out to the clubs. We go out every night. I have to steal from unlocked cars and phone booths to pay my way.

I go home to get my typewriter so I can type up a bunch of poems I've written. The days feel empty. At least Candy and I have a fantastic amount of sex. I classify as one of the horniest people to ever have lived and she keeps up with me.

In the suburbs my mother yells at me for not calling for a month. She thought I'd died or something. She gives me a huge list of all the times Cali has called wanting to speak with me. I feel pretty bad about that so I give her a call. She answers right away and asks if I can come and see her.

I turn up at Cali's house with my bags and my typewriter and she gets curious. I tell her I've moved in with a chick. She cries and begs me to give her another chance. We fuck a few times and as I leave she tells me she stopped taking the pill and she hopes she doesn't get pregnant.

Doing my best to hide my panic from Candy.

They let Reuben out of the hospital today! I call from the foyer and order a cab that can take a wheelchair. A regular cab shows up. Reuben calls the driver a wanker. Reuben hates cab drivers. This makes me happy because it means Reuben's soul stayed in his body when he died. I felt worried he might have split and left this swollen glum-looking shell for me to wheel around. Anyway, I get him out to the suburbs to his dad's house, this ugly duplex piece of shit deep in bogan territory. This place has clades of bogans. Without leaving the porch, you can trace their family tree right back to the first inbred who stole along the river and impregnated his sister.

I help Reuben into the house. We smoke a couple of bongs and play a game of chess that lasts about nine seconds because everything goes psychedelic.

Off the bus down at the beach, I decide to linger and sit on the rocks and smoke a cigarette, watch the pretty girls swimming. You can't go and jump right in the ocean here: you'll get killed in a few seconds by the Irukandji. These jellyfish can hide on a postage stamp and they shoot you with stingers from their bell piece. I read somewhere they have poison a hundred times more toxic than a cobra's. The beach has this thing they call a *stinger net*, developed by the university. It floats like a huge blue horseshoe inner tube, large enough for hundreds of swimmers. It also means that everyone swims in one spot. You never have to wander up the beach hoping to see a beautiful woman. Of course, you can't sit gazing forever without going into the water as you risk crossing the line between people-watching and perving. I sit awhile watching Venus and Suadela play volleyball. As I get up to leave, Gigolo comes along with his spray-can posse.

—Bro, he says, noticing the volleyball chicks. He gets tennis eyeball, trying to look at least two ways at once. His posse stands around, grabbing their balls and posturing.

—They let Reuben out.

—Seen him?

—Just now. Dropped him out at his dad's.

Gigolo bums a smoke off me. Struggling to light it in the wind, he takes my beaten-to-shit trilby off my head and uses it as a shield.

—Don't fucken burn that!

—Fuck … Looks like it died, he says, trying to straighten it out.

—I think I need a new hat.

He takes a few drags and, with one eye on me and one on Venus bending over for the volleyball, says:

—I need some help.

—Doin?

—Tonight me and the boys have planned a heist and we need a getaway driver.

—What kind of heist?

—Spray-paint.

—Where from?

—Don't worry. I just need you to drive.

—Bro, I dunno … I stopped this shit when I turned eighteen. They'll never get me in a prison cell alive and I don't wanna die just yet.

—You'll do it, bro. I know I can rely on you.

—Can't one of your dudes drive?

—Do you think Candy will let them drive her car?

—Candy's car!

—Yeah, bro. I dunno anyone else who has a car.

—She won't let me borrow her car to use in a heist.

—I already asked her if you can borrow her car tonight to take me to score some weed out in the burbs.

—You did?

—Yeah, bro. I've hung with these chicks for ages before you started shagging one of em.

We both get distracted when Venus loses her bikini top as she shunts the volleyball.

Candy has a gold Daihatsu Charade. She has super-rich parents, from what I can gather, so she can afford to have her own car. Her dad lives in Cairns, she thinks. Her mother and stepfather live in Papua New Guinea. Her stepdad works as an engineer on some new highway going through the jungle. Her mum used to own restaurants in Perth – a real social butterfly, one of those who gets involved in stuff so long as she doesn't get shit on her hands. You know the type: *Charity, dah-ling, the lifeblood of society life – titter titter – look at us collecting cash for retarded children while we swill thousand-dollar champagne and pretend to eat fucken risotto.* So they send their girls to live in Townsville because it has the most expensive private school in the state and they expect Candy to live here to keep an eye on them. They pay the rent and all the bills and tuition and shit. On top of this, Candy works at the bank and her sisters help her drink most of her wage every week.

I worry about Candy, though. She gets migraines so bad I have to take her to the emergency room because I think she might die. During an attack, she gets even tinier and squeezes herself into a foetal ball, and her lips go white as her clenched fists shake in agony. They always shoot her up with pethidine and renew her script for Panadeine Forte. She has developed an addiction. So much as a twinge of head pain and she swallows a couple of pills.

Gigolo arrives at 8 pm and Candy gives me her keys. We get in the Charade and head down to the beach to pick up Gigolo's posse. Six kids cram in the back.

—We have to make a stop, Gigolo grunts beside me.

We go to a smashed-up house in the Aboriginal part of West End. The place has wine-cask bladders for pillows on the couch. The carpet has cigarette butts dating back to 1930 crushed in there. The tongue-in-groove walls have fist holes and exposed electrical wires. The posse smoke about five thousand bongs each and drink a bottle of rum. I don't drink because I don't want to crash Candy's car. We get ready to go but before I know it the whole lot of them start examining a bunch of guns.

—Why the guns? I say.

A young Aboriginal posse kid who goes by the tag THC33 says, waving around a pistol:

—In case of guards. We'll have to shoot the cunts.

They busy themselves picking weapons. I say to Gigolo:

—Bro, that kid looks ten years old, waving around a fucken gun like a toy.

—You sound a bit toy, bro. Living with those three Witches of Eastwick making you a bit pussy, bro? He laughs: I've heard when chicks live together they synch up periods … Your rags synching up, bro? He says this loud, in contrast to my whisper. The posse piss themselves laughing at me. I jingle Candy's keys.

—Let's just do it then.

The now drunk and thoroughly stoned heavily armed kids bounce and sway in Candy's car as I drive them to the outskirts of town. Gigolo looks ready for anything, sitting there next to me. He had such potential. Years ago every other kid treated him like a star. He had style, flamboyance and charisma, and he could breakdance like Douglas Fairbanks could swashbuckle. But now he looks craggy and tired, and his eyes have a cornered desperation in them. I've noticed lately that when he smokes weed he gets paranoid and fidgety. He can't focus, and this makes him angry, or something, because he gets all aggressive and dominant.

—We have to adjust, bro, I say, above the beat of 'Funky Cold Medina'.

—Huh? He turns to look at me, eyes blank like a dead TV.

—Shit changes, brother. We can't cling to lost celebrity.

—What ya fucken talking about, bro? He shakes his head.

—I mean, bro, you outgrew this town … ages ago.

He looks out the window, pulling at his fringe. He used to spend hours doing his hair before we hit the city at night. Now it strings out from under his greasy baseball cap. His hat has *SOX* written on it. At first glance it looks like SEX.

—Fucken Tone Lōc. They should put on 'Fuck tha Police'. He shouts this at the radio.

—Fucken NWA, gangster as fuck! says one of the rabble in the back.

Gigolo has fallen on his spray can. Looking in the rear-vision mirror: two Aboriginal boys, mean-eyed and malnourished; three half-Aboriginal kids suffering from foetal-alcohol syndrome, seriously just off trainer wheels (one looks about nine); and one fat white kid rebelling against his rich Catholic upbringing, clutching a boltcutter like a teddy bear. I've seen this kid in the more affluent part of town. White bricks, two cars and swimming pools. Affluent. Not wealthy. They have swimming pools but you still see their dads mowing the lawn.

We cruise into an industrial suburb called Railway Estate. Yes, the railway tracks go right through it. Factories and warehouses in various stages of construction and demolition crowd up against the lines. A few decayed houses the army built in World War Two lie scattered around, now inhabited by bikies and amphetamine cooks. A hardware shop recently opened out here, a huge warehouse full of everything the home renovator could desire. Gigolo claims it has a whole wall-length display, about twenty metres long and two metres high, crammed full of spray cans, five deep. I slow near the gates and they all jump out. I watch them dart up, and the fat kid fumbles a bit and cuts the lock.

I slowly drive up the road and in a couple hundred metres do a real subtle U-turn in front of a servo. I make another pass and slow by the gates, which now swing wide open. I hear a window smash in the shadows of the building. Back up the road and around again, trying not to look suspicious.

Now the posse stand out by the gates and they each have one of those giant-size plastic garbage bins full of spray cans. They look agitated and impatient. I pull up. They try to cram the bins into the back seat. It won't happen. They get three in there and end up emptying the cans out of the other three right through the windows. No room for them now. Gigolo jumps in, perched on paint. The rest of them scatter into the shadows.

I drive back to the trashed house and help Gigolo unload. They have about five hundred cans. Back at Candy's place, I lie awake all night. Then I pace up and down on her veranda, smoking cigarettes. I exist on the distant peripheries of stupid. These kids will get busted as quick as that gecko hanging around the light bulb taking moths. Looks like a curtain call on this act. Townsville days. Cut. Wrap. Applause. I lean up against the balcony and flick my cigarette out into the street. I imagine an audience out there clapping. I take a bow and shout:

—Yeah, clap, you bastards.

Demeter goes wild, her growls and snarls and barks rumbling the house like Cthulhu calling from the deep.

Next morning the phone rings in the house and Marie sticks her head through the door and says to Candy:

—Mum … for you.

Pretty soon Candy comes back in crying.

—Shit! You okay? Rubbing my eyes.

—Mum has demanded I go see her in PNG.

—What do you mean *demanded*?

—Well, at first she asked me, but when I said I can't get time off work, she demanded.

—Huh?

—What she says goes.

—Why?

—What do you mean why? If I don't do what she says, she'll come here. Either way, my life has changed, again.

I sit up in bed. I must look confused because she starts telling me all about her mother.

—She went nuts, a while back, after her cancer scare, and from alcohol, and because of my dad. After the divorce she acted slutty, had troves of men visiting all the time. My dad used to have a fuckload of cash; he comes from a rich family. But after his brother died, he started drinking. He had a drinking problem in his youth but ended up fucked in hospital when he smashed a racing car, so he went off the piss for a while. Anyway, after my uncle died, Dad hit the bottle day and night. My uncle and my dad won all these prizes as kids, for maths. Both of them geniuses, worked for the navy for a while and then they made a fortune doing consultancy for engineering firms in Perth.

—How'd he die?

—Tongue cancer. A hair lodged in his tongue, from licking his moustache all the time. He'd always lick it; you couldn't stop him. He complained about having a hair stuck in it, but he never went to the doctor.

I've got out of bed by this stage, pulled on my filthy jeans and gone to the kitchen to make coffee, walked back into her room and out on the balcony to smoke a cigarette. She's followed me the whole way, talking. She stops as I light my cigarette.

—Not much of a genius, not going to the doctor, I say, exhaling.

She looks shocked for a second, but continues:

—My dad pisses me off. Gambled away all the money. She sighs and throws herself onto the day bed: So they divorced. Before, when they still had money, Mum had the whole society-dame thing going on … Hung out with Alan Bond's wife. We had a mansion in Peppermint Grove.

She glances at me to see if I look impressed. I guess she doesn't think I take punk seriously. I despise rich people.

—Lemme guess, the hell-rich part of Perth? I shrug.

—Yeah. Filthy. Like, eat the rich, filthy. Mum drove a Jaguar and Dad a Porsche. My sisters went to the best school there and I studied medicine at UWA. She sighs again: I miss UWA.

—You studied medicine?

—Yeah, made it to fourth year. Mum made me drop out to come here and look out for Marie and Blyth.

—What! I cough smoke.

—Seriously. As I said, she calls, my life changes.

—Why didn't you tell her to get fucked, or at least defer? I can't believe you dropped out on her command! My parents have an Eskimo's chance in the Sahara of getting me to do anything I don't wanna do.

—She'll cut me out of her will if I don't obey her. You don't raise your voice or act smart to my mother. No one dares. Anyway, I never wanted to study medicine; I want to study fashion design.

I really don't know what to say in reply to that. I honestly have not ever once thought about my parents' will. I don't want to think about them dying. I busy myself listening and smoking.

—She gets worse when she drinks. She glassed a waiter at one of her fundraisers, for mixing up the order of her cocktail. She asked for a Long Island Ice Tea and the bartender put in the gin before the white rum, and she lost her shit.

—Bloody hell. Does it even matter?

Candy shakes her head:

—Now she lives in PNG with her new husband, this Dutch-Portuguese bloke named Brian. He inherited a shitload of cash, so she hooked him right after she threw Dad out. Dickhead blows all his cash on her, though. He took this job in PNG to pay off her shoes.

I laugh, but she doesn't and I notice she has started crying again. I hold her awhile. She sniffles into my shoulder. What do you say to a chick who has a domineering mother as the worst problem in her life? Mind you, my mother suffered a similar fate. My grandmother subjected her to outright mind-control as she grew up. Mum told me once she had no choice but to devote her life to the cult because Grandma locked her out – emotionally, I mean, simply refused to talk to her or even look at her. My mum, the seventh and youngest, came along in Grandma's late forties, a change-of-life baby, a rare thing in those days. Back then you didn't want to get yourself abandoned by your family. They didn't even have electricity. Poor as shit, my mum's parents, like my parents now. Doesn't bode well for me.

Jesus Christ I hate money. Coloured paper printed by some swindler. Everyone else dies or kills trying to amass it. People who have money believe themselves superior, like somehow you owe them respect because they have more coloured paper than you. They act dismissive of the poor, like the poor have a choice. You always see the fucken royals on telly and in the paper. The pinnacle of their achievements? Born into a family that millennia ago slaughtered their neighbours and stole the livestock. Every time I see my grandma, I have to eat cow's tongue, and boiled chicken, and fucken pig's trotters. Real poverty, eating boiled pig's feet. I have poverty on every side of my family. Soldiers. Gypsies. Farmers. Convicts. I want to tell Candy about my life, I really do, some pretty personal stuff too. But whenever I talk about my life, growing up in a deranged apocalyptic cult that despises the world as the work of the Devil, no one believes me.

Candy sits bolt upright and says:

—I have an idea! Come with me to PNG!

PNG sounds like a good place to hide out while the shit goes down with Gigolo's posse.

6

At the airport in the duty-free Candy buys a couple of bottles of Frangelico, a hazelnut liqueur made by monks. The bottle kind of resembles a monk. I shouldn't have insisted on sitting in the smoking section on the plane; Candy's allergies flare right up. I put out my cigarette, but you can't go asking a bunch of fierce-looking Papua New Guinean tribesmen to put out their cigarettes when you sit in the smoking section. A couple of them have long thick cigarettes rolled with newspaper. Smoke, thick and acrid, cloys in the cabin. Last time I flew, I came home with a broken arm, from falling off a tank stand while trying to escape an oddly amorous cousin who insisted we touch tongues because it felt funny. I tell Candy the story, hoping to distract her from sneezing fits.

—Kinky bitch! When did this happen? Sneeze.

—Just kids … About nine or so.

—You haven't flown in a plane since then?

—Or before then.

—Wow! I've flown a million times.

—Dunno if I like it much, I say, looking out the window.

—Why? Sneeze.

—Trapped in an aluminium tube with jet engines attached, ten ks up, travelling at eight hundred kilometres per hour. Makes me paranoid.

—Statistically [sneeze] more people die in car wrecks than plane crashes. At uni every cadaver I cut up died in car wrecks, none from planes.

—You cut up bodies?

—Yeah … You get kind of detached after a while.

Sneeze times three.

—I've gutted animals … heaps of em.

—What?

—Yeah. Growing up in the bush, hunting: pigs, kangaroos, rabbits, birds.

—You killed birds!

—I ate em!

—Did you eat the kangaroos?

—No. Well, I've tried kangaroo and possum, goanna, snakes, wild rabbit, horse, donkey, and turtle, and crocodile. In fact I've eaten pretty much every native Australian animal.

—You have not eaten wombat. What sick fuck would eat a wombat?

—Okay, I haven't eaten wombat. You win.

As we touch down in Port Moresby, poor Candy has eyes like fertilised eggs and she looks like she used an angle-grinder on her nose, thanks to the aeroplane-grade tissues. We alight and walk across the tarmac into an airport shed. The customs officer has red-stained lips and teeth. When he asks me how long I intend to stay, he drools a long spittle of red down to the desk.

—From the betel nut, whispers Candy.

Candy's stepdad, Brian, waits on the other side of the rope. He has two locals with him.

—Bodyguards, Candy says under her breath as we approach.

Brian has strange eyes: brown, with a blue ring.

We walk outside to the car park and get into the back of a Toyota four by four which has caged windows. The two locals get in front and the passenger produces a rifle from between the seats.

—Why the bodyguards and the gun and the caged windows? I ask Candy as we roll through the centre of Port Moresby.

She doesn't need to answer. The place looks like a war zone, with ruined brick buildings, collapsed walls, rusted vehicles and fences buckled like soccer nets full of garbage. We stop at an intersection. I see a man walking on all fours. He has shoes on his hands, head down and swinging like something out of a Lovecraft novel. He looks up and he has an elephant-man face.

—See this, says Brian.

He sits opposite me, watching my horror with an amused look on his face, rolling up his sleeve. His forearm has a horrible purple scar from wrist to elbow.

—This happened last time I dared go out without guards. Machete. Shit has got worse lately, look! And he points out of the caged window at a line of about a thousand people jostling one another: About a month ago PNG got dollar scratchies for the first time … see that!

We slow as the throng spills onto the street. An old man clutching a goat hammers the bonnet of the Toyota with his walking stick. Brian points to a mountain of scratched-off tickets on the pavement. The bin next to the pile overflows too. A Papua New Guinean with a tusk through his septum and wearing a Nike tee pushes his face up against the glass as we crawl through the crowds.

—Crime has jumped three hundred per cent. Every bastard thinks they'll win on the next ticket. Gangs of rascals everywhere. Brian sighs.

—Rascals?

Candy pipes in through her sniffles:

—Here they call gangs of raping murdering thugs *rascals*.

—Full-on!

We motor through a few suburbs, past burned houses and smashed shopping trolleys, a juxtaposition of urban and tribal, poverty like I've never seen. Everywhere, looking down on this, giant billboards read:

7 Up
Drink Coca-Cola
Take the Pepsi Challenge

Candy's mum and stepdad live in a compound with an armed guard dressed in full tribal regalia.

—An ex-cannibal, Brian leans forward and whispers as the armoured gate squeals on its tracks.

The compound looks like a mini suburb of townhouses inside. At the front of one of them stands a stunning platinum-blonde woman with hair like Princess Diana's. We get out of the truck. A thousand dogs bark all over the place. Candy shouts something at me about the Frangelico. Her mum soaks me up, gives me a look like a judge at a pony show. Her gaze lingers on the duty-free bag.

—

I get the usual third-degree at dinner. Candy's mother, Margot, has the coldest eyes I've seen. She bores them right into me. They reflect the candlelight like facets from the hundred stones that glitter on her fingers. She made rice with some sort of leaf in it and I say, meaning it:

—Wow, this rice tastes incredible!

—Haven't you had curry-leaf rice before? she demands.

—Nope.

—Tell us about yourself, mate, says Brian.

—Um …

Candy cuts in:

—Brentley writes poems, has had a few published.

—Really? Where? Margot shows genuine interest.

—Two poems published, so far. One in a student magazine and another in an independently published anthology.

—Can you recite them? Do they have clever titles? I love clever titles! Margot titters.

—Um … 'Trotsky on Acid' and 'Opera of Destruction'.

—Trotsky? Margot snaps at me.

—Yeah, you know: the Russian revolutionary?

—I know all about Trotsky! She turns to Candy, who has sunk in her chair as if she intends to slide under the table: Have you brought home a fucken communist, Candy?

Candy glares at me, rises and disappears out of the dining room.

—We own quite a portfolio of property, you know! says Brian, his weird eyes like a dead eclipse: Don't we, darling?

—I don't have a problem with people owning property. If anything, you could call me an anarchist. I think people should have to utilise what they own, ya know, and not exploit other people's inability to own property … like landlords … I hate landlords.

Silence.

Brian stands, starts gathering up dishes. Margot watches him a moment and then says:

—Let's go into the living room.

No sooner do we get in there than, bless her, Candy calls down from atop the stairs. I apologise and get up the steps, probably too quickly. I thought Candy would reprimand me for stirring up her old lady, but instead she says:

—She had breast cancer, you know. So young too, only forty-three.

—God.

—You wouldn't know she had a double mastectomy.

—Full-on! I thought she looked well stacked and quite perky – for her age, I mean.

—She had a complete reconstruction, by the best plastic surgeon in Perth.

—Wow. Did they get all the cancer, though?

—It looks like it. Candy starts feeling her breasts for lumps.

We have really quiet sex.

—

Doing the tourist thing. Getting driven around in this fucken armoured car through ruined city streets. Everyone stares harder. We go to the markets in the centre of the city. As we get closer to the sprawling tents, we see more and more white people.

—Market safe, says the local guard sitting opposite us: Police, army, expats everywhere.

At the gates of the market sits one of those elephant men I saw yesterday. I try not to stare but holy shit. He sits there in rags with worn-out sneakers on his hands. A giant hunch thrusts up the rags, which fall over part of his face like a cowl. The various shades of filth on the rags and the way the peak juts reminds me of a Chinese landscape painting. As we pass, he looks up with a hideously deformed face, worse than Sloth from *The Goonies*. Candy chucks a one-kina coin into a cut-off Coke bottle he has clutched in his claw.

—Don't stare! Candy hisses under her breath.

—I can't fucken help it! Christ in a car crash.

—The poor bastard had leprosy.

What a burst of colour, like a crumpled-up rainbow deflated in the mud. Strange fruits I've never seen. Bows and arrows for sale, souvenir spears. Carved heads. The markets circle a sports field and a carnival has started up. Tribal music and singing. We wander down aisles of tourist crap: painted masks and etched pig tusks and postcards. Under every tree stands an overflowing barrel full of red spit from the locals' betel-nut habit. I want to try betel nut. Candy says she tried it the first time she came here and it made her sick and wired, like she'd drunk a thousand coffees.

We come across a woman sitting on a huge rug. She has a piglet suckling her left breast, and her wares laid out in front of her: a fan of those cigarettes rolled with newspaper and a bowl of betel nuts. She sits there chewing, red drool waterfalling. Some juice drips on the pig. I buy a betel nut and one of the weird cigarettes for one kina. When I choose the nut from the bowl, she snatches it out of my hand and with a rusted filthy knife expertly splits the husk. Inside it looks a bit like a hazelnut, but softer. She licks the knife, sticks a little seed on her spit and dips it into a jar of white powder. Then she makes a motion suggesting I put the nut in my mouth and lick the powder off the knife.

—What the fuck? I say to Candy, who stands there laughing.

—You have to do it now!

Fuck this. I squat down and take another seed out of the clay bowl shaped like a turtle, lick my finger and dip it in the jar of talcum-powder stuff, and cram the lot – nut and all – into my mouth. Not looking at the lady, or the pig on her tit. When I do look at her, she shakes her head. Candy laughs again.

—What?

—You have to chew the nut until pulpy, and then take the mustard seed and lime and chew it into the nut.

—Mustard seed? My mouth starts burning like hell.

—You'll burn your mouth with the lime straight on your tongue!

—Lime? I chew like crazy, trying to dissolve the fucken lime, and the thing grows larger with each chew.

—Probably builder's lime, too!

—Do you fucken swallow it? I ask, spluttering red stuff all over the front of my *Boys Don't Cry* t-shirt.

Candy laughs her arse off.

—Spit out the pulp as you go … Hahaha … The stringy stuff!

I run over to one of those teeming drums and spit it all out. Candy, behind me:

—You just wasted it. You don't spit it *all* out; you keep the centre bit and it slowly dissolves. The lime aids digestion, or something. They use cheap stuff, though, often not food grade.

—Fuck, I need a Coke or something!

—The Coke here tastes weird.

—What the fuck do you mean it tastes weird?

—I dunno, weird.

Margot and Brian arrive with the two bodyguards laden down with stuff they've bought for a picnic up in the highlands. On the way out I score a carton of Kool cigarettes for two kina and a bootleg cassette of a Prince album I've never heard of before.

Candy knows all about the Prince album, though. His third album, *Dirty Mind*, released in 1980, she says. She loves music. Her record collection weighs about three tonnes. What she doesn't spend on alcohol, she spends on records, clothes and shoes. She knows more about music than you'd think possible for one person. I spent months going through her collection while she worked at the bank. I've listened to everything recorded by Joy Division, the Cocteau Twins, Dead Can Dance, Echo & the Bunnymen, The Cure, Cabaret Voltaire, Clan of Xymox, The Birthday Party, The Jesus and Mary Chain, and The Wolfgang Press. I've never had any money to spend on records. Stealing LPs and Walkmans: two of the hardest things.

We drive up into the forest along roads about an inch wide. I don't feel well at all: a hard-edged rush comes on from the betel nut as the air thins out on Mount Hagen. To make it worse, at the picnic they have tuna in tins. My stomach turns. I get up and walk away into the forest to take a piss. Birds in the canopy. Crisp mountain air. On my way back I light up the cigarette I bought at the market stall. I take a deep drag and instantly vomit. Tobacco spins wrack my brain. I feel green and sweat like rain. Spitting like I sucked on the exhaust of a diesel train and washed it down with a chaser of sump oil, I vomit again and it comes out my nose.

—

Later that night my throat feels ruined. Trying to look at it burned and ulcerated in the mirror. I can hardly swallow. Candy has one of her infamous migraines. She lies in the room in the dark. I get one of our bottles of Frangelico and go downstairs. Smoke a couple of cigarettes down by the guard hut, but the cannibal doesn't make for good conversation. Back inside, watch television for a while. *For one kina you could live like a king!* says the Scratchie King. Rummage around the kitchen looking for a glass. Enter Candy's mother.

—You have Frangelico! Where did you have that hidden? Her words have a hint of mania on the edges.

—I didn't have it hidden!

—I would love a little drinky!

—Sure.

She gets two whisky tumblers from a shelf and a tray of ice from the fridge. We go into the living room and sit on the couch. I pour two double shots, spilling a few drops on the glass table. I rise to find a rag or something but she pulls me back down.

—Don't worry about it. She sniffs her glass.

Toast. She slams back her glass and SNAP. A fuzz happens behind her eyes, like television static, and then they sharpen again but she looks drunk.

—Did Candy tell you about my breast cancer? Her voice husky and intimate now.

—Um.

—Of course she did. Do you want to see?

—Huh?

She yanks open her blouse. I sip my Frangelico, trying to politely look. She has on one of those lacy low-cut bras that do up in front. She pops her bra open, slurs:

—Want to feel them? They still feel completely natural.

Her tits look fantastic, but I don't want to feel them, I don't think. She grabs my free hand and sticks it on her left tit.

I try to act nonchalant and take another sip of my drink at the same time but when I do you can see my damn hand shaking. The ice clinks. Her tit feels exactly like a tit. But then, completely by instinct, a subconscious sin, I drag my thumb across her nipple, and back, before I know what I've done. She gasps. I yank my hand away.

Leaving her tits out, she pours herself another drink, about five average shots. She smashes it back and stares at me with lust and hatred blended as perfectly as the hazelnut and the vanilla in the Frangelico. She leans forward, cocoa on her breath, and says, softly:

—I can't believe this … I shouldn't do this, and she puts her lips on mine.

My animal takes over and I kiss back, groping her breasts, and she gets hotter, climbs on top of me.

—Babe? Candy's sleepy voice rolls down the stairs: You down there?

Her mum looks like a five-year-old busted stealing chocolate, which morphs into sheer disgust. She gets her breasts back into her bra and her blouse done up and leaves the room in a blink.

Upstairs Candy has already crawled back into bed. I lie down next to her and sigh.

—You smell like alcohol!

—So?

She leaps up:

—Fuck me! Did you give any to Mum?

—Ha, yeah.

—You fucken what! she screams, stamping her foot.

I sit up.

—What … why?

—You don't give alcohol to a recovering alcoholic, you fucken idiot!

—Ouch! I guess she did act a little strange.

—What do you mean?

—Well, oddly amorous.

—Great … she tried to kiss you?

—After the breast thing and a few drinks she might have got confused. Nothing happened, though!

—What? What do you mean *breast thing*?

—She showed me them … You know, to show off her surgery, I guess?

—Fucken what?

—They feel totally natural.

So I started a war. Candy and her mother scream at each other until 3 am. When Candy comes back into the room, something has come over her. She seems resigned and distant. I say:

—Look … nothing happened, just a bit of drunken stupidity. I shouldn't have said anything.

—We have to leave, first flight in the morning. Massages her temples.

—Shit, that bad?

—What did you expect?

—I dunno. Doesn't she show everyone her boob job?

—She kissed you!

—So?

—Do girls' mothers always throw themselves at you … like some kind of fucken Lothario?

—Ha, The Impertinent Curious Man.

—See? I can't help but like you. Candy sighs and slumps her shoulders.

—What do you mean?

—Last guy I called a Lothario said, *I don't come from Italy*.

—I'd prefer you called me a Don Juan. Lothario doesn't cut it as a literary character, in my opinion, anyway.

—Great. She unzips her suitcase: Mum wants me to dump you … says you'll never amount to anything, not to mention the age difference.

—Fuck her. She didn't think me too young earlier.

—You should date Marie. You two have a lot in common.

—What?

She doesn't reply.

—What a strange thing to say!

Folding clothes, putting them in her suitcase.

—You want me to date Marie?

—You like virgins, don't you?

—What?

—You like virgins, yeah?

—Marie, a virgin? No way!

—I've only fucked one guy before you.

I shake my head, not sure if I've heard right:

—No, I don't have a thing for virgins, in particular, but you casually tell me you wouldn't mind if I started going out with your little sister … because your mother has a problem with our age difference?!

—I turn twenty-four in May!

—So-fucken-what?

—Blyth told me you two had sex.

Shit.

—Um …

—I don't care.

—We didn't!

—Blyth just turned sixteen, the self-discovery phase. She tries it on with every male I've ever shown interest in.

—Well, didn't work on me.

—Don't lie.

—I blame alcohol.

Banging at the bedroom door. The door opens. Her mum shoots me a look like she intends to get a hit man to take me out.

Screaming, until dawn, with the occasional softly spoken, reasonable interjection from Brian.

I've packed up all my stuff and resorted to smoking with my head out the window, waiting to see what happens. Soon, with the flames of dawn lapping at the night trees, I see a cab pull up at the gates of the compound. The bedroom door flies open.

—Get your things. Your cab has arrived, Margot screams at me.

Candy pushes in from behind her and slams the door in her mother's face.

—She took my passport, wails Candy.

—What?

—Won't let me leave with you.

—Fucken hell!

The cab horn blasts outside.

7

Only a week away and everything's changed. I visit Reuben at his father's place in bogan land. Poor bastard, his legs swollen so huge he can only wear a bathrobe. He chain-smokes. He has a bottle of whisky on the table with his Weet-Bix. He sees me looking at him.

—Yeah. Fucken sucks, brother. Not groovy, at all. I can't even wank.

He looks really sad. But he doesn't need sympathy; he needs to tell me where the fuck to find Gigolo. He shows me the newspaper from a couple of days after I left for PNG. *Graffiti gang busted after break-in*, reads the headline. Gigolo told Reuben the whole story. Gigolo has gone underground, police on his tail. The cops caught one of the posse kids tagging government property. They searched his bag and found his notebook full of practice tags and cans of the exact brand of spray-paint from the robbery. When they searched his house, they recovered one of the stolen giant bins full of cans, and he'd tagged the front of the bin *THC33*. All of them caught except Gigolo … and me.

—Fuck! Did Gigolo mention if they know who drove the getaway car? I push past his wheelchair and look out the curtains, paranoid.

—No. They had a car?

—Where can I find Gigolo? Do you know?

—Nope. Reuben shrugs.

I look at him for the second time since I arrived.

—You sure he didn't mention if I should go on the run too? Didn't give a hint where I can find him?

—Nah. Love Lane, maybe?

I get off the bus. Approaching the posse house, I see cop-tape fluttering in the breeze. Run back to the bus, trying to hide under my hat. At Redpath Street I find Candy's sisters packing up the house. They seem hesitant to talk to me at first. Their whole life has changed because their mother hates me and won't let Candy return from PNG.

When I track down Gigolo, he tells me the cops haven't identified Mr Risk. He says I didn't even come up in the interrogation, probably because I haven't tagged in so long.

—I'd get the fuck out of Dodge, though, bro, he says, with a frown.

I accidentally slept with Marie. I feel pretty sore about it, really; it just happened. I cried afterwards. The tears welled up out of nowhere. Candy has decided to defy her mother and come back. Yet still the sins of the flesh seduce me. I walk home in the rain to disguise my pain.

A year after my dad handed in his cop badge, he finally received his long-service-leave payout. Now he's decided on a trip to America for a white Christmas with Mum and Fliss. Best thing, he gives me two grand! Says *here ya go* and hands me a cheque for two thousand dollars. Melbourne, here I come.

I wait a week to draw on it, get some cash and kit myself out with some city-worthy clothes: new Doc Martens, new leather jacket and a rad new trilby. I go down to the bus station and price a one-way ticket to Melbourne: a hundred and forty dollars. Daylight robbery. Then a call from Blyth. Candy has escaped and will touch down at the airport in twenty-four hours! Like characters in a book, Blyth arranged the plane ticket and Candy convinced her parents' guards to accompany her to the airport under the guise of a shopping trip to the markets. So I go back down to the bus depot and buy another one-way ticket to Melbourne in Candy's name.

—We have to disappear, Candy says in the afterglow of her first night back. You do realise my mother will actually pursue me after this, and you … She'll figure out I've run off with you.

Candy makes me change the departure date, twice, while she packs up her stuff from the house on Redpath Street. This makes sense because my parents have gone away for six weeks, so we have their house to ourselves. She has a huge refugee bag full of antique plates and vases and shit she intends to take on the bus. I'll end up carrying the damn thing right across three states.

For two weeks we party non-stop. Blow the entire budget my parents left to look after the house expenses and to feed Jaz and me as they trek around America. Jaz has a heap of punk friends from school, and they pretty much move in, trash the place, pig out on everything in the fridge.

Harley comes to stay. Haven't seen him since he wrecked the Porsche. We sit around drinking whisky and smoking cigarettes, reminiscing about our school days until Candy's sister, Marie, comes to stay for a week while she waits for the keys to a new apartment. Right away Harley falls in love with Marie. She laps up his attention. *Do you mind if I fuck him?* she asks me, for reasons unknown. Since that night we accidentally slept together a few weeks back, I've seen her with at least a dozen different dudes. I guess she thinks it polite to ask if she can fuck my friends, given our history. *Um – should I?* I say, yawning. She shrugs.

—Cock yourself out.

—Ha ha! she sneers.

The whole house hears them, like you can hear everything in this house.

—How did you go? I say to her over our morning cigarette.

—Not so good. He has a hang-up … poor bastard.

—What hang-up? I say, surprised. I know of no hang-ups that Harley has.

—He has a big purple scar all around his cock. Childhood accident, he said, amputated by a wooden toilet seat … sewed back on. It works, it feels good. Dunno why he stresses.

—What? Holy fucken shit!

—Huh?

—Now it all makes sense. The scar he has between his eyes … kids used to tease him at school. They'd say he had a dick cut off his forehead, and he'd lose his shit.

—No fucken way!

—Shh! He'll hear us and beat me to death!

Marie claps her hand over her mouth, exhales smoke through her nose.

My parents arrive home from the States. They don't want us here. Mum makes Candy sleep in my little sister's room, to piss me off and get me out quicker. We now stay at Marie's new place, a converted garage with one room, a tiny shower and a huge king-size bed. Everything goes okay; we only have to spend a week here until Candy and I leave.

Saturday morning, days from departure, Candy goes off to get her hair done and Marie pulls out a bottle of Bénédictine. She belts a couple of shots and says:

—Do you mind if I paint in the nude?

As much as I don't want to, we end up having sex about a dozen times.

So I have to sleep in this bed with both of them. To make it worse, Candy starts rubbing up against me in the night and we have sex while Marie pretends to sleep. I think Candy does this because of some pretty bad feelings she has about the fact that her mum gave her car to Marie the day she worked out Candy had escaped. Marie didn't have any qualms about taking it, either. I like the car swap, because now the registration has changed, and the number plates, just in case anyone did see me driving an infamous graffiti artist sitting perched on a pile of spray cans.

Part Five
Lethe

I used to imagine adventures for myself,
I invented a life, so that I could at least exist somehow.
Fyodor Dostoyevsky

1

Haven't slept for two thousand five hundred kilometres. Feverish writing in my journal and looking out the window at the never-seen-by-me-but-totally-the-same-as-the-rest-of-Australia landscape slip by between Sydney and Melbourne. A girl gets on with that hippy, feral, slightly unwashed look and you can see her nipples through her top. Candy wakes up and notices me checking out her tits. She acts pissed off for the next hundred ks, refusing my advances, arching further away, until she falls back to sleep.

I've destroyed any hope for a long-term relationship with Candy. I can rationalise my indiscretion with her sister Blyth to myself. I slept with at least thirty chicks that summer – you know, one-night stands and stuff – before Candy happened. For all I knew, Candy would send me packing too. Blyth figures as an honest mistake any red-blooded eighteen-year-old male could make.

But Marie. Fuck. Last week we both went at it just because we could, just for the kicks. Real passionate sex too, and adventurous, no hang-ups. How do I explain that one? I can't. It simply happened. Besides, you didn't hear Byron or Kerouac complaining about women wanting to sleep with them. Like my heroes there, I have no complaints. But my relationship with Candy will die as soon as she finds out. You wouldn't blame any woman for calling someone who slept with both her sisters and pashed their mother the biggest bastard who ever lived. You'd walk right out. Love does it all the time, turns on her heel and leaves. I'd walk out on me if I could.

Look at it the other way, though. What kind of sisters do that to each other? Like the way Marie accepted Candy's car. Didn't argue the point. Didn't say *Mum, calm down. You can't just give me Candy's car.* Candy's sisters have it in for each other. Candy has no one in her corner. Her mum has disowned her for choosing me, and she doesn't know where her dad lives. I may as well do my best to stay with her and have some adventures. I have no one else either.

Look at Candy snoozing there: fine-featured, scowling, stunning little Audrey Hepburn replica. She has on ripped fishnets and a red and blue plaid skirt and you can see the straps from her garter belt peeking out because she has her knees up to her chest trying to get further away from me in her seat. She has on a Cocteau Twins t-shirt and one of the leopard-print fur coats you see hookers wearing in movies. This dude across the aisle has noticed Candy's suspenders and he strains to look sideways while pretending to look straight ahead.

Everyone stares at her all the time. That will probably doom us anyway. Love hangs around with chicks like Candy. I slept with her sisters to destroy any chance of it. I loved Billie-Jean and that faded like a polaroid left on a dashboard. Fuck you, Love, you middle-class fantasy. Just like rock stardom, you kill those who embrace you. In reality, people rarely attain you. Not people who have to fight to survive every damn day, anyway. As soon as some rich, better-looking, smarter, already successful and not just destined-for-greatness dude comes along, she'll disappear.

We steam and hiss into Spencer Street Station on the Greyhound. We soon find ourselves on our first Melbourne footpath, with our pile of luggage and Candy's huge bag of antique crockery. The city clangs around us. All I can see from where we stand: hotels, adult bookshops, bars and cafes. We walk about a block and check right in to a room at The Great Southern Hotel. We shower and fall into bed, and when we wake up twenty-four hours later we fuck and dress and head out into the city like excited children. We have about two grand between us and a credit card Candy received when she worked at the bank, with some special staff rates or something. We need to find a place to live and then we need to buy shit to set it up.

February 1991. We've rented this studio apartment on the third floor of 787 Park Street in Parkville. Right across the road sprawls a giant park, split into a sports oval with a tram rail going right through and, beyond that, the Melbourne Zoo. You can hear lions roaring in the night. You can also hear all of Melbourne roaring at football games at nearby Princes Park Stadium. The landlady of this place stinks like gin and her British accent slurs as the shadows of the day grow longer.

We live in one room, which has a bed alcove with curtains across it and a little private bathroom attached to it. It costs us eighty-five dollars per week. Melbourne has an anxious air, the trams and the frozen sky. I feel smaller here, invisible in the smog.

Down the road from our apartment we find a huge old pub called the Sarah Sands. Candy and I go and drink Flaming Lamborghinis whenever we can afford to. Other times we go into the city and eat pancakes. At home we live on noodles and soup. We both get the dole. It just pays our rent and electricity and gas. I need to get a job. Candy has an expensive habit of putting things on lay-by. She has more shoes than Imelda Marcos. I put a suit on lay-by at Myer. Every second Thursday we feel alive because we get the dole, and the night before we feel restless. Tomorrow we eat and get to drink coffee and spend the day hanging out in the city. I always run out of cigarettes; I can barely make a pack last three days.

My attempts to find work come to nothing, probably because of how I look. Not many people wear Doc Martens with a suit. I guess skinheads do mostly, but I have this rad new haircut, graded up the back and longer on the top and my fringe hangs down to my chin.

This actually seems to work in my favour today, though, because this old dame comes up to me on the street and flips me her card:

Melbourne Modelling Agency
School of Grooming and Deportment

I laugh.

She says:

—I think I can find you some work. You look great in a suit, and you have that alternative look everyone wants right now.

I figure *why not?* and agree to turn up to the agency's open night a week later.

At Melbourne Modelling on Queen Street. A bunch of dudes shuffle around in the foyer, hunching down into their collars. I get where they come from, trying not to look too confident. One dude has an interesting look – he has this whole Ian Astbury thing going on: shoulder-length black hair, denim jeans, leather jacket and Chuck Taylors. The others look like someone cut them out of a Country Road catalogue: too clean, too much cologne.

—Hey, man, I say to the rocker-looking dude, and I point to his James Dean belt buckle: Cool!

He shuffles about, getting deeper down into his shoulders.

—Cool Docs. They twelve hole? he mumbles.

—Yeah.

The old dame enters and she starts declaring our luck in getting *discovered* by her.

—I thought so, I say out of the corner of my mouth to the rocker dude.

—What? he hisses back.

—She wants us to sign up at her school here, man. This will cost us – pretty much a fucken scam.

—Ya reckon?

—Watch! Excuse me. Yes, I have a question.

—Yas, dahling? She looks at me like a slaver.

—How much does this training cost?

—We'll talk about that later, dahling … after I've told you everything I can do for you.

—Yeah, okay … but I, sort of, ya know, feel like I don't wanna waste your time because I don't have any money to give you.

—Only eight hundred dollars, dahling, for the full six-month course, two nights a week.

—Well, thanks anyway for the opportunity, lady, but see ya later.

I scoot out the foyer door, down the fire-escape stairs and up the street, and stop to light a cigarette. Behind me comes the rocker dude.

—Hey, man. Fuck that, huh! I say.

—Yeah, bro.

—Hey, you a Kiwi?

—Yeah … from Christchurch.

Silence.

—Wanna go for a beer?

—I dig chicks, man! he says, fast.

—So do I?

—Just checking … Some of those dudes in there looked at my cock area, I swear.

Josef: crazy thin-hipped dude with Hungarian and Serbian ancestry. The child of warring peoples. We drink all night. Compared with Josef, I don't actually smoke. I have around ten a day, maybe a whole pack if I feel stressed or hung-over. Josef smokes three packs a day. He's come over from New Zealand because of the terrible unemployment there, only to find Melbourne the same, in an economic slump and with a Gulf War budget sucking the life out of the system. Poor bastard lives out in the Dandenongs, at the end of the line, with his cousin. Takes him two hours to get into the city.

Regardless, we become regular drinking buddies. Candy tags along occasionally but lately she has withdrawn and says she wants time alone. Candy takes codeine tablets, drinks peppermint tea and reads fashion magazines all day. So I go out with Josef most nights and we pick up chicks. I end up with about a third more chicks because a bunch of them freak out when they hear his Kiwi accent. He also gets a touch moralistic for my liking, judging me because I have a girlfriend at home. Fuck that shit.

—Better to burn out than to fade away! I yell across the tram.

—But I like her, bro … Don't you feel like a cunt?

I shrug.

—You bad igg. He shakes his head.

—What did you say? I ask, laughing.

—Bad igg, bro. I called you a bad igg.

—What do you care anyway? You have a thing for her?

—No!

—Good luck, man. Have a go if you want.

—I would … but I wouldn't do that to a bro.

—Implying you'd actually succeed if you did try!

—I can have any chick. I have this game. I give chicks the heat and make them regret their boyfriends.

—The heat?

—The Josef charm, man. You jealous?

—Yeah, man, jealous of you and ya drug-fucked rocker look.

We both laugh. I reckon he might have a thing for Candy, but it doesn't bother me because I know she hates him for hanging around at our apartment all the time. What does bother me: I got all boasty/remorseful when seriously drunk a couple of weeks back and told him I've already destroyed my relationship with Candy because I accidentally slept with her sisters.

—

Josef has moved in. He gives us cash for groceries and shit, and he always has cigarettes. One thing sucks, though: spending all this time with him means I end up blowing all my cash on getting drunk. We aim to have as much fun as you can and still wake up. We wander around the nightclubs digging everything, go to see bands wasted. Candy doesn't give a fuck what I do with my money, because we've always had split finances. She starts coming out with us every night, and even though we end up equally smashed she has money left to pay her lay-bys. I dunno how chicks do it.

The best thing about Candy coming out with us: we have this system to party as cheaply as possible. In music stores you can find free passes to some cool clubs. Most of these clubs have dancing competitions for bar vouchers. Candy wins every single time, or comes second at worst. First prize at most places wins you a hundred-dollar bar tab. Candy can dance; you can't help but stare. She has the grace and magnetism of a film star. The way she dresses alone grabs attention. Then she glides out and dances like a Fraggle on acid navigating a waterslide on roller-skates. She waves her arms about so madly everyone around her clears a space. Especially when she has her hair teased goth-punk style and slam dances with herself. We get drunk, a lot, and it only costs us tram fare.

—

I try ringing my parents to beg for money, and my sister answers.

—Jaz!

—Oh, hey. Sounds bored.

—You all good?

—Yeah. The olds think you died or something, you know. You haven't called since you left.

—Yeah. They around?

—No. They moved out.

A tram clangs up Sydney Road and passes me in the phone box.

—What?

—They moved out! She shouts this time.

—I heard you. I just can't believe they moved out!

—Sorry, thought you couldn't hear me from the clanging bell rumble squealing roar behind you in the background!

—Yeah … trams. Used to em now. So they've moved out?

—Yeah, sucker. You left, and now I have a whole house to myself.

—Fuck you. Where did they go?

—They moved to Airlie Beach.

—Why?

—Dad started a security company there, or something, when they returned from America. Took Fliss with them. She has to do Year Ten.

—Wow!

—Yeah. Whole house – pretty solid. And you know what? They put in a spa, out the back of the master bedroom, which *I* now have.

—Fuck, cool and rad! Jaz … do you have any cash?

—No.

—Hey, how about the TV I rented before I left?

—I have your TV.

—Do you pay for it?

—No. I thought you owned it.

—Yeah. Can you send it to me?

—To Melbourne?

—Yeah. Chuck it in a box and put it on a bus. I'll owe ya one!

—Address then?

—Give me Mum and Dad's new number.

—Melbourne cool?

—Fucken freezing!

—Oh, ha ha.

—Yes, I seriously love this place, but I dunno how long we can afford to stay here. They booted me off the dole and I can't find a job.

—You still with Candy?

—Yeah. We have a flatmate too.

—You and Candy have become junkies, haven't you?

—No!

—You sound like a junkie: *Got cash? … Send me a stolen TV.*

—

Luck finally deals me an ace! I land a job at the Universal Theatre in Fitzroy. I work Thursday through Sundays. I turn up at about 3 pm and stock up the bar and the refreshments, open the box office down on the street around 4 pm and sit there selling tickets until the doors open for the show. I then get to sit around or even watch the show until the bar opens at interval. I love the building. Seedy and run-down rooms full of smashed props and broken cabaret letters from the old-school theatre billboard above the street.

A few weeks in, Candy and Josef arrive after the show like always and I slip them a few drinks while I clean up the bar. We decide to hit some clubs.

Then, out from the shadows of my past, at a club we have never patronised, in a part of town we've never visited, right there, burning up the floor with a crowd cheering his moves, Gigolo!

—The chances! I say as he sees us and clown-walks off the dance floor.

We can't hear each other in there, so Gigolo and I go outside and cross the street and stand around catching up. He says he has to front court in a few weeks so he's come down here to see his grandma in case she dies before he gets out of prison.

—Yeah, bro, some serious shit fell on me after the posse went down. They had a photo album of every tag I ever put up ... about this thick, man! And he puts his hands about a metre apart: Charged me with vandalism to public and private property with damages over one million dollars.

—Holy fuck.

Gigolo looks really sad there, so I say:

—I'd go to jail for my art! which cheers him up a bit. Then I say: Have you seen Reuben?

—Last time I saw him, he introduced me to some chick he knocked up ... I reckon already born by now. Anyway, he met this chick and then he moved to Brisbane with her.

—So he recovered then?

—He still limps.

We both laugh.

We all end up back at the Sarah Sands Hotel by our apartment for a late one.

Josef tells me while we collect cigarette butts in a car park at the end of another big night this same week that he wants to start a band called Quadrophenia, after the mod film by The Who. He reckons the world needs a new sound, to sum up our generation. I say:

—Don't you think The Jesus and Mary Chain or Jane's Addiction fill that role?

—Mary Chain need more speed – I dunno about shoegazing goth stuff. And Jane's Addiction … I dunno, man. That psychedelic, tie-dye, mystical shit just rips off Jim Morrison, you know. Josef stops to light a cigarette butt – for some reason he can't walk and light up. I wait for him to catch up and I say:

—Yeah, I agree. This generation has nihilism down as a lifestyle. No one has ever catered for us. Everyone just does their own thing.

—I wanna cross syncopated classical bass riffs with heavy metal lead and distorted rhythm guitar and punk vocals. I just gotta get an amp … You should sing.

—Nah, man, trust me, I can't fucken sing.

—Anyone can sing punk! You write really fucken good poems, some real dark shit, too. Use them as lyrics and put some effects on ya voice.

—Yeah, maybe …

I stop at a phone box and dump some coins into the slot with my numb fingers. I have Reuben's number from Gigolo written down on the lapel of my denim jacket. The phone rings out. Lonely phone ringing in a big empty Queenslander in Brisbane, on a warm early morning as crows caw in the backyard.

—What ya doin? says Josef, breath freezing on the glass phone box. Look at him: crazy, broad-shouldered, thin-hipped, skinny bastard with his lank black hair burrowed into his fur collar. Smoking cigarette after cigarette trying to get warm, dancing on the spot in his Chuck Taylors and torn jeans. He won't wear a beanie because he reckons it fucks up his hair.

—Making a phone call, you dumb cunt, I say, shivering.

—Obviously, dickhead. Who you callin? He huffs on the glass and writes *poof inside* backward in his breath mist.

—This old mate named Reuben. Got his number from that breakdancer dude we ran into a few days ago.

—What for? At fucken dawn on a Sunday? You inconsiderate cunt. You have a major problem, you know, with your inconsiderate cunt-ness …

sitting up all night writing while two other people try to sleep in the same room … fucken banging about like the loudest cunt on earth. So long as you get to do what you want, you don't give a fuck about the wasteland you leave behind. What a cunt. And he shakes his head and walks away towards home.

I watch him until he disappears into the morning fog. What a bass-playing Kiwi bastard. Thinks he has shit to whinge about. Poor him, hasn't had any cash since his parents went broke a year ago. Private-schoolboy ponce. He never wanted for anything all his life until now, and for the first time he gets out on his own and reckons he has it tough. I've a good mind to kick the bastard out. Probably sleeping with Candy too.

2

I finally get through to Reuben, just in time, he says, because he's moved all his stuff out to a new rental. He has a girlfriend now and they have a six-week-old baby boy. Reuben and a friend of his named Sean have opened The Bohemian Cafe on Elizabeth Street in the city. He reckons everything runs uber smooth.

—Get a load of this! he says on an exhale down the line: We've just rented this old brothel in Woolloongabba, up on the hill overlooking the city, right behind Boggo Road prison. The place has seven bedrooms, three living areas, an industrial-sized kitchen, two bathrooms, three toilets and a sunroom out the front. They've built in underneath … it has a bunch of seedy rooms with faux-pine panelling and a sink and a mirror in every one. I'll set up a home brewery and a grow-room down there, man. Weed and beer on motherfucken tap!

—An old brothel? I say, trying to picture it.

—Ya know … a house that had an illegal brothel, huge old Queenslander. We moved in last weekend … had a lawn picnic. We haven't had a proper house-warming yet. Plannin that shit now.

—Sounds fucken amazing, brother.

He senses the tension in my voice.

—You not having a good time, man?

—Yeah, just … so fucken cold down here. We only have a shitty heater, kicked me off the dole … can't find any full-time jobs.

—Who you with?

—Candy. She came too.

—Oh … groovy.

—And this dude Josef, who I met at a modelling agency.

—What?

—Long story … What else you doing these days?

—Fucking heaps of chicks who come into my cafe. The other day I actually closed up and Sean and I fucked these three French tourist chicks all afternoon. Brother … countless babe opportunities.

—Liberal girlfriend you have there, man!

—Jo? Oh, she initiates a lot of it. We have threesomes, foursomes and shit all the time … well, up until we fell pregnant.

—Man … you sure sound like you have shit worked out up there!

—You should come up, work at The Bohemian … rent some of our spare rooms … bring ya new mate, Josef.

When I get back to the apartment, I tell Candy and Josef I have a lead. Reuben can set us up with a job and digs in Brisbane.

Somehow, despite Reuben's new baby in the picture, we've decided to move north.

3

No writing in three months.

—

Busy livin all the poems I haven't written.

—

Blank.

—

Exist. Rush. Run. Faster. Obey. Consume. Contribute. Breed. Fear. Burden. Die.

—

Found a worm on the carpet and a remote control in the grass.

—

Josef and I sit here on Airlie Beach. The shadows of the past months have nowhere to hide in the midday sun. Josef drones on about his imaginary band. Cries of seabirds like feedback. Candy has a job interview in a newsagent on the foreshore. We bum around here under the palms, waiting for her. The gulls circle the tourists. A girl on the beach has all the male attention but Josef doesn't notice, talking about the bass line he dreamed of last night. I don't listen, though, because one of my rare episodes of worrying about the future has me firmly in its jaws. If Candy doesn't get this job, we will have to move back to Townsville. Jaz still has our old childhood house to herself. We can go live there, but Townsville seems a big backward step to me. Too many bad memories.

Candy comes out from her job interview and crosses to the beach. Josef has fallen asleep on the sand. She doesn't look hopeful. She shrugs:

—Owner treated me like a kid. Dunno if I'd wanna work there anyway. She notices Josef asleep on the sand. He has a lit cigarette between his fingers that has burned down to the point where he will leap awake screaming in pain very soon. Candy flicks the butt out of his hand.

—Aw, you ruined it! I say, disappointed: It would've hurt like hell!

She shakes her head, looking at the hot chick that ninety-nine per cent of the beach has their attention fixed on. Judging by the depth of the hot chick's tan, I'd say she does this a lot. She has the body of a goddess and she has her top off. She has an air of pride, about her breasts probably.

—Anyway, Candy sighs, flopping down onto the sand: Looks like we'll have to go back to Townsville.

—Yeah, my dad seems progressively more annoyed since we showed up … and the contract just ended.

—What has he said?

—Nothing … but I know his demeanour. The other night when I went around there for dinner, he sat there in silence and I got into a bit of an argument with Fliss and then, suddenly, he stands up and smashes his plate on the table.

—What? Candy shoots me an alarmed look.

—I've never seen him do anything like it.

Since we arrived unannounced at the house my parents rent while Dad works here, he has acted like a champion. After he quit the police force and received his payout, he purchased a Wormald security franchise in the tourist town of Airlie Beach. Despite the initial shock of his prodigal son returning home with two punk wastrels in tow, he gave me a job and an advance to rent an apartment. He has a contract with a new resort getting built down on the foreshore and he enlisted me to go and sit in the security hut and guard the construction equipment. I've had to sit there from 6 pm to 6 am six nights a week, for two months now. Many nights Josef accompanies me – because he has guilt, I reckon. He doesn't want me to notice his eagerness to get Candy alone, so he volunteers to sit up all night and keep me company. We sit out there playing poker, smoking cigarettes, messing about.

We grew tired of cards tonight and decided to go through some equipment lockers. I find a BB gun and a box of pellets.

—Let's go kill some shit! I say, excited.

—What? Josef looks alarmed.

—Don't tell me you've never killed animals?

—Maybe a fly or a mosquito, and a grub once.

—Fucken … what a panty-liner!

—Fuck you, cunt. Like you've killed anything more than your chances with Candy.

—What?

—Nothing. Did you just call me a panty-liner? He giggles at my insult, to distract me, I bet.

—I've killed countless native Australian fauna: birds, possums, kangaroos, pigs, snakes, turtles.

—Turtles? Why the fuck did you kill turtles?

—I dunno. Us kids used to throw rocks off this cliff and smash their shells, for kicks, I guess?

Josef looks horrified, busy messing around with the BB gun, trying to figure out how to load it.

—Give me that! I say, snatching the rifle.

—You'll get bad karma, man, shooting birds especially!

—What do you mean, you fucken hippy?

—You know, birds symbolise freedom, and all that. He shrugs.

—Depends which kind of birds you kill, man. This world works that way. I didn't know the difference until I got in big trouble for shooting a black cockatoo. Some birds people call pests and vermin, and others they protect. Think about that for a minute.

—You've lost me.

—I mean we shouldn't differentiate. Class ideology divides everything.

—Weird cunt. Josef shakes his head.

—Humans hold their values high, but they've gone off the rails. You know, black cockatoo or scummy city-square pigeon; national icon or flying rats; prince or homeless pauper: it pisses me off.

—You've gone on a rant, man.

—I reckon if you want to kill a bird, who gives a fuck what kind of bird? For example, here the law protects possums, but NZ considers them pests, right?

—You can get paid to kill em.

—Right, see! And I stalk outside with the rifle and Josef follows me out.

Smoke billows all around. The construction crew dug a huge ditch and filled it with all the unusable wood from the trees they cleared and set it alight. It still smoulders a week later. Lazy flames crawl up the sides of the ditch, licking the burned dirt.

—Look! A fucken possum. Fuck the possum, man. Fuck the laws!

I take aim at a possum which makes its way along the bough of a giant eucalypt preserved for its aesthetic stature. Can't quite get the angle right so I climb up on the tracks of a bulldozer, pump the air rifle, take aim and squeeze. An audible *thwack* as the pellet hits the possum high in the ribcage. It drops dead-weight from the tree and sends up a cloud of dust in the clearing. Still alive, it comes out of shock and scurries about in the dirt, wounded grievously. I pump the gun again and fire a shot into its skull. It only wounds the possum more, bone too thick for the brass ball bearing and I only gave the gun half a dozen pumps. It makes it to the foot of the tree and groggily attempts to crawl up. I grab a sapling and bash the possum to death.

Josef comes back into focus. He stands there, kind of frozen, his silhouette against the flames rising from the ditch behind him.

—Deranged cunt, he says, scrubbing out his cigarette butt with a beaten-up Chuck Taylor: What'll ya do with the corpse?

—I guess, throw it in the fire pit.

—Burn the evidence, he says, with a nod.

—Or it'll burn you.

4

Townsville, August 1991. We sit in Gil's shed drinking rum. I figure the rum may have something to do with why I feel despicable and as each day passes I grow to hate myself more. I remember this feeling from school, where everyone actually did hate me. I could feel animosity emanating from the crowd. Even I hated me. Some kind of strange freedom comes from that, though: hating yourself – not giving a damn if Consequence ever catches up and takes out your heart.

I've joined Josef's neo-punk band. The guitarist, Bolton, a friend of my sister Jaz's from school, has an obsession with a band named Nirvana. He has their album *Bleach* on repeat as we sit here in the shed in the blistering Townsville heat. Bolton says Nirvana have a new album out in September and he preordered it already. Bolton has his back to us, headphones plugged into his amp, trying to get his new guitar riff right, to show us. I didn't agree on calling the band Quadrophenia, but Josef already visited a copyright agency or something way back in Melbourne and trademarked the name.

Bolton and Josef hit it off straight away. Not as well as Josef and my sister, who started fucking as soon as we moved back, secretly they thought. The shitbox my parents designed way back in the eighties has flow-through acoustics. Fart in the kitchen and you'll hear it in the spa out by the carport.

Bolton told us about this dude still in school named Gil who he reckoned could out-drum anyone else in the whole town, so we aimed to convince Gil to abandon school for rock stardom. A funny guy, Gil. The day Josef and I met him, we turned up at his place, the only house at one of the busiest intersections in the city. We got by all the junk on the lawn and up the side of the house to find Gil's mum, a portly smiling woman, drinking a Four X on the steps.

—Sweetie! she sang out: You have friends visiting.

—Aw, Mum! came a voice from the window above us: Don't call me that in front of me mates! And then a stream of piss followed out the window.

As we bedlamed from the window, we saw a naked chick trying to cover up, and this dude with a Mohawk and a glistening dick pissing and laughing. His mum also laughed, shook her head, disappeared inside. Bolton didn't look shocked.

—Like I said, crazy. Bolton shrugged.

Crazy like Reuben those last days in Brisbane. He said *groovy* with expressionless eyes. *Man, I found a hundred bucks!* and he'd reply *Groovy. Dude, your son tore up your first-edition Kerouac! Groovy.* A few months after we moved in with Reuben and his new family, I arrived home to Abingdon Street in Brisbane one afternoon to find a woman sticky-taping an eviction notice on the front door. We paid our rent direct to Reuben every two weeks, and he'd dutifully go off to the real estate to pay, or so we thought.

Getting evicted didn't bother me; I'd gone through it heaps of times. The fact he went off to get wasted without me, now that bothered me. I wondered why he looked so happy on rent day. I don't know where he went or what he did with our cash, but he sure as fuck didn't pay rent.

Also, his business partner, Sean, started to blatantly sell speed over the counter at the cafe, and I expected the place to get raided any day. Sean became real creepy, too. He'd furtively slip you a bag of speed and you'd pick it up and he'd say *Two hundred and fifty bucks*. You'd go to hand it back and he wouldn't take it. *Cash only*, he'd say. Sean lived in the Rio Grande in West End, a run-down 1930s-style apartment building. Someone spray-painted *apostasy* on the gate. Sean owned a Triumph Dolomite and some nights after he'd snorted an entire bag he'd take us driving, his jaw set like a hood ornament, speeding through the backstreets of Brisbane with the headlights off.

That three months happened so fast I didn't get a chance to write any of it down until now. Candy and I, and Josef, decided to bail on the whole situation. We waited for Reuben to leave one morning, and for Jo to gather up the baby and go for a walk, and we hastily packed our suitcases, called a cab and skipped out to the bus station. We bought tickets to Airlie Beach. Sitting around in the bus station, I had the guilts real bad and decided to go down into the city to the cafe and tell Reuben I had to leave. As I walked in, he looked anxious to see me, standing behind the counter like a tired cowboy slumped against the saloon bar.

—Hey, brother, I said, sad.

—Hey.

—Man, we have to leave. I hate to do it like this, but …

—I know … Jo rang and said you'd all packed up and bailed.

Silence. His blue eyes too far apart, like somehow his lower face had sunken and his upper widened.

—Sorry, man. My voice broke a little.

I really did feel sorry. I cleared my throat to say something else – I don't know what: something – but a crowd of people came into the cafe.

—Groovy, he said, shifting his gaze to the patrons.

About six hours into the bus trip north I realised we'd left behind my television, which by now, for sure, the company I rented it from would have reported stolen. Candy curled in on herself like a nautilus shell again. She had a mental breakdown during a foursome with Reuben and Jo. Stood bawling in the shower for two hours. On the bus all the way north her hand felt like a birdclaw.

—Right! says Bolton, throwing off his headphones, yanking the plug out of his amp: Got it. Listen to this shit! He cranks it to ten and starts with some melodic picking and then launches into a jangly storm, furiously stomping on his distortion pedal. The shed shakes and stretches.

—Fucken-A, screams Gil above the roar, and leaps onto his drum kit. He has a Besser brick in the bass because he kicks so hard it keeps slipping off the piece of astroturf he has his kit perched on.

Josef slowly rises, takes off his shirt, ties it around his waist, lights a cig, picks up his bass, and starts playing along. Before long I start singing, making up lyrics as I go, shouting through Josef's bass amp, which he convinced my sister to buy for him with a university loan. My voice sounds fucked, but who cares. The song sounds a lot like Nirvana, only with a shit singer. *Neon Jesus shine on me, neon Jesus set me free ... plastic churches coloured lights you can pray day or night ...*

We jam like this for hours into the night, until Gil's alcoholic old man comes shuffling into the shed and tells us he will murder us unless we stop right away.

—

The days of my fucken life. Shit has turned sour again: what a surprise. My dad kicked us out of the house in Townsville because we didn't pay rent for the whole five months, and a dude turned up and served me a court-attendance notice for a stolen television. I had to convince Josef to sell his prized 1968 Gibson twelve-string sunburst for six hundred bucks to pay the TV rental company to stop proceedings.

I had sex with Candy's sister Blyth in the spa one afternoon and I think Candy saw us, but she never said a thing. Frosted over, went shopping. A chill in the space between us, like a dead park between two skyscrapers, a place the sun forgets to touch. Blyth only spent one night with us, en route from Port Moresby to Sydney for a job interview. Mad chick wants to join the air force. Josef and I picked her up from the airport. I smiled and waved as she walked through the arrivals gate. She looked Josef and me up and down and said: *Jesus, you dudes look like junkies.*

5

A few weeks drag by. We busy ourselves looking for a new place to live. We look for two-bedroom apartments, but we can't find anything. Discouraged by this, and because the band has fallen apart, Josef decides to go back to New Zealand. He calls his mother, she buys him a ticket and he leaves. I've never heard anyone talk to their mother like Josef talks to his mother. He doesn't even listen. He holds the phone away from his ear, even puts it down sometimes. You can hear his mother's thick Slavic accent buzzing on the line. He sits there slapping his bass while watching television or something and occasionally says *Yeah, bitch*, or *Whatever, you silly hag*, and then, when you hear the poor woman say *Eh larve yah, Josefzzy*, he says *Yeah ... fuck off ... bye*, and drops the phone on the cradle.

—Dunno if I'll ever see you again, you weird-kneed cunt, he says at the airport: Have a nice life.

Crazy bastard. I don't know why, but I love him like the brother I never had.

Candy and I move in with two chicks we met at a nightclub. One has moved in with her boyfriend, but she signed a two-year lease with her mate, Trina, a dental assistant. Trina says they have a room for rent in an older-style apartment building on Fryer Street, up on the hill right above the city. Cheap, moderately stylish. I set up my typewriter in the sunroom, looking out to the ocean, and feel right at home. I only have to walk three hundred metres to hand in my dole form.

Candy hangs out topless, wearing only a sarong around her hips, because of the heat, and pretty soon so does Trina. Self-consciously at first; her breasts look easily double-D. I don't mind.

Hanging out in the cafes, I run into Bolton. He has this smoking-looking hippy girl named Angel with him. I keep running into Angel, at the shops, at the library, randomly in the mall. We flirt with eyes and smiles. Today I stop. She likes that I have written a collection of poems and I like her photographs.

—Want to come to the cemetery and take photos of the tombs as the afternoon shadows wash over them? she says.

Then, hours later, after sharing a joint in the cool of a broken family crypt, dew sparkling on the grass between the graves, Angel says:

—Want a blowjob?

I've avoided her for several weeks. Then, this afternoon, out of nowhere, Candy answers a knock on the door.

—Hello? says Candy.

—Hi … Angel … Candy, right? I see a hand stick in the door. Candy shakes the hand.

—Yeah. Do we know each other? She turns to look at me coming down the hall.

Angel spies me and says:

—Hi, Brentley!

Candy's face starts to contort.

—Hi. Bolton with you? I say, innocently.

—I came to introduce myself to Candy. I hate everyone in this town and you look interesting, says Angel, and she sounds pretty damn genuine.

I listen awhile and then I make an escape to my typewriter. About two hours later, as the darkness comes and shouts of patrons en route to Friday night stop my poem mid-stanza, I walk into the bathroom and find Candy and Angel naked.

—Um … I say, as I notice both of them no longer have pubic hair, and they giggle at my surprise.

—Just exfoliating, says Angel.

Angel has something written in runes tattooed under her left breast and a sun tattooed around her belly button, and she has both her nipples pierced. Both of the girls, naked, like a Norman Lindsay painting, with the late-afternoon Queensland light dappling shoulders through louvres. I try to not look interested at all and make my exit.

Later they both emerge fully dressed, all made up with nice hair and everything, and announce they want to go drinking.

—Wanna come? says Candy.

—Holy-fuck-yes! and I rush to throw on my jeans and boots and catch them halfway up the street already.

We go to The Bank and inside they immediately hit the dance floor. I stand around watching, because I don't dance, and then I see this dude who visits Trina sometimes. He invites me to join him. He has a jug of special house-mix spirits. We find a table and he says:

—Mind if I spice it up some?

—With what? I shout above the music.

—Temazepam, he shouts back.

—The pharmy?

—Yeah!

—What does it do? Never tried it!

—Fucks ya up, man! he screams in my ear so it crackles.

I give the *sure, why not* shrug and he squeezes the liquid from half a dozen green gel caps into the rocket juice. Just then the crowd in the club get rowdy. The DJ says over the mic under no fucken circumstances will he play Nirvana's 'Smells like Teen Spirit' in this nightclub so stop fucken requesting it. Half boo and half cheer, and the music starts up again, a dance track.

My glass of Liquid Ecstasy has a temazepam capsule floating in it. The cocktail alone creeps up on you: Bacardi, Midori, Blue Curaçao, lemon juice and pineapple juice in that order, eight serves of it, in a jug.

Probably six hours later, Angel and Candy come sweating off the dance floor to where we sit smashed out of our gourds. Candy leans over the table and yells:

—Two males, two chicks, we should all go home for group sex.

People from three tables away turn to gawp and the dude perks right up, not sure if he heard right, and shouts:

—What? Fucken oath. I'll come!

—Just joking … funny bitches, I holler into his ear, and I scamper out of there with the two girls.

They make a show of it all the way up the nightclub strip, stopping to pash and grope. Right in front of a group at a taxi stand Angel puts her hand up Candy's skirt, her fingers to her nose and says *Mmm, pussy scented.* Soon as we get in the front door, the girls lose their clothes and run into the bedroom. By the time I get in there, because I can hardly walk, I find them in a sixty-nine, getting very vocal. I slump onto the mattress on the floor and watch, at times fighting to remain conscious from the temazepam cocktail. The very air I breathe feels soft and scented. Then they turn on me. Candy pulls off my jeans and takes my cock in her mouth. Angel sits on my face. Then Candy rides me near to oblivion while Angel goes to the very verge of suffocating me with her cunt. Then Candy says *Get on his cock* and Angel says *You don't mind?*

They both scream the house down, the most vocal sex anyone has ever attempted to describe.

Morning. I untangle myself from limbs and fuck-stained sheets and get a coffee off the stove. I sit on the front steps to smoke. Magpies on the fence behaving badly. The chick who lives downstairs comes out, on her way to work I bet, and, spying me, says:

—Someone had a helluva time last night, huh! Laughs down the path.

After that, Trina moves out and Angel moves in. Candy and I never discuss this. We share a bed, each other and everything else. We don't always have threesomes. Sometimes one of us might not feel like sex – well, one of the girls, anyway, because if I don't feel like it, which means I died or something, watching the two of them has me feeling like it pretty quick. We don't care who knows. In fact we revel in making it known. It lasts several months, until one morning, spontaneous as it started, it ends. Angel says she has to go, packs up, kisses us goodbye, and leaves.

And just now, as I sit on the steps, talking to this guitarist who lives downstairs named Simon, Marie walks up the garden path. My heart drops. She looks as hot as ever, but, honestly, I haven't even thought about Candy's family since Blyth breezed through on her way to the air-force interview.

—

Turns out Marie escaped from Port Moresby. Trapped for an entire year in one of the seven levels of hell. I have a phobia of jungle since visiting that place. Marie didn't come to Townsville alone. She has Blyth in tow and also John, the girls' biological father. My secret hopes of never meeting the man dash like a kid's teeth on the edge of a swimming pool.

Candy claims her small stature results from a childhood disease which afflicted her while growing up. Her father, however, torpedoes her canoe when he turns up with Blyth not ten minutes after Marie trips up the path. Candy's dad stands, at most, five feet short.

He also has this generic alco skin the Australian sun has beaten the living shit out of, a leathery deep-wrinkled look that would only flatter a goanna. And he has a super-skinny body, like Candy, but with a beer gut like a garden worm swallowed a marble some kid left on the lawn. On top of all this, despite the dried-up buffalo-turd skin and old-man hips, he has a weird youthfulness about him, a mischievous mouth, sparkling eyes, like Pan telling you a hilarious joke while pouring you another cornucopia of wine on a sunny mountain slope somewhere in Ancient Greece. He looks like an old kid. Sixteen or sixty?

Now I can see where Candy gets her eternal-girl look. Nearly twenty-five but looks at most fifteen. Her driver's licence has worn paper-thin it comes out of her purse so often. People give me disapproving glances in public. She makes me look like the oldest twenty-year-old in history.

The panic has already set in Candy's eyes. Me, I've never experienced gradual change. My life perpetually earthquakes underfoot, and Candy knows now this rubs off if you hang around with me. Not five minutes later they've gone to the pub to celebrate the reunion, but I have no intention of breaking my five days off, twenty days on alcohol rule, so I decline and sit down to do some writing.

About an hour later Marie comes back from the pub by herself, undresses in the doorway and says:

—I don't think we need to tiptoe around the fact that I need to fuck, something serious.

Here I go again, walking on edges.

The next day John has already rented us a new apartment, given Candy a shitty blue Datsun 120Y and made it obvious he will live with us for a while.

We move into a two-storey brick piece of shit in a building of twenty identical flats surrounding a slimy leaf-choked swimming pool. Two blocks back from Townsville's main beach, the pool serves no purpose. Candy and I share a room with Marie. Blyth has her own room and John sleeps with his carton of beer on the couch downstairs. Blyth has made a successful application to join the air force, and she has a few months to party before she begins.

Candy devises a plan to escape the family chaos she despises and enrols in a TAFE course for chefs. She reverses the Datsun 120Y out at eight every morning. John leaves the house at ten, when the pubs open. Blyth goes off to the beach to work on her tan. Marie gets into bed with me and we fuck until about midday and then go to Cafe Nova to hang out. We get home about four. If no one has beaten us there, we blow each other in the living room and fuck on the stairs.

Blyth wants sex also, when somehow we end up alone. She says stuff like *Let's see how far we can go without actually fucking*, and we fool around for a bit until we end up having full-on sex anyway.

Lethe, your eyes effulgent from the fall, look tenderly upon me. I've lost so much already in this oblivion of lust and fury.

Months of this.

I know something bad will happen.

Part Six
Untitled Plane Crash

O son! did you not ever go on your knees and pray for deliverance for all your sins and scoundrel's acts? Lost boy! Depart!
Jack Kerouac

1

We pull up outside Maggie's house and she looks hell-pleased as she runs down the driveway. Stuffing her bags in through the window, she leaps in like her life depends on it.

Out of the city now. The lights of Townsville disappear over the horizon behind us. Maggie uncoils her shoulders and breathes like a weight has lifted.

Spinning down through the black in a crappy blue Datsun. Maggie holding my hand for the past two hundred kilometres, interlacing her fingers with mine, resting on the gearshift. I finally get the rusted-out crap-box of a car up into fourth, hovering around a hundred ks an hour as we roll down the ranges south of Townsville. Dark sets in and Candy stretches out, falls asleep on the back seat. Everything we own, we have crammed in. The interior of the car looks like a kid's fortress made out of dirty laundry.

I haven't slept with Maggie yet. I met her a week ago, in a nightclub. She said she needed to escape an abusive relationship. I shared our plan to take off in the dead of night to Brisbane, to escape a generally fucked-up situation ourselves. She offered to put in for fuel.

Then the headlights go out. Pitch black, travelling at a hundred ks an hour. Maggie screams, which sets Candy off. I pull over safely, swap a fuse, and we make it to Mackay right on midnight. We pull in to a bus terminal car park and settle in to get some sleep.

As dawn comes with onions on the wind from some breakfast fry joint, I awake to a security guard tapping on the window with a flashlight. I wind down the steamed-up window and he gawps at Maggie passed out with her skirt up in the back seat, and then he gawps at Candy curled up in the front passenger seat with her tits sticking out of her singlet, and then he gawps at me rubbing my eyes and fumbling for a cigarette and says: *Move it along, buddy, before the cops find ya with that half-naked underage chick.*

The girls wake as I start the car, and we roll out of there, heading for Brisbane.

—

Candy doesn't like Maggie. I told Candy I found our petrol buddy for the trip to Brisbane and Candy looked suspicious of her dancer's body right away. But, as far as Candy can see, Maggie looks like the first and best option to help us get the fuck out of Townsville as soon as possible. Out of the blue Marie did her nut at me one afternoon, sitting around playing Dungeons & Dragons. Bolton had shown up with our old drummer Gil's girlfriend's sister, a real cute punk-rock chick named Bonnie, whom I can't help but flirt with. Suddenly Marie starts screaming at me, calls me *the biggest cunt on earth.* She turns to Candy and says:

—Brentley and I have had sex about two hundred times since we've lived here, and about a dozen before that.

Then she rises. You can hear her arse drag on the carpet in the shocked silence of the room. She goes upstairs and bangs around while I try to decide whether I should chase Candy, who slammed her way out the door so hard the window cracked, or run fast in the opposite direction. Then Marie thumps down with a suitcase, goes out to the kerb, hails a cab and disappears.

John gets home to find Candy a sobbing heaving mess at the front of the building and then Blyth comes back from the beach right on his tail. I have a huge fight with John, to the point where he takes a couple of swings at me and I dance around, not wanting to hit the papery old bastard, denying everything, saying Marie must have had a psychotic break because we've never had sex, certainly not two hundred times.

2

December 1992. Candy and Maggie and I roll into Brisbane in the wheezing blue Datsun. After scouring the newspapers at a cafe, Candy realises the two of us can't afford a rental on our own. I see the telltale signs of a migraine swelling behind her eyes. Candy suggests Maggie rent with us if she has no other plans. We find a private rental above a family of Italians. A two-bedroom place with high ceilings and a large sit-in kitchen and a balcony overlooking a ratty lawn full of mower parts and broken concrete birdbaths.

I spend a good few weeks trying to seduce Maggie. She leaves the shower door open a couple of times when Candy goes out. She lets me massage her through her underwear and play with her tits but slaps my hand away as soon as I lift the elastic.

Josef shows up to find me living with Candy and Maggie opposite the train tracks in Bowen Hills. We have a merry time. For my twenty-first birthday my dad gives me a thousand dollars, which he says took him twenty-one years to save. Josef and I blow the entire wad getting drunk at The Beat nightclub in Fortitude Valley and getting lap dances at a strip joint called The Red Garter.

When we get home that morning, Maggie has just arrived back herself. She goes out every night dancing to techno music. She looks like a club kid, she dances like a club kid, and she picks her moments like a club kid. Josef and I flirt with her, mucking around, trying to see up her skirt and shit like that, when suddenly she grabs my hand and sticks it right into her knickers and Josef's hand and puts it on her tits. The precise moment she does this, Candy walks out of our bedroom all messy-haired and groggy-eyed and sees me fingering Maggie in the kitchen while Josef gropes her under her t-shirt.

—Great, she says, turns on her heel and slams the door.

Maggie goes into her room, comes out with a suitcase and leaves.

At Chalice House cafe in South Brisbane a poet named Rey plays master of ceremonies and a rabble turn up for the open mic. I sit with an old artist named Graham who reeks of rabbit-skin glue and a poet with a master's degree in physics named Francis. A poet named Sando turns up every week and recites his Shelley-inspired verse, which gets my head drooping like a dead rose. Francis has only one poem and he only reads it when some new chicks show up in the audience, staring right at them. He has a tremulous voice which vibrates on the edges like double-bass strings. A poet named Rebecca gets up every week and reads poetry which gives me visions of someone pulling their intestines out of their vagina and stringing a harp with them.

A couple of poets here look like they came in on the tail of a beatnik's dog. Drunk, stoned, debauched poets whom I can't get enough of.

One poet named Damo keeps drinking right through to breakfast. He tells me a story about catching herpes from a chick he fucked on a bus he got on by mistake which took him to Darwin when he should have landed in Melbourne. He shows me a beautiful poem he wrote on the back of a summons for drunk and disorderly conduct (urination in public). He says he woke with three verses formed perfectly in his head. He tells me he had one hell of a night because he got laid and can't remember it. *Woke up with crunchy pubes*, he explains. The poem on the court summons, written in a drunken shaky hand and covered in red circles from the bottoms of wine glasses and rubbed in cigarette ash, reads:

Untitled Plane Crash

Visionary man
imbalanced
by the hit and run
of destiny,
accidental fate.
Poet without a pen
you ve dared
to live your life
deeply, as the
oceans decree.
Valker of edges
you ve felt the
lip crumble
beneath uncertain feet.

He has a whole collection of these poems, written on things like needle-exchange-program leaflets and beer coasters. A guy who lives like him could die at any moment, and he knows it. Fragile soul, beaten mercilessly by the third dimension, like a leather flower bud he blooms to suede. Real poets have no sword, no horse and no army. They face the Beast alone.

I've started painting and visit Gilchrist Galleries on Brunswick Street at least once a month and show the art-dealer chick my work. She does this little *oh god, him again* forehead wrinkle as soon as she sees me. Candy and I consider ourselves in an open relationship. We have a few more girls in our bed, mostly suburban chicks who come into the Valley to experiment. Then Candy meets the artist Davson. She gets the idea from a friend at fashion school to do nude modelling for art students. She does a couple of jobs at the TAFE college and then along comes this famous prick.

—He calls me his new muse, Candy gushes at me: Says he'll pay me a hundred bucks an hour … five times more than the college art department pays!

—Yeah, I mumble.

I go along to Davson's studio in the Valley to pick Candy up on the first night. I turn up early. He has a shop front, looks like temporary digs, the windows covered up with newspaper so you can only vaguely make out shapes moving around inside. I peek through a ripped corner and Candy sits there with all the modesty of a Babylonian-temple whore. Legs about ten metres apart, her shaved vulva and gleaming clitoris ring aimed at twenty drooling guys all pretending to draw her. One of the hottest women I've ever seen, sitting there, not just naked but on display, with the same amount of shyness as she has clothes.

Candy gets rich quick, has an inch of fifties in her purse. We only pay eighty bucks a week for this run-down shop. It has just one room but extremely high ceilings, with French doors through to a miniature bathroom – a shower cubicle, a toilet and a vanity crammed in there. A tailor ran a shop out of here, on the second floor, from 1956 to 1985, the landlord said as he gave us the keys. The landlord retains a flat below us; we see him about twice a century.

The inside of our flat looks like the Palace of Versailles, filled with expensive designer clothes and kitchenware, coffee cups and jugs and lamps and shit like that. Candy has a thing for non-utilitarian utensils. I bought her some flowers to put in one of her new vases and she put them in a Milo tin. *What about the new vase?* I said. *You don't put water in that vase!* she shrieked as I carried it to the tap. You could serve me coffee in the bottom of an old cut-in-half milk carton and I wouldn't give a shit – honestly, I wouldn't, unless the coffee tasted like pus or something.

I guess you could say her popularity with life-drawing classes and artists came as a blessing, though, not only because she bought me clothes and art supplies and a second-hand electric typewriter, but also because, when our Benny Hill look-alike landlord turned up one afternoon and told us he intended to tear down our building, we paid cash for a much classier rental, only two doors down on Bowen Terrace – a three-storey, art-deco, red-brick building named Ravenswood.

3

Josef returns from living with a black metal band in Lismore.

—Shit got weird … fucken drummers, he says after I let him in and we smack backs. He rents our spare room here in Ravenswood, not that we need the cash this time. Davson throws so much money at Candy. The classes crowd as word gets around that Davson has captured a real-life Sheela-na-gig. I even saw a newspaper article about how popular his art classes have become.

Josef coming back doesn't lift the black slump that's come over me lately. Lying in the dark, crying. Candy goes off to fashion school every morning and I stay in bed all day, or sit on the back steps smoking, watching crows shit on the concrete. A lot of people describe depression as an animal which creeps up on them and pounces. It doesn't happen like that for me. My spectre sends omens in advance. Like light gleaming from the coin in a street magician's fingers.

Not light in a binary sense, though: you know, light and dark, war and peace, love and hate. I disagree with absolutely everyone in that last case. When Love turns her back, you'll find Despair. My writing condition stops, like the tremors after days without whisky. Doesn't incrementally fade or happily boil to death. Dries right up in an instant. All the time, before Despair comes to visit, I hear voices in my head. But they don't bother me. Sometimes they cajole me, but most often they goad me into action. When Despair comes, she switches off the radio and gives me time to feel the world for a while. When she leaves, though, she lingers, like perfume in a hallway. Crawls out of me like those dark spirits in the film *Ghost.*

The shadows lift a little and I manage to sit up straight at my typewriter.

I compile all the notes and journals I've kept since way back in Greenvale. I type up a couple hundred pages of everything that's happened right up until now, and my damn typewriter dies. Fucken electronic piece of shit Candy bought me from the Salvos. I stride out of the house and fume up the street, intending to hurl the machine through the front windows of the shop, and I run into the poet Sando, from Chalice House. I bitch to him, saying that right in the middle of a major inspirational maelstrom of writing my typewriter packed it in.

—What ya writing? New collection of poems?

—Nope … a novel.

—What about?

—Nothing … everything … life. About a boy who fears Love and desires impermanent possessions. I shrug.

—Nutshell me the plot line, man. He squints through the yellow glasses he wears for dyslexia.

—It has no plot … life has no plot.

—I like that! You can use my computer to finish it if you want.

—

I've spent the last month in Sando's living room, hunched over his computer, transcribing so fast from my notes that I knocked off the Z and the O keys at one point. An Eiffel Tower of cigarette butts and empty takeaway coffee cups fouls up the desk. Whenever I burn out, Sando and I go and drink at Mellino's cafe in the Brunswick Street Mall. Sando says:

—You have a lot of girlfriends, huh, and you have threesomes and stuff with Candy.

—Yeah.

—How do you do that? I can't figure out women at all.

—I don't think about it.

—What do you mean?

—You know how people say: it happens when you least expect it?

—Yeah.

—Well, stop expecting anything, ever.

Just then I notice this dude I keep seeing everywhere. He hunches down as I stare at him. He has on a sky-blue suit, a chambray shirt and a white straw fedora. He looks like a Smurf.

—Fuck! I say under my breath and melt into an alcove.

—What? says Sando, peering over those yellow glasses at me in the shadows.

—That dude that looks like a Smurf … I see him about fifty times a day and he keeps staring at me.

—What, a Smurf? Where? says Sando.

I peer around the edge of the shop door and the dude has vanished.

—Probably the acid, man, says Sando and he pats my shoulder.

We see Vincent and his little babe of a girlfriend named Rose and an old wizened-looking woman walking down the mall. Sando has a relationship of some kind with Rose's mother. Vincent's poems always conclude with a thinly veiled metaphor about Rose's cunt, so everyone listens carefully. Sando invites them to join our table. Before long I get into an argument with Rose's mother because I say that I believe in total personal freedom. I just finished telling Sando and Vincent that the poet Yuri and I spent three nights and four days awake, drunk and on LSD, writing a manifesto called *The New Decadence*. We decided, Yuri and I, that destiny has decreed we have no choice but to embrace a life as dissolute as possible. Cursed by the Fates and born with the souls of poets in a time which regards us as redundant, and in a country which regards us, at best, as drunken wastrels, well, we'll do what everyone expects of us.

—Can I read it? Do you have an axiom? says Sando, putting a fourth sugar into his short black.

—Yeah: total personal freedom. Lighting a cigarette.

—Bullshit! coughs Rose's mum: No one acts outside of personal interest.

—I don't fucken care, I reply.

—If you really believe what you say, you'd get up and go over there and kick that window in. She laughs at me.

—Why would I do that? I don't want to hurt my foot.

—If you have real conviction in your beliefs, you'd go kick it, she challenges.

—Nah. I know that tactic: demonising my argument. Most people say, *What, so you can just kill someone if you feel like it, with no repercussions?*

—Exactly! says Rose's mum.

—Yeah, but you can rape and murder someone now. What stops you? Not *just* the law, I hope!

—What then? she huffs, annoyed now.

—Predators have walked among us since the dawn of time. They always will, hiding like tigers. If one has sized you up as prey, or one wants to randomly attack you, they will do it, laws and cops or not. You know, their animal has taken over, stamped out the little angel on their shoulder, like a cigarette butt, or a spider.

—Don't get him started on a rant. I warn you, says Sando.

—Smart-arse. She shakes her head, studies me a moment: Do you believe in God?

—Not particularly.

—Either you do or you don't.

—Why?

—Why what? You can't sit on the fence about these things.

—I know I don't believe in *Man*.

—Huh?

—God specifically forbade following the laws of man ... you should only observe the laws of God. I chuckle at her confusion.

She stubs out her cigarette, wipes some hair from her face with the back of her hand, regards me with those old worn-wise eyes hippies of her generation have. Says on an exhale:

—Did you just use a religious defence for anarchy?

—I guess.

—Clever.

—Don't patronise me.

—I didn't mean to patronise you. Why do you think that?

—You put yourself in a position above me by commenting on my ingenuity.

She shoots Sando an accusing look, before saying:

—You don't need to get aggressive, darlin. She scrapes at the milk-scum cappuccinos make when the froth goes hard on the edge of the coffee cup.

—Me, aggressive! You suggested I kick in a window to prove my beliefs.

—Look … I didn't mean to offend you. Obviously I have. I have no problem with people who believe in God.

—I don't *believe* in God. Not today anyway.

—You talk a bit like a Christian … like someone who had fundamentalism beaten into them. She slurps her coffee.

—Told you: psychic! Rose cuts in.

Sando blushes. He knows all about my upbringing in the cult. I told him this last month while sitting in his boarding-house room, writing my novel on his computer. Obviously he has told Rose. This pricks her mum's ears and she appears proud and suddenly interested.

—You grew up in a cult? She starts rolling a cigarette.

—Yeah … I don't really like to—

—Oh? Which cult? Sparks her durrie: I've studied cults. I actually work with some victims. I bet I've heard of it.

—The Truth.

—Well, I'd like to know, but total personal freedom and all that … You can lie if you want. She shrugs, sarcastic, sits back.

—No … They call themselves *The Truth*.

—Never heard of them.

—Spiritual Israel, The Way, The Light.

—They sound Calvinist.

—Exactly … worse.

—Like Amish? says Rose.

—Far stricter.

—Bullshit! says Vincent, finally adding to the conversation.

—You kinda sound like you still believe in God, man, says Rose.

—You do believe in God, when you find it convenient, gloats Rose's mum: You still have extremist views, not much better than a Christian. Pffft, disregard man's laws ... If you really believe what you say, you should kick in that window.

—Nah, fuck that, I say, annoyed now: Who cares if God exists or not? I prefer the *possibility* of God, rather than the self-appointed authority of man. Man calls himself an intelligent animal, and, sure, I agree, but these two parts conflict unlike any war ever waged before. Man, prone to animal fits of passion, will never find the stability his intelligence seeks. I see man as more than an ape who figured out how to light fires and build wheels. I see us as part animal, part angel. Why? Well, because I have a bizarre fascination with the Romantic poets, but also because it seems logical to me we didn't get here on our own. I lived in a house with a baby, and, from my observation, humans would never have survived in a cave with a screaming kid when sabre-toothed tigers roamed the land. Anyway, sure, people make fun of Christians and other devotees all the time, myself included ... but if you live by the fundamental teachings of the holy books – don't steal other people's shit, don't trespass on their person and don't kill anyone, whether they deserve it or not – you can live peacefully with your neighbours.

—I warned you, says Sando to the now silent table: Don't get him started on a fucken rant.

—Pah! says Rose's mum, with one eye squinted because she got smoke in it and that stings: I smell bullshit, son. All words. I've heard it all before. Action: now that speaks louder than words.

—Fuck your cliché, I yell, smashing my coffee mug on the pavers before I get up, skip over to the sliding glass door and give it a real hard kick.

I met Yuri at a poetry reading at Zane's Cafe in the basement of the Metro Arts building. He emulates the Beats but he has his own style about it. As we try to navigate the Story Bridge under the influence of some particularly potent LSD, I say:

—Yuri, you sum up the living embodiment of a neo-beatnik … I mean, you even hum jazz when you write poetry. Look at you, man!

The damn bridge has gone all soft, and halfway across we both freak for no real reason and can go no further. We hide behind a balustrade because no one feels more paranoid than us right now, except maybe for Josef. Josef has a double doctorate in paranoia. He sleeps fully clothed, wearing sneakers, in case he has to bail in the dead of night.

—What? says Yuri, trying to look at himself, twisting like a tongue trying to taste itself.

—I mean … look at you, man. You look like a short homeless Kerouac.

—Fuck you, man! He looks all sore for a second.

—No, brother. I mean it as a compliment.

—I don't feel great, he says, suddenly taken with his hands: Oh, man … I haven't had a very fantastic diet this past month … mainly Midori and nachos … and the fucken room above the pub in … man … I dunno even what town … somewhere that has sugar cane and the ocean nearby … the fucken room near killed me with this draught and Soph … the chick I lived there with while I tried to write a novel … man, what just happened to the moon?

—What about her?

—Who?

—The chick … Soph.

—Um … did I say that out loud?

—I dunno.

—Fuck.

—What happened, with the chick?

—Man … we knew each other from school. Her, my old friend Gerhard and me … We also hung out with Soph's brother. We dated awhile, me and Soph, and then one afternoon her brother died in a car crash. We went to the funeral and later that night, real bummed out and shit, Soph says *Let's have sex, my brother would have wanted it.*

Yuri smokes two whole cigarettes while he tells me this story and, as he flicks the butt from his second off the bridge, he looks pretty sick with memories.

Recently Yuri took over running the Chalice House poetry gig from Rey. I go to Chalice regularly and Yuri comes to the Valley for the Rose Croix at The Zoo. About twenty poets show up, and we have a captive audience. The Zoo puts on free Spanish wine for us and not a sober soul leaves the building after the final poet has torn out their heart and doused the crowd in arterial bliss. I bought a book of vintage erotic bondage photography, wrote *Rose Croix – Poetry at The Zoo* on a few of the images, photocopied them and hung them on every lamp post and in every bookstore window in Brisbane. One image had a woman getting spanked by another woman, and had a plinth with an open book on it in the background. I modified the page to read *Thou Shalt Not Read Poetry.*

Now that we both run separate poetry readings, Yuri and I start a third poetry reading together, at Bitch Cafe. We envision a reading every night of the week. This way, we have a good reason to get drunk every night, not that we need one. Yuri and I keep the monks who make green chartreuse in alms for the next century. I see Yuri pour it on Weet-Bix one morning, instead of in his coffee. He realises, shrugs and puts some in his flat white too. He makes me laugh. If he gets into an argument while drinking wine, he always ends up smashing his glass to emphasise some point or other.

4

A knock on the door of our apartment at Ravenswood and my sister Jaz stands there, distraught. I haven't seen Jaz in over a year, nor spoken to my parents or my little sister Fliss.

—Bren, she says, grabbing me: I feel like death. I don't know what to do. Her heart breaks right on my doorstep.

I get her inside and Candy hugs her while I make coffee, and we calm her down enough for her to begin the story. Jaz doesn't say anything about us having no couches and she eases herself onto the floor. Most people give us shit about having no couches.

—Mum's fallen seriously ill … probably an undiagnosed injury from when Dad ran her over with a tractor.

—Your dad ran over your mum with a tractor? Candy snorts into her Alessi coffee cup.

—What … you don't know this? asks Jaz, looking at me.

—No! Candy exclaims, also looking at me.

—She fell off a tractor on our grandma's pineapple farm, Jaz explains: She should have died, they said.

—For a while there I thought he'd run her over on purpose! Candy laughs.

—Put her in hospital for a year, I say, also laughing.

—Yeah, sniffs Jaz.

—You know how she … She turns to Candy, who's pulled her knees up to her chest, sitting on the carpet: Mum's always had migraines. Made her a real bitch as we grew up.

—Not to mention the no-holes-barred religious brainwashing she afflicted us with, I snarl.

—I still feel physically ill with guilt … to this day, says Jaz.

—Don't you mean no *holds* barred? says Candy.

—Nope. No holes … no vagina, arse or mouth. Those tramp preachers fucked some kids in the ear, I swear.

—Anyway … I tried saving for a bit to get back to Townsville to see her. I've spent the last year in Melbourne, living with this guy Dad hates, so I didn't call home much. She takes a sip of coffee, adjusts her position on the carpet.

—So, about Mum … Should we worry? I interject there, tapping a cigarette on its box. I go to light it and Jaz says:

—Can you not? She fumbles with her cup.

—Why?

—Pregnant.

—Holy fuck! Crushing my cigarette.

—Does your boyfriend know? asks Candy, sitting upright now.

Jaz starts sobbing all over, chest-heaving sobs from a place deep down where pain has brewed for a decade.

Poor Jaz. Pregnant, and she found out after she realised her relationship had all the chances of Tony Montana living to forty. *Bastard fucked a stripper*, she wails. *A stripper!* She fears Mum will kill her. Mum most likely will kill her, or publicly disown her, which Jaz probably finds worse.

We put Jaz in our bed and, sometime around four in the morning, Candy falls asleep in there too. I sit up until dawn, writing this down, drinking coffee, trying to remember where I put my old tobacco tin of weed when Jaz's knock came so early in the morning. I've decided to take the plunge and call home, to see what I can find out about Mum not feeling well.

And just as I think this, someone knocks at the door again! Loud as hell this time, and I near fall over trying to find the tin of weed to hide before I realise that if I spent five hours searching for it unsuccessfully, no one else will find it. I answer the door to find, standing there, the dude I've seen following me! In a different suit this time, but with the same chambray shirt he wore when I last noticed him. He says:

—Brentley?

Honestly, I near shit myself. I just stand there, with my mouth open too, I bet.

—Do you live here with a young woman named Candy?

—Fuck, I squeak.

Then, over his shoulder, peeking around the red-brick corner of the foyer, out by the postboxes filled with glossy catalogues, crudely photocopied handyman flyers and leaves blown in from the street, I see platinum-blonde hair, in a Princess Diana cut, and the unmistakable *fuck you, pauper* glint of diamond earrings. Candy's mother.

—

She hired a private detective to find us. I've seen him in my peripheries for over a year.

This all started because, somewhere, on a mine site in the deserts of Western Australia, Candy's uncle, her mother's brother, picked up a copy of *The Picture* magazine, leafed to the Home Girls section and saw Candy there, naked, explaining how good her clitoris piercing makes her feel. Her mother freaked, assuming I'd started whoring out her daughter to pay for my heroin habit, and she hired a private detective to track us down, so she could rescue Candy. I don't have a heroin habit, but I have rent. If I stop paying rent, I could die. It happens for me like that. I open a door and my reality comes crashing down. Everything goes south, fast, like a 747 at full capacity, drifting in silence ten ks above the Pacific. Blue sky and the gentle rush of ice vapour over the flexing wings until, suddenly, the fuselage tears apart. Then the deep blue, divers recovering victims still strapped into seats, naked from the freefall, bodies all bloated and the same.

She starts with her evil right away, screaming at Candy about her behaviour. Finally, after inspecting the entire house and all the cupboards, she leaves with the private detective. Candy stands looking at the closed door and says:

—You know, she called me a lesbian, after seeing Jaz in the bed.

Margot has Candy's sister Marie living in our spare room by the afternoon. It takes Marie two days to sleep with Yuri and three days to sleep with me, despite my resolve. I don't trust Marie anymore, not since she told Candy all our secrets.

Then things get worse. When Marie moves in, she moves all the old manuscripts and paintings I had in the spare room. In there I had a letter this poet named Masha sent to me after we pashed one night at a party. I met her at the Hub poetry reading. A new face on the scene, she'd recently returned from studying in Europe. We argued about Joyce. She said:

—No better writer will ever live.

—Don't count on it … but the dude did have the advantage of Idiot Savantism.

—What?

—No one can write like that unless they have a mental condition.

—Do you have any favourite writers?

—Yeah: Baudelaire, Rimbaud, Lautréamont, Byron, Twain, Genet, Miller, Burroughs, Kerouac, Céline, Salinger.

—Pfft. Joyce shits all over them.

—Like fuck! I said, and so on until later at a party I pashed her under the stairs, right after this other female poet named Vesna announced to the party exactly how much of a misogynist she finds me, for putting my arm around her during a conversation.

The letter had nothing incriminating about it, at first. Masha wrote about literature and poetry and stuff like that, but then, at the end, in this Joyce–Plathean metaphorical kind of way, she talks about how wet she got when we kissed that night. The letter sends Candy over the edge.

Nightsweats in a dream. A thousand tortured angels chased me down in a fugue of sleep. A masquerade party in Hades. Agony dressed as Love. I fucked her under the drooping porticoes of a broken temple on the outskirts of grief. An angel in the hall said to me: *If you look deep into my words, you can speak with me across time and space and we can laugh like old friends in a warm cafe on a cold day.* The ancients lent me tragedy to hold as my own dying bouquet. Metaphysics and her breasts forming in the clouds. Day and night entwined like a killer's laughter. Then who comes knocking at my door but Fortitude, wounded by her charge. I soap her wounds but she dies quietly in my bath. I awake in a clairvoyant dawn burdened with ancestry. The sempiternal Odysseus, an immortal and divine vagabond who dances in this cabal, but not to your music. Desire's psalmodic eyes, her holy-oil covenant aching in a jaundiced sky. She toasts me with a glass of Melancholy's blood. We drink like Pasiphaë the bull's deathly seed. The serpents which lick my wounds turn blind like worms in the fallen clay of our ancestors. I have come to know Waiting and her many charms, the madpale garden of her skin. Only the blind can observe this burning, the epilepsy of the soul against creation's cage. I lose myself in the ruins. The chartreuse moon, my green priest in a bottle, elucidates on his night-subject of loneliness.

Then comes the anticipated change. Candy's mother says to us at dinner:

—You'll come with us to Perth. We'll rent you an apartment if you look after our dogs while we do our month-on shifts at the mine.

Candy wants to go. I ask Candy if she wants me to come. She doesn't pause when she says *Of course*. If she'd paused, I would have packed a bag and left her that night.

—What about my university studies? Trying to find a way to excuse myself from going to Perth with Candy's family.

—You can fly over to your residentials. You only have three a year, right?

—Yeah.

I dared walk with a wayward wolf, wandered into her company lair.

5

Fliss's new husband has an air of beautiful doom about him. Obsessed with Jim Morrison. So much so, I call him Jim. He towers above me, skin pale as a gecko's belly, masses of waist-length red curly hair, in keeping with his Scottish ancestry. You can imagine him in a kilt, blowing some crazy bagpipe on the shores of a loch. We take acid together in Townsville tonight. New Year's Eve 1996, two days before Candy and I board the train to Perth. The trips have a cartoon on them, Fat Freddy's Cat from the *Furry Freak Brothers* comic. I spit hallucinatory fur balls. Candy has a bad trip, says *I hate myself* over and over. Jim grins through the whole thing and sips wine from a pewter mug in the shape of a dragon's foot. The LSD turns out the strongest I've had by far. Things start getting strange.

We sit watching *Rage* on television. The film clip for 'Paint It Black' by The Stones plays and I swear Mick changes into a lizard. I turn to look at Jim, and it must've taken me about an hour because everything has morphed into some sort of viscous liquid marble. I open my mouth to say *Jim, holy fuck, Mick turned into a dragon*, but Jim says:

—I hear you write poetry. Spits out a hair ball: I write poetry too. He turns to me, flickering television on his impossibly pale skin.

—Really? I say, a three-sixty-degree band of light emanating from everything at about waist level.

—Yeah ... listen: *If the shoes I really want to wear hurt my feet ... should I walk at all?*

—Beautiful! Marvellous!

We each watch our own private lightshow for a while.

—I envy you, he says then, out of nowhere.

—Really! Why the fuck would you envy me?

—You seem … so, *alive* … and free.

—My freedom comes at a price, man.

—I'd pay it. How much?

—Love … forever.

He laughs.

—Seriously, I say, trying to figure out why I can't light my cigarette: Think about this, right: no one alive gives a flying fuck about you.

—Thanks! He looks hurt.

—No … I mean you, me, any person.

—Really? Do you believe that? Don't you love Candy? He spreads his hands a bit and his fingers split into rainbows with little birds pissing on them. I shake my head some, which doesn't help at all.

—I almost love her, but I broke it … on purpose. Anyway, people hold themselves back because of love, or some other incarnation of dread and hopelessness that comes in the lonely hours. People think other people care what they do … they don't. Everyone plays the game for themselves. Most of the time no one notices if I get up and leave the room. You can spend your life living right on the edge of the blade while everyone bashes their brains out against the blunt of the handle trying to impress other people. In that realisation lies a tremendous amount of personal freedom.

—I wanted to live on the edge … but I went and got fucken married, before I turned twenty, man. He sighs, shrinks three feet and then rotates somehow.

—Brother, I have a motto. I made it up one night stranded on a highway somewhere west of Neverland, with my friend Josef.

—Yeah? Cough it up then.

—Huh? Thinking he meant one of the phantom chunks of Fat Freddy's Cat in my mouth.

—The motto, man.

—*If you want to live on the edge, learn to balance first.*

At this point I realise I've spent the entire time trying to light my lighter with my cigarette.

—I like that, he says, the boy with far-away eyes.

—

Five days on the train across to Perth rattles something loose in my brain: seven thousand kilometres of clack-clack clack-clack. To drown it out I have all three Mazzy Star albums. I've used half a pack of twenty double-As in my Sony Discman already. Playing 'Wasted' on repeat. Candy and I sit in cattle-class, right down the east coast of Australia. Townsville to Brisbane on *The Sunlander*, a landscape I long to escape. We change trains at Roma Street in Brisbane and board the XPT down to Sydney. Familiar territory. At Central Station in Sydney we board the *Indian Pacific* to Adelaide. West, across inland New South Wales through the Blue Mountains to Broken Hill, to the other side of the range, where the real outback starts, where the history of boom and bust imbues the dust. All alien territory to me. Slightly south-west to Adelaide then the great southern deserts, the Nullarbor Plain, thundering through mallee scrub. Here the ghost gums and eucalypts have an eerie symmetry, like battalions crowded along the tracks.

The train stops, for reasons unknown, at Maralinga, where, in the late fifties and early sixties, the British government dropped nuclear bombs on the Dreamtime. Everyone crowds off to take photographs of themselves posing in front of a huge sign announcing the brutal past. We stop then in Kalgoorlie-Boulder, the end of the Great Eastern Highway and home of the Super Pit, a huge mine that operates around the clock. Then onward, off the edge to Perth, a city built on sand.

6

Perth, not knowing what to expect. This apartment that Candy's mother and stepfather rent for us, on the proviso we care for their dogs six months of the year … nothing more than a converted carport under an actual house on Scarborough Beach. Beneath some rich-looking arsehole who drives a collectible BMW. We live opposite the dog beach. We can't run Candy's parents' dogs out there, though. The wind from the Indian Ocean blasts the sand like a machine. You could buff a car down there. I reckon the pair of retarded guinea pigs they call dogs would get blown clear to the desert.

Invited to Uncle Mike's for dinner. An apartment on the beach. Next to the pampered fluff of Candy's mother, Uncle Mike looks like a bikie. I know he already hates me. He thinks I pimped out his niece to the Home Girls pages of *The Picture* magazine. I sit down beside him at the dinner table and he strokes his Chopper Read moustache, aggressively cracks me a Jack Daniel's and cola premix. Candy looks nervous. I sip the Jack. He rumbles:

—Tell us about yaself, mate. Takes a mighty slug of his premix, looking at Candy's mother.

—Sure. I write, and now I study philosophy too.

—Poetry, I've heard. He drains the can, crumples it in one hand.

—Yeah.

—You look like a faggot.

—Uncle Mike! Candy yells across the table.

Her mother titters. Brian looks concerned.

—Sorry, mate … just joshing ya! And he slaps me on the back, hard.

I finish my can and he cracks me another. I say, into the silence and the stares:

—You work the mines, yeah?

—Yeah … drive big rigs.

—Cool. Getting real interested in the can of Jack Daniel's.

—Why cool?

—You know, a valid profession.

—Look out! Big words. Why don't you *elaborate*, sport? He laughs his arse off at his own funny cunt-ness.

—Someone has to do it, drive the trucks. I smash half the can in one gulp, try not to burp.

—You havin a go at me, mate? Better drivin trucks, I say, than a useless poofter profession like yours!

—Don't call me gay, man! Instantly regretting saying that. The pain bottled up from where he near broke my shoulder blade came out as a hiss in my voice, like a cornered kitten standing up to a werewolf.

—Fuck you, you … cunt! He leaps to his feet, chair screeching on the faux wood floor: I oughta belt ya one for what ya did to Candy!

—You fucken … degenerate! screams Candy's mum, spilling wine everywhere, eyes boring into me.

I look to Brian. I don't know why. He avoids my gaze, dabbing at his mouth with a napkin. Candy bursts into tears, stands, screams at her mother:

—Great! Now you hate him again! And she storms off to the balcony, slams the sliding glass door.

—Get the fuck outta my house, you faggot, says Uncle Mike with real menace on the edges.

I raise my hands, stand, drain my third can, try to catch Candy's attention on the balcony but she has her back to the room, looking like Virginia Woolf out over the Indian Ocean. I stumble out of there, drunker than I realise, and find a bar down on the beach.

In a window seat, smoking and drinking a chartreuse. Perth feels like another country. The wind rips across the Indian tonight.

Hundreds of rabbits on the beach, where the grass meets the sand and where Love first punched me.

—

Candy enrols at the University of Western Australia, to study palaeoanthropology and forensic archaeology. She went from chef, to fashion designer, to nude model, to Indiana fucken Jones in five years. Our relationship strains to breaking. I busy myself smoking marijuana grown by a botany student, sitting on the esplanade, exhaling into the Fremantle Doctor.

—

On my way to university. Away from Perth and five months of nights punctuated with shouts and breaking crockery. The middle of winter in Armidale. Josef offered me a couch. He lives with another black metal band now.

I get off the bus from Sydney and Josef fails to show. I walk around in the freezing Armidale night looking for a phone box and finally get his address. When I arrive, a real sombre mood has the place in a grip. The day before, an electrician, come to fix their roof after a storm, died right in front of them – fell into their car park, fried.

I pick up a sexy Greek woman named Miki in the student refectory on campus. She says she has to sleep in a tent for the whole residential. Back at Josef's place after drinking whisky. Just as she finishes giving me head, Josef walks in and loses his shit. Screams at me about disrespecting him and his friends, that I shouldn't treat Candy like that. *I consider Candy one of my closest friends!* he snaps at us as we leave. Miki and I get a room above a pub. I watch her piss in the sink. I cry as she blows me again.

—

A nightmare. Awake in a sweat with the feeling someone has died, or something has ended. Down the hall in this flophouse hotel, Despair's perfume lingering in every corner. I walk in the dawn and, after smashing off ice from the telephone receiver, call Candy. No answer. It rings out five times. I walk until I find an open cafe, drink a coffee, call again. She picks up:

—Hey, I stammer, a feeling of dread rising up my oesophagus.

—Oh … hi.

—Why didn't you answer earlier?

—Huh?

—I called, five times, half an hour ago.

—Oh … I guess I fell asleep upstairs.

—What?

—I went to a party upstairs last night.

I vomit on the phone box.

—You okay? she asks, meekly.

—Yeah.

A motorbike roars by on the road behind me.

—I slept with James, if you want to know.

—Who? And I don't wanna know.

—James who lives upstairs … He has some moves!

—I thought we agreed on the train over to give monogamy a go … try and save our relationship!

—But I wanted sex.

—Did you use a condom?

—Yeah. He went to put it in and I remembered you said to use one.

—You only used one because I asked you to?

—Why else would I?

—Um … disease?

—You get so paranoid.

—You got that serious thrush that time!

—Yeah … from anal, probably.

—Did you do anal with this guy?

—Private … none of your business.

—That prick owns the collectible BMW, right? Didn't I see him in an army uniform?

—Reserves. So?

—Says a lot … You had sex with a trained killer.

Silence.

—I don't think I should come back, I say with an actual heavy heart.

—Yeah.

—Yeah … what?

—Yeah … maybe you shouldn't … Unless you tell me the truth. Perhaps we can save us then. But I sincerely fucken doubt it.

—The truth about what? I cough there, trying to smoke my cigarette like Reuben, without touching it once, because I have both freezing hands in my pockets and the receiver cradled between my achingly cold neck and seized-up shoulder.

—About my sisters. Do you have anything to tell me?

—No. Trying to spit the butt out but finding it frozen to my lip.

—Why keep lying? I just told you I fucked someone last night and you still won't fess up! She sounds angry and over it.

—What do you want me to say?

—A normal male would try and hurt me right there … but you keep up the lie, you … you cheating piece of shit.

I imagine myself there as a pile of steaming shit, getting stepped in, waiting for her to slam down the phone. She doesn't.

—You know which chicks I fucked … you helped me. I haven't gone out on my own!

I could've thought of something better to say, but it fell out of my mouth. I feel pathetic saying that. It sounded pathetic, a lie. She knows – I know it. Pretty soon I'll freeze to death in this phone box. The sky's gone green. It looks like it might snow. I've never seen snow.

—Does the sky go green before it snows? I say.

—You fucked that chick Louisa … and Chrissy!

—I didn't fuck Chrissy. I only went down on her!

—So you did fuck Louisa.

—You asked one of my best friends for sex!

—What … *who?*

—Yuri.

—He told you!

—Yeah.

—He rejected me.

—Bruise your ego, did it? I say, not hiding my sarcasm.

—No more bruised than yours right now.

—Seriously, sometimes your inner moll comes crawling out, hey.

—Fuck you, she says, tired and resigned.

The early-morning traffic drifting in.

—We spent so many years together, running from our families, I say above the din.

—Yeah, you know … She sighs again, the way you sigh when you feel hesitant about sharing something: I realised recently that for seven years we never spent more than a couple of nights apart … we rusted together.

An old man shuffles up to the phone box and stands behind me, breathing heavily. I spark another cigarette. Striking the lighter hurts my frozen fingers.

—So you wanna break up then … get it over with?

—I don't know. She takes a deep breath and sighs: Sometimes I think we broke up ages ago and we stay together out of habit. Will you ever learn to reel in your sex addiction? She sighs again, sounds tired.

Banging on the phone box. The war veteran attempts to bounce on the spot but his old-man hips have frozen up.

—You still there? She sounds kind of sad now.

—Yeah. Some old dude banged on the phone box. I don't have a sex addiction. Does that even exist?

—Yes you do. You have a compulsion around attractive women … some of them not even attractive, like Louisa. You fuck any woman who aims her vagina at you.

—No I don't … though every woman does have something beautiful to offer the world.

—Why do you cheat on me so much? You make me feel ugly and inadequate.

—I don't want to wake up one day all beat and grey and regret what I didn't do, all the art and drugs and poetry and beautiful women naked in the morning light. I'll never turn down an adventure, a title, or a free lunch.

She doesn't reply. I can see her on my private screen, clear as a Swarovski swan, thousands of miles away on the west coast, on Scarborough Beach in Perth, in our shittily converted double garage, that rich soldier naked next to her in our bed. She raises one of her sculpted eyebrows and does this pout which means she wishes I'd disappear.

—Ya know, she says: nothing can save us now.

—Yeah, I saw what you said.

I sound far away to myself, my words down the line like zeros lost in static.

—Huh?

—Nothing.

Silence.

Then she says, angry now:

—I've met some damaged people in my time, hey … but you—

I run out of coins there. As I walk away, a VW Beetle rolls past, Iggy Pop's 'Candy' blaring crazy lyrics on the wind, like her last angry sigh.

7

Not a single person on earth gives a damn about me. Returning from the University of New England I get off the bus at Central Station in Sydney. I call Candy a dozen times and the phone rings out in our converted garage. Candy doesn't want me home. I throw my return plane ticket to Perth in a bin outside the terminus and sit in Belmore Park. The storm in my soul rages and the revolution in my heart becomes a pogrom against Love. Love writes Despair in cursive on the cafe window as she passes. You have to feel it, to feel it. I sit here for about ten hours, without thinking anything at all. A poet without hope, running from Love. Through the lies of our dreams we find ourselves alive with gorgeous tears. How like the little monsters to come now, regret interloping on my resolve. I must face the Beast alone and never surrender to her charms.

As Sydney crashes and rumbles around me, I feel totally and utterly alone in the universe. I can't feel a single person out there who has a spare thought for me. The sun vanishes beyond some menacing-looking clouds, rumbling in from the ocean. People rushing past but no one there, only bodies, minds elsewhere, rehearsing interviews, troubling over chores and bitching inside. I don't care anymore. All along and probably since the dawn of time no humans have given a shit about each other, only one-sided egotistical attachments, like love, and family. A hundred years ago an entirely different set of people lived out their lives right here and no one alive now gives a damn they've all gone.

Thunderclap and cloudburst. Under a shop awning now as the heavens open up and rain squalls across Railway Square. Pigeons unbind their tongues.

We need the idea of God to fill the void, to hide the truth: that we can never connect with one another. Souls sealed in bone and touching with no contact. I feel zero pity for fools who pray for rapture when the bible warns of slaughter.

Back in Townsville. My darkest days in one of Australia's sunniest cities.

A month sitting here in the dark by myself, caretaking a building full of everything but residents. I sit around with the curtains drawn and only venture out to buy tobacco. I think the darkest depression ever has descended on me. That lingering perfume of Despair in every corner of every hallway, trapped between the fire doors on the escape staircase. I have bad dreams every night. Bellies with mandibles. Scabs on walls. Petal couches and suede flowers. Nightmares of outback highways curling like burned cassette tape. I sweat so much I awake dehydrated. Afraid to sleep. I can't stop thinking about Candy, like Joan of Arc leading her own personal sexual revolution.

The phone ringing. The first time in four months. Candy on the line. She in Perth, me in North Ward, not three blocks from Redpath Street, where it all began.

—Hi! Pleased to hear from her, despite myself.

—Hey. Very flat.

—I miss you. Mentally punching myself in the face.

—Do you? Incredulous, sarcastic.

Silence. A humming on the line.

—Why did you call? I say, cold now too.

—Where do I send your stuff? You have a bunch of shit here you left behind. Icy crackles in her voice.

—You mean everything I own in the world. You told me not to come back. I only had my duffel for the residential. I've worn the same clothes for months now.

—Gross.

—Thanks.

—Where do I send it? Your books will cost a fortune.

I give her the address on Landsborough Street in North Ward and she says:

—I know that building. I used to walk Demeter by there. You live at a boarding house for retards?

—Not retards … mentally disabled. They all moved out to live in the community, a new initiative by the foundation.

Candy yawns:

—Anyways, send me money for the removalist.

—Okay. So, you all good? I sniff.

—Like you care. She sounds far off, distracted.

—I asked, didn't I? Now I sound resigned.

—I had the best sex I've ever had last night. This French guy I met at a party after the Blur concert. She sounds truly happy about it.

That did it for me, just there. Since limping back, licking my wounds, to my parents four months ago, after nearly dying of cold on the streets of Sydney for three weeks, hitching north to Brisbane, sleeping in parks and on friends' couches, drinking too much with a belly dancer whose boyfriend showed up to one of our drinking sessions and threatened to gut me. Then seeing Gerhard, Yuri's old friend, smiling in the mall with a gorgeous woman, in love and getting married. Another bus trip north, the same old route, up the coast, through numerous towns you can never imagine living in and then further and further up the coast into the dry tropics, where the tourists don't get off. Then the *Warning Estuarine Crocodiles Roam These Waters* road signs and the *Warning Irukandji and Box Jellyfish Infest These Waters* signs picketed along the beachfront, the mosquitoes getting thicker on the bus windscreen as the mangrove swamps start.

Followed by my parents with the *I told you sos* choked back with their sarcasm because they can see the pain in my eyes and hear wounds on my sighs as I drag myself around their house, looking for somewhere warm, hoping the block of ice in my chest will thaw and let me breathe. And then sitting out in the middle of nowhere alone on my parents' farm for weeks on end while they travel abroad, drinking all day and crying with each sip. Feeling totally, fucken, lost.

Now, after sitting in the dark for so long, trying to remember myself, nose full of the stink of despair, mind crowded with visions of myself strung up in a cupboard in this abandoned boarding house … fuck her. I put the receiver in the cradle. I get up, shower, put on my jeans, my boots, a decent shirt, and walk right into the city, into the Exchange Bar, order a pot, and throw it back before I've even exhaled from slamming down the phone.

I've barely left the building, only a couple of times when Fliss's husband, Jim, came by and we went driving around the suburbs, trying to score weed. He drives too fast. Tool's *Ænima* album on the stereo at a minimum of eighty in the dark. I have flashbacks, Harley and the Porsche, crumpled like the poker cards an outraged cowboy throws in the face of a cheater. Not that I care if an enraged cowboy empties his Smith & Wesson into my chest. I feel dead already. I simply stare ahead while Jim barrels down the streets in his marital chariot, my little sister at home, cursing me for taking her pale angel out into the storm.

Yuri comes to Townsville to visit, just as I fall headlong into debauchery of Sadean proportions. I spend all my wages on weed, chartreuse and cigarettes, in that order. I can't afford to eat. You can only drink a quarter bottle of chartreuse before your frontal lobe starts to misfire and you end up biting your tongue and poking yourself in the eye all the time. I drank half a bottle one night and woke up naked on the beach. I have no idea if I walked the four blocks nude or what happened to my clothes. They say alcoholism starts when you drink alone. I started drinking alone at nine years of age, swigging Charlie's rum in our fortress on the hill behind the Greenvale medical centre while I waited for The Wreckers to come for a midnight jaunt, if they ever came at all.

I haven't seen Yuri in a year. He has a new confidence in his step as he bounds off the bus in Townsville. I hail a cab out the front, where years ago I left Reuben after our spectacular Cairns adventure and he went off and tried to permanently stop his pain. I think of finding him near death in the cupboard. That whole scene pushed Gigolo over into whatever abyss he'd stood on the edge of for so long. Yuri runs an art gallery in Brisbane now with his artist friend Gerhard and another painter I've not met named Niko. He tells me this in the cab on the way back to the complex I caretake.

—You? Yuri says, winding down the window. The cab driver smells like a dead whale on a beach.

—I landed a job caretaking an abandoned building. It has forty rooms.

—Abandoned? Why?

—It housed intellectually disabled people … run by the Endeavour Foundation. They all moved out, something to do with not wanting them to feel institutionalised. Now street kids and park people try and break in all the time.

—Park people?

—Abos, interjects the cab driver.

—What do you do there all day? asks Yuri, leaning forward.

—Writing, drinking, smoking and fucking … in no particular order.

—Ha! he says from the back seat.

I turn around and give him a grin. The cab driver shoots me a look.

—I've got a girl … serious … marriage material, Yuri says.

—Yeah? Megan?

—No, we split up after she found out I slept with Marie.

—How'd she find out?

—Read my journal.

—Bitch.

The cabbie chuckles.

—Hey, you remember Gerhard?

—Yeah!

—Gerhard asked this chick he only just met to marry him … a super hot babe, so I don't blame him.

—Yeah. Natalie?

—Natalia. How'd you know?

—I ran into him in the Queen Street Mall in Brisbane, right after I came out of that pub under the mall beneath the Wintergarden. I got smashed down there with this chick I met on the bus back from Sydney. I get on the bus in Sydney and she has the seat next to me. Before I even sat down she said *I will never cheat on my fiancé, so don't even try*. I didn't even want to try, until she told me she belly dances for a living. Anyway, yeah, I ran into him and Natalia and he looked happy … too happy. He looked pinned.

The cab stops at traffic lights outside the old Townsville General Hospital. It has a construction fence around it now.

—Look at that. Twenty-six years … full circle back to where I started. Changing the subject.

—You born there? says Yuri, looking up at its art-deco balconies.

—Yup … right after Cyclone Althea. The whole roof got blown off … most of this whole town pretty much decimated.

—Maaate, says the cab driver: Christmas Eve, 1971: the whole sky screamed like a fighter jet in a tunnel. Eighteen-foot waves crashing through the estuaries. I remember the news saying over six hundred thousand tonnes of roofing and signage got dumped in Platypus Channel!

—Platypus Channel? I say.

—Yeah … off the port, says the cabbie.

—Never heard of it! I grew up here and I've never heard it even said?

The cabbie shrugs as we turn onto Redpath Street.

—Candy lived there when I first met her.

I point to number ten, now overgrown, and it looks a lot smaller concealed beneath the trees.

—You heard from her? She still in Perth? Yuri leans a fair way out the window, checking out the old Queenslander as we roll past.

—Nope. Don't care. We split up, over the phone. I never went back. Last I spoke to her, she told me all about a dude she picked up that gave her the best orgasm she's ever had. Candy can go to hell. Right now I've got four chicks on the go.

—Four! His head comes back in the cab.

The cabbie shoots me another look.

—Yeah, man. Mandy, Hayley, Tana and Tiffany. Tiffany I've only just started getting somewhere with. The other three … well, put it this way … a couple of weeks back we had a foursome.

—Bullshit! says the cabbie and we all laugh.

—Don't make me show you the video to prove it, man, I say, as the laughing stops.

—Video? says Yuri.

—Mandy studies film-making at uni. She insisted on filming the whole thing.

—I wanna see the video … Wait, do I? laughs Yuri.

—Mandy has it, says we should take turns having it in our possession. But it starts in the pool, well before any of us even had a clue where it'd lead. Then it cuts to me naked pulling a bucket bong and then cuts to Mandy and Tana full-on going at it in the shower … I filmed that bit. Then it cuts to me reading from *Juliette* by Marquis de Sade and then it cuts to Mandy eating out Tana as I fuck Mandy doggy, which Hayley filmed, then to Hayley and Mandy and me, which Tana filmed, and then we set the camera up on a chair so all four of us could—

—This the address? The cabbie cuts me off there, blowing the scene.

—You live here! Yuri says, eyeballing the three-storey built into the cliff.

—Yep … I get paid to live here.

—Lucky bastard, says the cabbie, shaking his head.

Part Seven
Collapse

Not all those who wander are lost.
JRR Tolkien

1

Brisbane, February 1998. Josef works at a mattress factory. He gets home angry most nights. Last week I thought he'd died. I picked up this chick at an art exhibition and she invited me to see Derrick Carter, a DJ from Chicago, at a swish club down by the Botanic Gardens in the city. Josef said he'd come. I scored an ecstasy tab from this dude in the toilets. Josef begged to share. I didn't mind. Only, after it came on, I realised we'd taken a *tripstacy*, an E with a drop of LSD on it. I'd wondered why it'd turned mushy in the clippie. I lost Josef. He vanished. I went home with the chick and we had sex in her bathtub, but I lost connection with my body. I felt dead. I worried about Josef. I didn't think he'd taken LSD before, and drugs work on him weird. Give him a joint and he'll bounce around, talking and excited. Give him some speed and he'll curl up on the couch and go to sleep.

He came home today, three days later. He walked to Byron Bay, tripping along the freeway. Says he went to visit Miki. I have no idea how he knows where she lives. Last I know that he saw her, he kicked us out of his house in Armidale, right after he walked in on her blowing me in his living room.

Not long after Josef visited Miki, she visits us. Josef gave her our address.

—Hi, I say as I answer the door, hesitant, because the last time I saw her she told me we shouldn't see each other.

—Thought I'd come visit you and Josef … needed to get away from Byron for a bit.

—Josef's gone away for the weekend.

—Oh … Oh well. We can have some fun, can't we?

—Sure, I shrug.

Phoebe, the chick whom I've spent the last month or so having sex with, only wants sex, which under normal circumstances I don't mind at all. Except about a week ago I thought Death had come for me. My little sister Fliss, who feels strangely absent from my life, came to visit. We went out for kebabs and beers and hung around digging the Valley on a Friday night until the dawn, because I wanted to spend as much time with her as possible. Soon as I got home, I started shitting lava, came down with the worst case of food poisoning imaginable. My organs had turned to acid and my stomach came up my oesophagus. The third day found me still so weak that Josef, concerned, had come home from the mattress factory with a brick he'd found, to hurl through the window of the kebab joint. *For trying to kill my mate*, he told me, with not even the spirit of a grin. Phoebe came around on her lunchbreak. *I need a fuck!* she demanded. *I can't even open my eyes … someone poisoned me!* I said, attempting to rise on an elbow from my sweat-soaked bed. *Oh*, she said, and left.

So Miki and I venture out, but I can't get my heart in it. Sitting at the bar, contemplating my drink and chain-smoking while Miki flirts with the bartender and the living dead dance around their handbags. Then, seeing my heart has already left the party, Miki says, *Let's bail … I'll take you home and cheer you up*. But at that exact moment Phoebe comes staggering into the bar, grabs me and sticks her tongue in my mouth.

—Who … the … fuck? Phoebe demands as, embarrassed, I pull away: You fucken … She points into Miki's face but she sways like a buoy on a wave.

—Just a friend from uni, says Miki, calm in the swell.

—I should take you home … to sleep it off, I say to Phoebe, trying to defuse the situation now that the entire bar has stopped staring at us.

—Fuck, yes … cha cha CHA! yells Phoebe, attempting to do some sort of bebop dance mixed with house-music rave shuffling.

Miki and I get her home as fast as we can because she gives lip to everyone we pass: cheeky, bitchy, a mix of both. I take off her platforms and lay her down on my bed and she vomits. Copious amounts too, an entire all-you-can-eat smorgasbord. Seeing she hasn't choked to death but looks in a coma or something, I haul her out of there into the bathroom to put her in the shower, and Miki sees me from the living room, dragging an unconscious chick down the hall, trying to get her dress off as I go.

Miki gets up and leaves, permanently, I can tell. Gorgeous woman, our ride in the same direction didn't last very long. I disembarked in the Land of the Lost. She calls me foolish and shakes her head with a sad smile as the bus pulls away.

Josef moves on again. He never stays anywhere long, kind of lily-pads his way around the country. His mother lives in Australia now; this time he moves in to her garage in Albion. He wants to save to buy a new bass guitar. *I can't afford rent*, he said as he left.

2

I now share a flat with Yuri, on the corner of Harcourt and Brunswick streets in Fortitude Valley. From the front balcony I see a woman standing with her back to a twenty-four-hour laundromat across the street. She hunkers down in her coat, cold in the early-morning light, and sways there awhile. A car crunches over to the kerb. Taillights and exhaust fumes. She doesn't move. The car pulls away. She squats down, knees apart, rocks on her stilettos. Removes one shoe and pulls off a fishnet stocking. Stands again, one leg naked, struggles to get her shoe back on. Another horny shark thunders at the kerb. *Fuck off*, she screams and the car fucks off. She squats back down. Scratches her vulva. Wraps the fishnet stocking around her upper arm, tight, and pulls it with her teeth. She doesn't look for voyeurs, doesn't notice the cab driver watching her at the traffic lights, nor the bleached-looking dude in the laundromat folding his old-man pants. She shoots up, chest heaves, she vomits, loses balance from her squat, falls back against the glass, legs out, spread-eagled. She urinates; it streams across the footpath and over the lip of the gutter. Joins the refuse.

Winter took me by surprise. Came with a mist of freezing wind across the Story Bridge. Like the stranger who haunts me now and again. He stands on Brunswick Street in a shop doorway, all day, every day. He has a beard down near his waist and a look in his eyes like he saw Hitler committing atrocities firsthand. Sando told me one day that this dude has stood there for twenty years, waiting for his wife to come home. I don't know where his wife went, if she came home or if she died, or what. Anyway, this reminds me of Candy and the last time she telephoned me. I haven't heard her voice since.

An ambulance and some cops turn up to take away the dead junkie across the street. Red and blue flickers in cigarette smoke.

—

Small world, miniature cosmos, or just the same old neighbourhood? On the staircase I run into the chick who runs Gilchrist Galleries, the art dealer I used to go and hassle all the time when I lived on Bowen Terrace, before my Perth misadventure. She looks at me in the dark musk of the old hall and says with squinted eyes:

—Do I know you?

—Nope … probably seen me around. I live in number two.

—Jodie. Number three, upstairs. She sticks out her hand.

—Brentley. I shake her hand.

—Oh … I do know you. You still painting? When did you move here? Didn't you go to Perth? I saw you in the *Northern News* a couple of years back. You write poetry, right?

—Um, yeah.

—I've got to run. We'll talk later. The door slams behind her.

—

Adrift on a pointless ocean. The other two survivors have already resigned themselves to the fates: Despair shakes like a little old lady drinking milk on a train; Hopelessness at wrist readies a blade. Yuri comes home tonight late and fumbles with the lock. I get up to let him in. He falls in the door crying, drunk and confused. I try to console him. He won't stop sobbing.

Life hasn't worked out so well for Yuri lately. His art gallery closed, the building scheduled for demolition to make way for some apartment buildings down on the river. His friend the painter Niko had some sort of breakdown after a man landed directly in front of him on the pavement one afternoon, a jumper from thirty storeys above. Then Yuri's girlfriend started acting strange and distant, didn't invite him to move in with her when he found himself homeless. Then, out of nowhere, right after he exited the stage at the Queensland Poetry Festival, not seconds after he finished reading an ode to his muse, she dumped him, right there, side-stage, on the riverbank in West End.

Now, I don't know what horror has visited him. I get him into a chair and make him a hot Milo on the stove and light a cigarette for him and he sobs:

—Natalia, the girl Gerhard wants to marry. She died in a car wreck on the M3 this morning. Asleep on the back seat, man. Didn't stand a chance.

My heart broke a little there, for her beauty and her youth, and because, not three nights earlier, as I left an art exhibition at Soapbox Gallery and drifted down Brunswick Street, I glanced into Ric's Bar as I passed, and I saw her there, leaning up against the bar, alone. She smiled and waved and I didn't go in.

Life works like that, one of the many paradoxes on offer. Soon as you let go, give up desiring something, it comes in abundance. Some sort of cosmic joke, probably. I say this to Eliot. Eliot lives upstairs with the art-dealer chick. He makes light sculptures for a living, installs them in cafes and strip joints. Since I moved in downstairs, we talk in the hallway. He needs an assistant. Pays me fifty bucks for a few hours' work here and there. It pays for some weed. For a long time I haven't had cash for weed. Smoking gets me out of the front room and away from watching the prostitutes and slipping into a Dostoyevskian depression. Eliot has a world-worn beatnik look; he has really lived. He has a street-earned charisma about him, too. Hanging out with him as his unofficial apprentice has me laughing most days – a good thing, probably. He lives hard, like William Burroughs junkie hard. He doesn't do anything by halves. He doesn't even smoke weed like normal people; he uses what he calls a rocket. We sit in my front room watching prostitutes clocking in on the corner.

—Let's smoke a joint.

—Fuck that, he says: Let's get stoned.

—Yeah, I'll roll one up.

—Nah, man. Ya doin it all wrong.

I laugh.

—Ya got a cone piece?

—Yeah. And I go and fetch the cone from a brass pipe Josef left on the picture rail above the kitchen door.

—Gotta Coke bottle, with the lid still on?

—Yeah … and a bucket, right?

—Nope.

He busies himself getting the cone through the lid by melting the plastic with his cigarette lighter and twisting the thread of the cone piece through. I don't think I could do that with my girly poet's fingers. Then, instead of cutting off the bottom of the Coke bottle to have bucket bongs like normal, he punches a hole in the side, down the bottom, with a screwdriver that he fishes out of his Tardis pockets.

You wouldn't believe some of the stuff he keeps in those pockets. On one job I near fell off a ladder I laughed so hard. He looked up at me from the floor, where he'd laid out these brass rails which go up on the brackets I'd screwed into the ceiling, and said:

—You seen my hammer, man?

—Nah, I replied, looking down at him.

He stood, hunted around a bit, kicked some cardboard boxes, then started feeling his pockets, before saying:

—Oh, here we go. And he pulled out a claw hammer.

Another time, he pulled out a forty-centimetre stainless-steel ruler – not a flat one, either, but one of those that have a liquid level built into it. Damn things weigh a kilo.

Now, he sits crumbling up some hydro we scored off some lesbians who live down on James Street.

—To the sink! he says, leaping up.

At the sink Eliot puts his finger over the hole in the side of the bottle and fills it with water. He screws on the cap, with the cone threaded into it loaded with hydro, gets out one of my cigarette lighters, sparks it up and lets go of the hole. The gravity of the escaping water pulls the smoke into the bottle.

—Oh … I've heard of a gravity bong, I say.

—I call it a rocket, man … kinda like main-lining the cone. See, when the little light goes out.

As the coal fades, he makes a *ding* sound, unscrews the cap and inhales, hard and fast. He straightens up, pale, sweating, exhales and instantly fills the sink with vomit, in one barely audible yack.

—Looks extreme! I say, hesitant.

—Naw, man. Happens to me sometimes. Probably won't happen to you. Trying to jam the vomit chunks down the plughole with his magically appearing screwdriver.

—

This happens, when you come through slaughter and witness the symbiosis of ghosts. Comb the hubris of your collapsed universe and you will find a more effective self-definition. When I do battle with my demons and I win, I strut around like a peacock. I met a woman today who shooed away my bravado. I sat across from her and the space between us crackled. We met and I got lost in her right there. Her wit countered mine. I couldn't shock her, no matter how hard I tried. She followed my brilliant one-liners with sassy-talk.

Earlier today I ran into Jodie on the stairs.

—Wanna earn fifty bucks? she said.

—Sure. Doing what?

—Stuffing envelopes for the next exhibition at my gallery.

—Sure. Need anyone else? I said, thinking how desperately Yuri needs fifty bucks.

—No. My assistant, my sunshine, will help us.

And so I met her assistant: young, redheaded, stunning, noble-looking. She shook my hand and said *Sunshine*, and I said, *You call yourself that?* I'd never met anyone named Sunshine before, and the way Jodie had said it I hadn't heard it as a name. She said *I prefer Sunny*, and then I stuffed my whole leg, boot and all, in my mouth and said, *Do you have a real name?* She said *Yeah … Sunshine*, and gave me this cute-incredulous look, like I had *idiot* stamped on my forehead, but in amusing lettering. I felt like my spine had fallen sideways when she told me her age. Like a nineteen-year-old would have any interest in someone seven years older than her. Sunshine: not even a metaphor for her personality and blinding wit, more an outright simile. She says:

—A poet, huh?

—Yeah.

—Jodie told me.

—I have poetic ambitions.

She laughs.

—You find poets funny? I say, mock hurt.

—Not funny … pretentious.

—Ouch! Real hurt.

—I bet Byron rocks your universe.

—Big fan!

—Byron … Ha, what a fucken prat.

—What?

—I read him at uni. Nancy boy, foppish rich-boy blues.

—Holy shit.

—Truth hurt? She laughs again.

What a laugh. Somehow, the timbre in her voice when her green eyes sparkle mid-chuckle, it makes me feel good, like when a bone cracks in your back after bothering you for weeks, or when you come in from the cold with frozen hands and you warm them over the stove as you make coffee, laughing about something with a friend you met on the street. I don't even care that she dissed a hero of mine. She makes me laugh like I have never laughed.

—How do you know Jodie? she asks.

—Oh … ha. Years ago I used to hassle her to look at my paintings. Now I live downstairs from her and Eliot. I actually work for Eliot. How do you know Jodie?

—She sells my mother's paintings. I worked for her once before, and recently, totally by chance, I ran into her celebrating her birthday at The

Beat nightclub, and she told me all about this new gallery space and offered me a job as her assistant.

—You have an interesting name. Never met anyone called Sunshine before.

—Blame my parents, bloody hippies. I grew up in a cult: the Hare Krishnas. You've heard of them, right?

—Yeah, I worked for a dude who got kicked out of the Hares. He used to push speed on people all the time. He'd randomly hand it to you and refuse to take it back. *Cash only*, he'd say … dodgy dude!

—Ha … interesting. Last night I took a truckload of speed. Haven't slept … chopped off my tits. And yeah, Hares do that: give you something for free then demand payment of some description.

—I grew up in a cult too. I know how they operate.

—Really!

—Sunny! cuts in Jodie: Watch out. Poets should come with a warning label, you know!

—I can look after myself. Sunny laughs that laugh again, winking one of those emeralds.

So Jodie brought Sunshine and me together, and we turned yet another corner in both our lives. Don't look and you might find it. I sit across the table from Love now and I don't smell Despair's perfume anywhere.

Later, we sit on the stairs in this rich apartment owned by the gallery partner. Sunshine asks me if I have a girlfriend, and I say *Not really … just this chick I use as a bed-warmer*, trying to shock her again. She replies *Poor starry-eyed poet-ho*, and I think I fall in love with her.

I can't stop thinking about her, seeing her occasionally on the stairs. Then I jump at the opportunity when Eliot offers me work as a general hand on the new gallery construction site. There I can see this angel every day.

I don't mind working, but it interferes with living. You always have in the back of your mind that you have to go someplace and get there on time. Working a menial job gets people looking forward to death, which results in the whole vicious cycle I've spent my life railing against. Commitments kill – I've come to this conclusion.

Then of course you have the problem of bosses. I hate people who think of themselves as a boss. All bosses have a genetic predisposition to sadism. No one can put me in a box, and that pisses bosses off. They hire me for personal amusement, to try to break me, make me jump through rings like a lion at a fucken pony show. It'll never happen.

You have to fight to stay conscious in this crazy world. I lose myself and fall into a trance all the time. Rushing to work, troubling over the bills, crowded out by the music spilling from cafes and fashion stores. I catch myself, headlong on the path, and I slow, stop on purpose and get a coffee. Forget about excuses for the boss. Write a poem and smoke a few cigarettes, watch the people racing to their doom.

Once, right after I got a job, the boss asked me to tell everyone about myself. I said:

—Six feet tall, brown eyes – not poo brown, more mud brown – crap hair. I used to have some fucken out-there haircuts but now I keep it short … probably all the dyes and bleach and shit killed it. Skinny but not bony, more sinewy. I've got pretty bad teeth from living in gutters and garrets and only eating crap. I can't even tell you how many times I've come up five cents short when I'd kill to eat …

—Ah … mate, I meant tell us about your character! said the boss.

—Oh … okay. Self-indulgent, slightly dodgy, but loyal if I like you. I dig hats. I smoke too much and drink more than Bukowski. Easily distracted … I go off on tangents all the time. Ya know, they didn't have diagnoses for ADD and autism and all that when I grew up. I had a girlfriend who said she thinks I suffer from a mild form of autism, or something … I mean, I do have repetitive behaviour patterns. I can't sleep if I don't write, and if I write I don't sleep. I always get mighty distracted by beautiful women and other interesting spectacles. My parents taught me manners and put the fear of God in me, but I rebelled against all that and now, well, Mr Boss, I'd help myself to your wife, your wallet and your fridge without feeling at all terrible about it.

Thankfully I don't have to worry about Eliot firing me if I sleep through the alarm. Eliot knows I don't even own a clock. Most mornings I rise early anyway, to try to make myself look like I don't sleep on a discarded mattress on the floor of an apartment with only books as furniture. By the time Eliot trundles down the stairs and hammers on my door, I don't answer because I've made it outside to the footpath already. Then I get to give him shit about running late, claiming I've stood around waiting for at least half an hour. The truth of it, though: I just want some Sunshine.

3

Out of nowhere came an invitation to the 1998 National Young Writers' Festival in Newcastle, for me, Yuri and six other Brisbane poets. Both of us feel pretty elated. I have a bit of trepidation about travelling with Yuri again, though. Last festival we went to, after we swore to stick together to pool our cash, he abandoned me as soon as we arrived in Sydney, for the first offer of a couch that came his way. Niko lived down there then, and Niko said I couldn't stay because his girlfriend hated me. I ended up in a shitty backpackers' hostel, one where you sleep in a room with a dozen other stinking travellers, and the very first morning there I got caught smoking weed in the showers and got kicked to the kerb. Broke and alone, I had to cut out on my gig and go home early on the bus.

Thing that bums us both out, though: while the invitation to this festival includes accommodation, it doesn't include transport or alcohol. We mope around for a couple of weeks, trying to figure out ways to get some cash together which don't include skipping our three weekly meals or cutting back to one pack of cigarettes a day. We put off accepting the invitations to the very last moment.

Just as we lose all hope, Sando knocks at apartment two, 54 Harcourt Street. Sando has skills with computers, and lots of people have them now. He has a job working for a charity organisation fixing their PCs, or something like that, and as part of the job he gets a car. A good road car too: a Falcon. He says, even though he'll get fired if they find out, he will drive all of us down to Newcastle for the festival.

We drag him out right there. We hug him in the street, we light his cigarettes and pay for his drinks, and when he gets too drunk to walk, we leave him there, on the couch at Ric's Bar, to sleep it off. We figure he'll understand. No poet's charity extends to other poets who can't handle their piss. We agree on this, Yuri and I, staggering down Brunswick Street as the morning sun beats the crap out of the drunks sleeping it off on benches. Roaming the mercury-gas-lit streets, hungry for it, willing to crawl through a sewer for a fix, but I don't know of what.

—

Sando, strange waif of a man, looks a bit like Michael Hutchence, if Michael Hutchence really did wear clothes from a thrift shop. Sando has big sad eyes and a mouth way too sensual for a boy. Lots of chicks befriend him because he has an air of post-traumatic stress in his countenance, with a dash of vulnerability. He reminds Yuri and me of the poet Shelley. Not quite Byronic and dangerous enough to hang with us because we fear breaking him, though still a genius who deserves respect.

But he surprises us now. He screeches to a halt in the no-parking zone at the front of our building and keeps his hand on the horn until we emerge, get our bags in the back and enter the car, and he opens it up on Brunswick Street. Points his nose to the road and tears across the Story Bridge onto the freeway south like he took lessons from Neal Cassady himself.

Four of us in the back: Yuri, Masha, Rey and me. Yuri on the floor, legs all over him. Sando driving; Vesna, his girlfriend, riding shotgun. I haven't managed to smoke enough weed with my coffee this morning to straighten out from the LSD I shouldn't have taken right before a road trip. Last time I did that, I spent three days on the highway jumping at shadows like velvet lizards. I curl up as best I can among the excited banter. They make jokes about Sando crashing on the freeway and killing the best of Queensland's Generation X poets.

I dream most of the road trip to Newcastle. Trying my best not to think about the slight indiscretion Masha and I had a few months previous because damn she does look sexy there smiling in the midday rays coming in with the overpasses' strobe on us all contorted in the back. Honestly, I don't know whether I only find her sexy because she has red hair like the chick I've fallen in love with. And damn! Did I just say I've fallen in love? Fuck love. Bitch has only ever pissed in my eye from afar. I hunch deeper into my envious pockets when I pass laughing couples kissing on park benches. It begins with lost hours in each other's eyes and ends up with arguments about dirty dishes and bills. Young love turns into old devotion. Which poet wrote that? Surely some poet has written that down.

Look at Masha and Rey now. It looks like love. Rey said he'd fallen in love with Masha the night we all first met her, at the Hub poetry reading. I kissed her first, under the stairs right after Vesna called me a misogynist arsehole. That night as I left, I found Rey on the front lawn, striding up and down, slugging from a bottle, mumbling to himself. *You all right, man?* I said, and he looked at me, crying. *I've fallen in love with Masha.* I didn't believe Rey that night. Love at first sight: what bullshit, right? Then, of course, for the first time in, wow, I don't know how long, I think of Candy.

—Damn! I say out loud, and the whole car, which has fallen into silence, out of fear for their lives as Sando tries to put the accelerator through the chassis, says *what?* in unison. I dumbly reply, like a complete romantic frilly hanky of a human:

—I've gone and fucken fallen in love. All the pain of my past doomed relationship slipped away when I met this woman and I only just realised it!

—See! says Rey, to no one and everyone: I told you all! Brentley, as bad as everyone says, actually has a post-romantic soul. Beautiful reckless boy, he says and uncorks a bottle of wine, pours it in a tin picnic cup and toasts me across the car.

—Cute, says Vesna, turning around from the front passenger seat: You made the woman-hater blush.

—I don't hate women!

—Like fuck you don't, she snaps.

Vesna has that way about her. I don't know her story, but I bet she has reasons for her extremism. Someone once said her family had to flee atrocities in Serbia, so, you know, I don't blame her.

—Feminazi, I mumble.

—See, she laughs back, looking triumphant.

—Seriously, though. Why do you think I hate women?

—Really? You want to know my opinion? Wow. He wants to know a woman's opinion, everybody!

Laughing.

—The way you treat women like … like fuck-toys! She had a hard time saying that, I know, because the last time we argued, one afternoon at Sando's house, we all sat around talking about poetry and I said she should say *vagina* or *cunt* or *pussy* in her poems instead of referring to her genitalia as her *woman-hood*. Vesna did her nut at me, saying I have no right recommending she use oppressive patriarchal language, and I, with serious intent of pure comic irony, said *No need to get hysterical*, and she all but smashed me in the face with her fists, her hatred of me came out so strong.

—What do you mean how I treat women? What did I do?

—The way you treated Masha, for instance.

Both Masha and I squirm right there, because of our fear that Vesna has constructed a giant road sign to point at the elephant in the room: our recent indiscretion. I see Rey's ears burn and he turns to look out the window, very interested in the pine plantation outside. When I first arrived back in Brisbane, I went out drinking with the poets. Masha and Rey had lived together for a while by then and planned to get married. Honestly, I hadn't even thought about the letter Masha wrote me, the one Candy read, which effectively ended us. That night, back at the old haunt at Ric's Bar in the Valley, we all drank too much, and Masha and I got talking about that letter.

Rey and Masha had an argument, something that if you ask me had brewed there for some time. Pre-wedding jitters, I reckon. Rey stormed off; Masha could hardly walk. I took her home to Harcourt Street. We didn't fuck, despite what everyone might assume. We got down to our underwear. We cuddled under the sheets, drunk as Hemingway. I fingered her awhile. I remember not much else, but her waking, looking embarrassed, horrified, mortified even, at what Rey would have woken up feeling like without her there, alone in the late-morning light. She rushed off. We never spoke of it.

Thankfully, though, Vesna brings up the night I supposedly tried to hit on her but ended up making out with Masha and she called me a misogynist. Yuri pipes in at this point, saying that, on the morning after that party, he walked in on me getting a blowjob from my girlfriend's sister, which doesn't help the scene with Vesna at all but outrages everyone else enough to draw attention away from the fact that Vesna hates me and always will.

—What about what you said to Dorothy Porter? Vesna cuts in again.

—What? says Sando.

—At the regional poetry festival in '95, Brentley told Dorothy Porter to go fuck herself!

—It had nothing to do with gender! I scoff.

—Tell me about that! said Sando, looking for the first time away from the road, long enough to glance at me in the rear-view mirror.

—Okay. A bunch of us had readings lined up in the New Voices section, and right before our part Porter gets up on stage and talks about us. You know, saying how we should have the support of the older generation of poets, signifying our importance, yadda yadda.

—Yes, says Sando, somehow impatient.

Look at him there, crouched over, one with the steering wheel now. His corduroy jacket with the leather elbow patches conceals the tension in his fishbone-thin shoulders. I like Sando, but we never gravitated towards each other, instead circling each other like opposing magnets. I spent a month in his living room, awake all day and night. I broke his keyboard trying to write my novel, but he never said much, about anything. He looks like someone built him out of Meccano, thin and flexible as a sheet of tin punched full of holes. He reminds me of an anorexic Atlas, holding up a planet-sized burden in his head, but he has the surprising strength of Meccano, too. He holds the world there, on his shoulder, gazing down into the universe below. No one else says anything, so I continue:

—Then … at the break, right before our readings, I see Porter getting on her motorbike in the car park. I wander over and I say *Hey, you not sticking around for the important new generation of voices you just spoke about?* She says – no paraphrasing here – *Fuck no, I need to get to the pub.* So I said *Why don't you go fuck yourself, then.*

Much laughing, but the scene ends with Vesna snapping:

—Some of your attitudes belong back with the dinos, and then she hisses *vagina dentata* at me, which I know – because, believe it or not, I do read quite widely – implies that I have a fear of the vagina, which, of course, I don't. I'd go swimming in a tank of them, no worries at all. Instead of saying that, though, I shout, probably because of the LSD:

—Arggh, a Vagosaurus … help me! with mock terror in my voice, but I must have yelled it too loud because no one laughs much after that.

Then we arrive in Newcastle, to perform at the National Young Writers' Festival. Eight of us – Masha and Rey, Sando and Vesna, Yuri and I, and another poet, Bodhi, and his girlfriend, Mary, who travelled separate to us – all crammed into a cold, damp, concrete broom closet full of creaking lumpy bunk beds. Bodhi towers over everyone. He has a giant beard and waist-length dreads and he wears oversized clothes. His poems have a nice mix of beauty and depravity. A lot of them portray his sexy girlfriend, Mary. I'd never make a pass at her; Bodhi looks like he'd demolish any bastard who tried. Anyway, if you ask me, Mary and Bodhi look like they have long-term written all over them. If I did get suicidal and make a pass at Mary, she'd not even notice. That happens when couples devote themselves to each other.

I don't know if Rey wants me dead or not. He never says much, but you can tell by the way he watches everything like a bird enthusiast, with the slight curl of a smile they get when they see something rare. You can tell he soaks up the world as material for his poems. Rey reminds me of a Junior Woodchuck from Donald Duck comics. The Junior Woodchucks hang in the forest, still as the stump they sit on, and after a while the animals pay them no mind and get up to their antics. The Woodchucks watch everything, noting down behavioural abnormalities.

Tonight Masha defused the tension between us, anyway … perhaps I imagined the whole thing. Everyone bails out in a big hurry to eat but I stay behind to shower, feeling a bit shaken by Vesna's outright hatred of me. As I get my jeans halfway up, Masha walks into the room, obviously to retrieve something forgotten, and sees me standing here in my boxers – the very same boxers I wore that drunken night when we stripped down and got under the sheets. She makes this sort of involuntary titter, blushes and hurries back out. Obviously she finds her memories of that night amusing.

I try hard to party, to pick up chicks, to get drunk and stoned and dig everything like the future holds any real hope for lost wastrels like me. But I had a terrible dream last night. Love herself came to visit, and I ran away. Love and I sat on the porticoes of an old slumped mansion in Hades, invincible to fire, and Love told me secrets, about the ancestral animals, our body and their knowledge. I dreamed fitfully about the aristocratic-looking gallery assistant Sunny, listened for her laugh in the crowds at the bars and on the Newcastle streets, staggering in the dawn with drunken poets.

Damn hey, Sunshine, what a name. I've spent countless hours inventing new metaphors for the moon and the night, the dawn sometimes but never for the sun. Half my mind on poetry and half on her green eyes. Half my heart in a bottle of whisky and half in her palm. What if D-day has arrived? I slam the door shut in Love's face and she might never visit again. What have I gained anyway, running from her? Sitting here in a bar in Newcastle while all the other writers of my generation from this part of the world get along like Verlaine and Rimbaud. I've had it this way all my life. Treated like an outsider. But then, just now a pretty girl asked me to dance and I shrugged her off. All my own doing, all of this. I feel pretty damaged at the moment. See myself in preschool, sitting on the outside of the ring. Not singing along. I feel too damn self-conscious for that.

4

Dusk all the way back from Newcastle. Shops closed in every town we pass through. No one says much for the whole trip. Sando drives painfully slow, like he feels no hurry to return to Brisbane. I guess we all went within, reflecting on the events of the festival. Yuri and I got drunk with a few real-life published writers, up-and-comings. We initiated Nick Earls into the wonders of green chartreuse. We had a long conversation about the New Decadence with Luke Davies, a writer from Sydney. My gig went okay. I read my poem 'Plastic Daffodil' and the artist Ben Frost came to compliment me on my use of metaphor to describe killing native fauna for fun and profit.

The truth, though – and I can hardly bring myself to admit it – I feel like a husk, like a cicada shell discarded on a ghost gum. I've floated above this road on rubber so many times since 1987, when Reuben and I went hitching, without the kicks, that I feel like I've had enough. What have I learned? I mean, really learned? I don't think I'll ever find God. I don't think God wants me to find him. I think God hates it when you look for him. I've denied that love exists, dismissing it as a fancy of the leisure classes, psycho-candy invented by aristocrats pretending at real poetry. Perhaps I have denied Love at my own peril? She may have come knocking, but I ignored the call, too busy writing a poem about her. What do I know? What do we as humans know about ourselves? Someone in my philosophy class pointed out, at university in Armidale, years ago, that our brains have no idea how they work. The same applies for our definition of ourselves. Who the fuck called me a human? Other humans! Who called them humans? And so on. Perhaps Truth doesn't come pre-packaged, has no instant magic. Maybe Truth grows like a new puppy, a little every day – so you don't notice. Other people do, though. They come to visit and they say *Wow! How the puppy has grown!* And you say *Really?* Because the puppy looks the same as it did yesterday, it shat on the rug same as yesterday, damn thing chewed my boots, just like yesterday.

I keep thinking of a poster Candy had in her room all those years ago, a large glossy photograph of The Sisters of Mercy. It had a quote from the lyrics of their song 'Some Kind of Stranger'. It said: *All I know for sure, and all I know for real is knowing doesn't mean so much.* I've listened to that song a million times and every time I cry. Candy, some kind of angel in the hall outside. Has anyone ever said a truer thing? Except for maybe Buddha, or Bill Hicks?

Yeah, emulating your heroes leads to heartache. I bet my heroes drowned in loneliness and cried into their absinthe as soon as the biographer looked away. I tried to live like I have the starring role in a film about my life. I treated other people like cameras and did my best to not look at them, listened only to their voices as cues for my own lines – always busy ducking dollies, aware of stage left, tempted to break the fourth wall – like a crazy person in a supermarket queue, demanding we all look at them, addressing the audience. For certain, the universe has rhyme, but you'll never find any reason. I feel like I've graduated the School of Life with a PhD in ennui.

Then, as the last of the afternoon rolls itself out like a long child, Brisbane's mercury-gas lights flickering on, Sando ghosts us to the kerb of Harcourt Street. As I exit the Falcon and stretch, I look up; I don't know why. A psychology student once told me people hardly ever look up. Sunny sits up there in Jodie's apartment window, smoking a cigarette. She beams down on me, bright as the tundra in an Arctic summer. I go right up to Jodie's apartment without even dropping my bags, knock on the door, and Sunshine answers.

—

I told her everything, my whole damn life story, without even stopping at her *reallys?* and her *bullshits!* I opened up and ranted at her through the night and two packets of cigarettes. We went out as the pubs opened and sat in the back drinking beers while I kept on ranting. The whole damn story too, including realising I'd fallen in love with her on my way to Newcastle, right up to here and now. I even told her that I thought about her the whole time down there in Newcastle. I didn't care if it sounded creepy.

I read Sunny's tarot. The Lovers comes right up, inverse, which gives me a shock at first, because upside down it means two people will come together for purely earthly purposes, the Angel of Love chained to her own carnality. Sunny looks suspicious, like I rigged the deck of life. So I ask her to shuffle and choose different cards, and The Lovers comes up again, only the right way up this time, and I accidentally let out an audible sigh of relief.

—Did you rig this deck? she asks, checking for tells.

—Yeah. You don't know this? Every night I have a show, The Great Brentovsky, the worst magician who ever lived.

She titters. I do a coin trick there, so transparent she laughs her arse off. I probably told her too much, because even though she comes down to my apartment for the night and we talk up a tsunami, joke about The Lovers card, right after I tell her about Candy and her sisters, she says she has three sisters of her own. She remains clothed in bed, but lets me hold her.

I shouldn't have mentioned Candy and Marie and Blyth, or sounded boastful when I talked about sex with them. I touch Sunny through her t-shirt and she turns her back to me, says:

—I can't possibly sleep with you … not yet. I haven't read your poetry. I'd never sleep with a terrible poet.

We lie here on the floor of my bare rented room on this old lumpy futon mattress Josef rescued from a factory dumpster, and I feel at peace, for the first time since I don't know when.

The next morning we go to work at the art gallery, and Jodie, spying us arriving together, says:

—See, I told you … sparks!

Nothing happens for weeks. I see Sunny slave-driven by her boss, so busy she stops giving me smiles across the worksite from the office. I assume I've blown it with my story of anti-heroes, sex in overdrive and claustrophobic roads. I made it sound like I have an enormous sexual appetite, and that I feel pretty proud about making it known. Ha, call me insatiable but not proud. See, I can't help but get hyperbolic and purple. Sunny doesn't know this, though, that I often fall prey to exaggeration. I conclude that I've shocked her, due to her age. But this doesn't make me feel better. What if she dismisses me as a dirty old man? I feel dirty and old at twenty-six. Remorse, get thee behind me!

A little beam of hope shone this afternoon. An attractive, intelligent blonde chick came up to Eliot and me in the gallery. I swear I've seen her somewhere before. She says:

—Brentley? Only she looks a little angry. Eliot and I point at each other and say:

—Him … he did it! and she laughs, not angry at all, and says she wants to meet me.

—Stella, she says, winking: Sunny and I go way back, old school friends. She told me to come say hi.

Later, on my way home, kicking up Brunswick Street, past the old boarding house where Sando used to live and I attempted to write my novel, past the doorway where the stranger who haunts me used to stand, I remember I have seen Stella before, at a Nick Cave concert, years ago. She had on a handmade t-shirt emblazoned with *Lady, love your cunt.* You see, I might suffer from a bit of name deafness, but I never forget a face, especially not a pretty one.

Then, because once long ago I cursed God, Tiffany shows up. Remember her? I do, from Townsville. I'll have to read back through my story to see if I told you what happened with her. I assume I didn't, though, because of how embarrassed I feel about the whole situation. She came and sat down at my table at Ric's Bar before I even saw her. I probably would have run if I had seen her. Last time I saw her in Townsville, I blew the scene. I hate that. I don't mind when other people force an edit, because all the other players have their own director: who cares if they fuck up? When mine yells *Cut!* it really pisses me off.

Tiffany came around at two in the morning. I spent about three months smiling at her in nightclub queues. A chick way out of my league – you can tell she comes from generational wealth. Society warns girls like her about bum-poets and scoundrels before they've learned to talk. Upstairs, looking around for a bottle of whisky I stashed someplace, I'd turned to find her naked, closing curtains. She launched at me, knocked the bottle out of my hand, pinned me on the bed and sat right on my face. She could tell something went wrong. I spent about an hour in the shower until I heard the door slam as she left.

Now, here at Ric's, right when I couldn't give a flying fuck about any woman except the one who has crept into my heart like a lone sunbeam through a dusty curtain, here comes Tiffany.

Wasted. Going through the motions. At least this time I rise to the occasion. But the whole thing bores me. Tiffany feels rigid, like her rich-girl upbringing won't let her go. She hardly moves. I don't remember sex feeling this cold. I've got Sunshine on my mind. Tiffany manages to squeal as she comes. Enough to wake Yuri. I hear him moving around in the kitchen, trying not to listen. Poor little rich girl, come for an adventure on the poverty side of the line. She falls asleep after a while. I go out to the kitchen, find Yuri there, reading Rimbaud, puffing a cigarette, smoke rising in the morning as it breaks on the windows.

—Sunshine! Yuri whispers, giving the thumbs-up, jerking his head at my bedroom.

—No. Tiffany. I give the disappointed mouth shape.

—Man … he says, shaking his head: I thought you and Sunny had it going on? Not two nights ago you got drunk and ranted at me about finding love and her not wanting you. This won't help.

—Yeah. I feel like I cheated on Sunny and we've never even kissed.

—Weird, man, sighs Yuri, turns a page.

I want Tiffany out of my house, gone, out of my life. And she shouldn't take it personally. She sleeps until early afternoon. I wake her, pry her out of my bed saying *Starving … let's eat!* She takes about an hour to shower and dress, and I get her down the hall and out the front door and Sunny's face rises over the open boot of a parked car. Like the light of truth, catching me there, in the shadows of my old ways. I want nothing more than to prove I can change, to myself, to Love, in case she ever comes around again.

Sunny sees Tiffany and me coming down the steps and through the gate and she looks hurt, but proud, and the hurt runs away to the edges of her face and hides under her red curls, along her jawline smooth and beautiful as a marble bust of Helen of fucken Troy. She puts the artist portfolios or whatever she has in the car and says:

—Hi!

—Hi, I stammer. Red, then sickly pale.

As I pick through my Fatboy's Cafe all-day breakfast and Tiffany chit-chats happily about her plans and aspirations while in Brisbane, I remember, as a teenager, fishing on a beach somewhere with my father's brother. He hadn't spoken for hours when he suddenly said *Sorry, kid ... lot on my mind ... real dark days, depressed ... But hey, look on the bright side, my psychologist told me, she said you don't have to believe everything you think.* And I dumbly said, like any teenager who knows everything, *What, you only just realised that?* Obnoxious? Maybe, but true enough, at least for me – because I've never believed my own bullshit, positive or negative. People do, though; I can't imagine why. Walking around thinking themselves important, treating friends like paupers and strangers like kings, in case said stranger can help them get higher up on people's heads. Or they walk around with saddle-sore shoulders, wisdom-aching through their days and dreaming of dying. I resolve right here, sitting like some clown in a sitcom of errors, I won't lie to myself and I won't expect Sunny to believe my bullshit either. I'll tell the whole unabridged truth of it, or die trying, dammit.

Later that day, at the gallery, somehow I manage to get Sunny alone on the balcony. A bunch of artists and collectors and well-to-dos have come together to eat risotto and tapas and to celebrate the new showrooms. I say to Sunny, above the clamour of the party:

—Can we please go on a date?

—Hmm … she says, sipping champagne.

—Please?

—What about the chick I saw you leaving your apartment with?

—Look … scout's honour. I make the scout three-finger-sign thing: That chick means nothing to me … simply a dark corner I turned while fleeing my shadowy past.

—Fucken poet, Sunny laughs. She takes out a cigarette, taps it on the packet. She lights up, exhales: I think, if we do this, check out each other and see what happens, I think we should agree to make it exclusive … until we know how we feel.

—Absolutely fine by me.

—Shake on it … and I *might* read your poetry tonight. Winks.

I put out my hand, laughing, nervous.

—No … spit! she says, and she spits into her palm. Challenges me with that blue-green sparkle which makes me feel like I struck it rich, like a famous actress asked for my phone number, or I got more than I paid in change.

I understand it now, beautiful ideas that kill, the spiderwisp of promise pregnant with morning regret. The elegant agony of Truth you can never articulate. I understand Love – Love doesn't care if you don't want her. Love didn't come searching for you, either. Love looks just as surprised as you when you bump into her on the escalator, rushing to the game of life, lost in your preoccupations, afraid to miss the kick-off. We all sit alone in a cinema behind our eyes, dreaming of at least a walk-on part, rehearsing our lines so we don't disappoint our viewers, while outside Life runs past laughing. I understand Love now. She came along as literal sunshine and brushed aside my Svengali act like webs across a garden path. I see her and I smile, relax inside, give over to the ebb and flow, spit in my hand – and surrender, for the first time, ever.

Author's Note

I have changed people's names in this true story to protect their privacy.

Fliss's husband 'Jim' died from a heroin overdose in Melbourne, 1999. RIP, brother.

In the year 2012 'Reuben' received a life sentence for murder in the state of Tasmania, Australia. The news stated that the killing happened during a fight over an eighteen-year-old girl.

I composed this book, in its entirety, using a literary constraint known as English Prime. No tenses of the verb 'to be' (am, are, be, been, being, is, was, were, plus contractions) appear in the text (excluding attributed quotations). For more information on this constraint refer to my doctoral research paper, 'Beyond Is: Creative Writing with English Prime', published in *TEXT* journal, April 2016 (available online).

Acknowledgements

Love and gratitude to these beacons in various dark harbours: Sún, Jack and Vivienne. My parents and my sisters. Everyone I journeyed with. Lindsay Simpson, Nigel Krauth, Anthony Lawrence, Annette Hughes, Maggie Hall, Martin Edmond, Caroline Overington, Cheryl Akle, Lou Johnson, Alexandra Payne, Kevin O'Brien, Ian See and University of Queensland Press. Thank you.